THE CABINET OF IMAGINARY LAWS

Returning to the map of the island of Utopia, this book provides a contemporary, inventive, addition to the long history of legal fictions and juristic phantasms. Progressive legal and political thinking has for long lacked a positive, let alone an imaginary project, an account of what improved institutions and an ameliorated environment would look like. And where better to start than with the non-laws or imaginary legislations of a realm yet to come.

The *Cabinet of Imaginary Laws* is a collection of fictive contributions to the theme of conceiving laws in the vivid vein of jurisliterary invention. Disparate in style and diverse in genres of writing and performative expression, the celebrated and unknown, venerable and youthful authors write new laws. Thirty-three dissolute scholars, impecunious authors and dyspeptic artists from a variety of fields including law, film, science, history, philosophy, political science, aesthetics, poetry, architecture and the classics become, for a brief and inspiring instance, legislators of impossible norms. The collection provides an extraordinary range of inspired imaginings of other laws. This momentary community conceives of a wild variety of novel critical perspectives. The contributions aim to excite reflection on the role of imagination in the study and writing of law. Verse, collage, artworks, short stories, harangues, lists and other pleas, reports and pronouncements revivify the sense of law as the vehicle of poetic justice and as an art that instructs and constructs life.

Aimed at an audience disgruntled with the negativity of critique and the narrowness of the disciplines, this book will appeal especially to theorists, lawyers, scholars and a general public concerned with the future of decaying laws and an increasingly derelict legal system.

Peter Goodrich is Professor of Law at Cardozo Law School and Visiting Professor in the School of Social Science at New York University, Abu Dhabi.

Thanos Zartaloudis is Reader in Legal History and Theory at Kent Law School and Visiting Professor at the Center of Hellenic Studies, Harvard University.

Part of the DISCOURSES OF LAW series

series editors

Peter Goodrich, *Benjamin N. Cardozo School of Law, USA*
Michel Rosenfeld, *Benjamin N. Cardozo School of Law, USA*
Arthur Jacobson, *Benjamin N. Cardozo School of Law, USA*

For information about the series and details of previous and forthcoming titles, see https://www.routledge.com/Discourses-of-Law/book-series/SE1036

The publisher gratefully acknowledges the support of the Jacob Burns Institute for Advanced Legal Studies of the Benjamin N. Cardozo School of Law to the series *Discourses of Law*.

A GlassHouse Book

THE CABINET OF IMAGINARY LAWS

Edited by
Peter Goodrich
and
Thanos Zartaloudis

Routledge
Taylor & Francis Group
a GlassHouse Book

First published 2021
by Routledge
2 Park Square, Milton Park, Abingdon, Oxon OX14 4RN

and by Routledge
605 Third Avenue, New York, NY 10158

A Glasshouse book

Routledge is an imprint of the Taylor & Francis Group, an informa business

British Library Cataloguing-in-Publication Data
A catalogue record for this book is available from the British Library

Library of Congress Cataloging-in-Publication Data
A catalog record has been requested for this book

ISBN: 978-0-367-56659-3 (hbk)
ISBN: 978-0-367-56658-6 (pbk)
ISBN: 978-1-003-09882-9 (ebk)

Typeset in Bembo
by Deanta Global Publishing Services, Chennai, India

CONTENTS

AUTHOR BIOGRAPHIES

James Attlee is a freelance writer, editor and publishing consultant living in Oxford. He is the author of *Under the Rainbow: Voices from Lockdown* (And Other Stories, 2021), *Isolarion: A Different Oxford Journey* (And Other Stories, new edition 2020), *Guernica: Painting the End of the World* (Head of Zeus, 2017); *Station to Station* (Guardian Books, 2017), shortlisted for the Stanford Dolman Travel Book of the Year 2017, and *Nocturne: A Journey in Search of Moonlight* (Penguin, 2012), among other titles. His digital fiction *The Cartographer's Confession* won the New Media Writing Prize in 2017.

Aristide Antonas, is a Greek architect, philosopher and literary author and a visiting Professor at the Academy of Fine Arts in Vienna and the ETH Zurich. His art and architecture work have had solo presentations in museums in Switzerland, Austria and France while they have been featured in international shows as the Biennale of Venice and documenta 14, Kassel. His published works include novels, short stories, theatre scripts and essays.

Swethaa S. Ballakrishnen, is a socio-legal scholar whose research examines the intersections between law, globalization and stratification from a critical feminist perspective. Particularly, across a range of sites and different levels of analysis, their work interrogates how law and legal institutions create, continue, and counter different kinds of socio-economic inequalities. Ballakrishnen's writing has appeared in, among other journals, *Law and Society Review, Law and Social Inquiry, Fordham Law Review, International Journal of the Legal Profession*, and the *Journal of Professions and Organization*. Their first book *Accidental Feminism* is published by Princeton University Press (December 2020).

C.F. Black is an Intellectual Explorer travelling through both cyberspace and the ethereal legal world of the oldest traditions of the world. She is a descendant of the indigenous Yugambeh-speaking peoples of South East Queensland, Australia. Her scholarship brings a unique perspective to studies in legal theory. Her recent works shine a light on the potency and potentiality of Indigenous legal traditions to play a major role in helping the West come to terms with the impracticality of an affluent lifestyle in a time of growing economic inequality. Her major publications include *A Mosaic of Indigenous Legal Thought: Legendary Tales and Other Writings* (Routledge,2017) and *The Land is the Source of the Law: A Dialogic Encounter with an Indigenous Jurisprudence* (Routledge, 2011). Much of her work including her articles and chapters have been taught in universities around the world including Sciences Po, Cornell University, Kent University, McGill University and University of New Mexico. Her latest project with her colleague, legal philosopher Jan Mihal, is to write a book which creates an innovative wormhole into the algorithmic digital vortex. As Associate Professor adjunct at Griffith University, Australia her work ventures into the world of sea rise and warnings emanating from popular literature. She has given many keynotes and public seminars on Indigenous Jurisprudence. Her burgeoning creative writings include short stories, political plays, poetry, and sci fi fantasy novels for youth. Her art, photography and performance have been exhibited in New York, Beijing, Denver, and various cities in Australia. Her interests include plant consciousness, quantum physics, algorithmic decision making and ancient myths, symbols, and laws.

Chiara Bottici is an Italian philosopher and writer. She is Associate Professor in Philosophy and Director of Gender Studies at The New School for Social Research and Eugene Lang College (New York). She is the author of *Imaginal Politics: Images beyond Imagination and the Imaginary* (Columbia University Press, 2014), *A Philosophy of Political Myth* (Cambridge University Press, 2007) and *Men and States* (Palgrave, 2009). With Benoit Challand, she co-authored *Imagining Europe: Myth, Memory, Identity* (Cambridge University Press, 2013) and *The Myth of the Clash of Civilizations* (Routledge, 2010). She also co-edited the collections of essays *The Politics of Imagination* (Routledge, 2011, with Benoit Challand), *The Anarchist Turn* (Pluto 2013, with Simon Critchley and Jacob Blumenfeld) and *Feminism, Capitalism and Critique* (Palgrave 2017, with Banu Bargu). Her short stories have appeared in *Il Caffe illustrato* and *L'immaginazione*, while her feminist experimental writing *Per tre miti, forse quattro* was published by Manni Editore in 2016 and is forthcoming in an English translation with Bloomsbury.

Niall Brooks practiced for many years in the UK as a solicitor-advocate, specialising in criminal defence and prison law. He has since dedicated his life to writing poetry and fiction under various pseudonyms, including Otto Loser and Anton Matins. He lives with his wife in central Europe.

David Campbell has taught at a number of British universities and in Australia, Hong Kong, Japan, New Zealand, Spain and the USA. He currently is a Professor in the Lancaster University School of Law, UK. He has written on a wide range of legal and social scientific issues in leading UK, Commonwealth and US journals. He is one of the leading contributors to the formulation of 'the relational theory of contract'. His books on this theory are *Contract and Economic Organisation: Socio-legal Initiatives* (ed. with P. Vincent-Jones, 1996); I.R. Macneil, *The Relational Theory of Contract* (ed. D. Campbell, 2001); *Remedies in Contract and Tort* (with D Harris and R. Halson, 2002); *The Implicit Dimensions of Contract* (ed. with H. Collins and J. Wightman, eds., 2003): *Changing Conceptions of Contract* (ed. with L. Mulcahy and S. Wheeler, eds., 2013); and S. Macaulay: *Selected Works of Stewart Macaulay* (ed., D. Campbell, 2020). A book which restates the relational theory of contract entitled *Contractual Relations: A Contribution to the Critique of the Classical Law of Contract* should, circumstances permitting, appear early in 2022.

Justin Clemens works on psychoanalysis, European philosophy, and Australian poetry at the School of Culture & Communication, The University of Melbourne. His most recent book is *Limericks, Philosophical and Literary* (Surpllus, 2019). With Thomas H. Ford, he is writing a book about Barron Field, a colonial judge in NSW, who, in addition to formulating the Australian doctrine of terra nullius, also published the first book of poetry in that country in 1819.

Elizabeth Cowie is Professor Emeritus in Film Studies at the University of Kent in Canterbury. She was co-founder and co-editor of *m/f a feminist journal* 1978–1986 (now open access online), and published *Representing the Woman: Cinema and Psychoanalysis* in 1997. She has subsequently written on film noir, on the horror of the horror film, and on the cinematic dream-work. In *Recording Reality, Desiring the Real* (Minnesota University Press 2011) she addressed documentary film as to how it has been simultaneously understood as factual, as story, as art, and as political. Recent essays include "The World Viewed: Documentary Observing and the Culture of Surveillance", in *A Companion to Contemporary Documentary*, 2015; "The time of gesture in cinema and its ethics", in *Journal for Cultural Research* 2015, vol. 19, No. 1; "The difference in figuring women now", *Moving Image Review & Art Journal*, vol. 4, nos. 1 & 2, 2016, a special issue on feminism and women's art; "Feminism and Film Theory Now", *Re-Reading the Monstrous-Feminine: Art, Film, Feminism and Psychoanalysis*, eds. Nicholas Chare, Jeanette Hoorn and Audrey Yue, London, Routledge, 2020 , pp. 66–88; and "The Certainties of difference and their difficulty: desire and the symptom", in *Femininity and Psychoanalysis: Cinema, Culture, Theory*, eds. Agnieszka Piotrowska and Ben Tyrer, Oxford: Routledge, 2019, pp. 8–36.

Frederick M. Dolan is Professor Emeritus of Rhetoric at the University of California, Berkeley. He taught at UC San Diego, UC Irvine, and Princeton University (where he was awarded the Ph.D. in 1987) before joining the Berkeley faculty in 1988. His interests include political and moral philosophy, philosophy of art, and American political thought and culture. Some of his work can be accessed via https://frederickdolan.academia.edu

Stacy Douglas is Associate Professor of Law and Legal Studies at Carleton University in Ottawa, Canada. She has published work on constitutionalism and legal theory in *Law and Critique; Law, Culture and the Humanities*; the *Australian Feminist Law Journal*; and *Feminist Legal Studies.* Her book, *Curating Community: Museums, Constitutionalism, and the Taming of the Political* (Michigan 2017), argues against the centrality of sovereignty in our political and juridical imaginations. Her current work explores narratives of law's violence in popular culture, as well as activist campaigns for individuals facing extraordinary charges. Her plays have been staged at Markethall (Peterborough, Canada) and at Theatre Passe Muraille (Toronto, Canada).

Daniela Gandorfer holds a PhD in Comparative Literature from Princeton University and is the co-director of the research agency *Logische Phantasie Lab* (Loφ Lab). Currently, Daniela is a Postdoctoral Researcher at Princeton University. Her research focuses on a materialist ethics of thought and the matter(s) of legal theory, understood as a material-discursive practice of sensing and sense-making. Daniela has worked on various collaborative and international projects such as "Synesthesia of Law," and "Reading Matters," and is currently co-editing a special issue of *Theory and Event* (Johns Hopkins Press) on "Matterphorical" as well as the *Research Handbook in Law and Literature* (Edward Elgar Publishing).

Adam Gearey is a Professor of Law at Birkbeck College, University of London. He teaches courses on jurisprudence, social justice and property law. His most recent publication are *Poverty Law and Legal Activism* (London: Routledge, 2018), and "'You May Find Yourselves Changed in Unexpected Ways:' Literature and Poverty Law", in Law & Literature 2017, 29 (3), pp. 405–423. Past publications include *Islam, Law and Identity,* with Marinos Diamantides (London: Glasshouse 2010), *The Politics of the Common Law: Perspectives, Rights, Processes, Institutions,* with Wayne Morrison and Robert Jago (London: Routledge 2008) and *Justice as Welfare*, (New York: Bloomsbury 2012). See also 'Welfare, Law, Solidarity' 2013, *Law, Culture, Humanities* 8). His current work concerns property law and the critique of political economy; see, indicatively, 'Re-Reading Capital: Notes Towards an Investigation of Law, Politics and Pensions' in De-Sutter, L. (ed.) *Althusser and Law,* Abingdon, UK: Routledge, 2013) and "The More He Argued, The More Technical He Became": Trusts, Surplus Value and the State Finance Network" , in *Critical Trusts Law*, eds. Nick Piška and Hayley Gibson (London: Counterpress 2020).

Peter Goodrich was the founding dean of the department of law, Birkbeck College, University of London, where he was also the Corporation of London Professor of Law, then Professor of law at Cardozo Law School, Yeshiva University and a Professor of Law at New York University Abu Dhabi. He has written extensively in legal history and theory, law and literature and semiotics and has authored 12 books. He is managing editor of *Law and Literature*, and was the founding editor of *Law and Critique*. His most recent books are: *Schreber's Law: Jurisprudence and Judgment in Transition* (Edinburgh University Press 2018); *Imago Decidendi: On the Common Law of Images* (Brill 2017); *Advanced Introduction to Law and Literature* (Elgar 2020); and *Vision and Decision* (forthcoming with Oxford University Press 2022). He also co-wrote and co-produced the award-winning documentary "Auf Wiedersehen: 'Til We Meet Again" (Diskin Films 2012).

Piyel Haldar born to Hindu parents, was given a Catholic education at a boarding school near Hereford. As a consequence, he was raised and nourished beneath the sign of three sacred bulls: Hindu, Papal and Herefordshire. Always destined to profess a recondite subject, he came in from the pastoral in order to enter legal academia. He grazes the metropolitan fields as a senior lecturer at Birkbeck College. He is currently researching the sentiments of anti-legality and equity in early customary practices.

Valérie Hayaert, is a French historian and humanist researcher of the early modern European tradition. Her particular interest lies in the images of justice, on judicial rites and symbolism as well as its role in contemporary courthouse building. She received the EUI Alumni Prize for the best interdisciplinary thesis in 2006. Her first book *Mens emblematica et humanisme juridique*, Geneva, Droz, was published in 2008. Her subsequent work looked at the aesthetics of justice in courthouses of the early modern period until today. Her publications include: *Allégories de Justice: la grand' chambre du Parlement de Flandre*, Paillart, Abbeville, 2014, with a foreword by Robert Badinter, co-authored with French magistrate Antoine Garapon, 2014 and "In the Orbit of Lady Justice", an essay for the catalog of the exhibition Call for Justice. Recht en Onrecht in de Kunst vit de Nederlanden 1450–1650. *Art and Law in the Burgundian Low Countries* – Hannibal, Antwerp, 2018. Valérie has taught in Cyprus, Tunisia, England and France and held various positions and fellowships. She is currently a research associate at the Institut des Hautes Études sur la Justice, Paris. Her next book, *Allegories of Justice* will be published by Edinburgh University Press in 2022.

Hayley Gibson is a lecturer in law at the University of Kent. Her research focuses mainly on the critical application of philosophical archaeology and theories of the archive to jurisprudence and legal theory. She also has research and teaching interests in law and literature, and theories of private law. She sits on the boards of *CriticalLegalThinking* and *feminists@law*.

Bernard Keenan is a Lecturer in Law at Birkbeck College, School of Law, University of London. His research interests lie in the study of law, political power, and secrecy (with particular reference to contemporary questions of national security), digital media and legal techniques, the immigration system, and social theory. Prior to his academic career, he worked in radio at the BBC in Belfast.

Pierre Legendre is Professor of Roman Law and the History of Law and Directeur d'études honoraire at the École Pratique des Hautes Études - Section des sciences religieuses (Sorbonne); Espaces canoniques du christianisme occidental. Some of his work can be accessed at https://arsdogmatica.com.

Linda G. Mills, serves as Executive Director of NYU's Center on Violence and Recovery and the inaugural Lisa Ellen Goldberg Professor at New York University. Her scholarly work develops a new theory and practice of treatment for rethinking our response to violence in intimate relationships. Mills has been the Principal Investigator on two National Science Foundation (NSF) studies in Nogales, Arizona and Salt Lake City, Utah, focusing on treatment programs for people convicted of domestic violence crimes using restorative justice principles. She is also the Principal Investigator on a National Institute of Justice qualitative study related to restorative justice and domestic violence. Mills' work has been published in *Nature Human Behaviour, Journal of Experimental Criminology, Cornell Law Review, and Harvard Law Review*, to name a few. Mills is also an accomplished filmmaker. Her films have premiered at the Tribeca Film Festival and the Los Angeles Jewish Film Festival, among others, and her film, *Of Many: Then and Now,* was seen on ABC. Her latest documentary feature film, *No Contact* (2020), builds on 20 years of research on intimate abuse. In addition, Mills is Vice Chancellor for Global Programs and University Life at New York University.

Phillip Mitsis is A.S. Onassis Professor of Classics and Hellenic Studies at New York University and Affiliated Professor of Philosophy, as well as Academic Director of the American Institute for Verdi Studies. He is a past president of the Society for Ancient Greek Philosophy and a Fellow of the New York Institute for the Humanities. He works on Greek epic and tragedy, Latin poetry, and ancient and early modern philosophy. Recent publications include *Wordplay and Powerplay in Roman Literature* (De Gruyter 2016); *La Teoria Etica di Epicuro* (L'Erma di Bretschneider 2019); *The Oxford Handbook of Epicurus and Epicureanism* (OUP 2020).

Andreas Philippopoulos-Mihalopoulos is an academic, artist and fiction author. He is Professor of Law & Theory at the University of Westminster, and Director of *The Westminster Law & Theory Lab*. He works with performance, installation, video, photography and text, and his work has appeared at the 58th Venice Art Biennale 2019, the 16th Venice Architecture Biennale 2016, the Tate Modern, the Danish Royal Cast Collection, Arebyte Gallery, Palais de Tokyo, and currently collaborating with Danielle Arnaud Gallery London and Venice. His fiction *The Book of Water* is published in Greek (Thines 2017) and English (ERIS 2020).

Pierre Schlag is University Distinguished Professor and Byron R. White Professor of Law at the University of Colorado (Boulder). He teaches torts, constitutional theory, jurisprudence, and assorted seminars. He completely disavows authorship of "A Confidential Private Placement Memorandum," published herein and offers as usual no explanation.

Bernhard Schlink, Professor Emeritus of Public Law and Legal Philosophy, Humboldt University Berlin, is a lawyer and a writer. His scholarly work focusses on fundamental rights, the role of the police, and the meaning of justice. His latest books in English are *Guilt about the Past*, a collection of essays, and *Olga*, a novel. He lives in Berlin and New York.

Karsten Schubert is Lecturer in Political Theory and Philosophy at the University of Freiburg. His work focuses on contemporary critical political theory and social philosophy: radical democracy, legal critique, Michel Foucault, biopolitics, queer and gay theory, and intersectionality. Currently, he is researching at the intersection of radical democracy and theories of identity politics. His book *Freedom as Critique. Social Philosophy After Foucault* was published in German by transcript in 2018. Major articles in English include: "Freedom as critique: Foucault beyond anarchism." *Philosophy & Social Criticism*, and "The Democratic Biopolitics of PrEP" (Biopolitiken – Regierungen des Lebens heute, 2019). You can find out more about his research and download texts and videos at: www.karstenschubert.net

Tobias Smith is interested in law, punishment, and words. He is currently convalescing from a Ph.D. and has never visited Buenos Aires.

Jake Tilson is an artist, graphic designer and author. His work is rooted in everyday culture with a pervading sense of place and is held in public collections including the Tate Gallery and the Museum of Modern Art. He published the influential arts magazine *Atlas* (1985–1993), and wrote and designed the award-winning cookbook "A Tale of 12 Kitchens" (2006). He was an early adopter of the World Wide Web as a medium for art through his website "TheCooker" (1994). He exhibited at the Venice Architectural Biennale in 2012. His current studio works focus on the Tsukiji Fish Market in Tokyo which was shortlisted for the Tokyo 2020 Biennale. The Italian art critic Gabriella Bassano is currently writing a book on Tilson's work entitled "Art Works in the Third Person - Cryptic Narratives and Hidden Histories", to be published by the Tokyo Urban Press.

Tiziano Toracca is Visiting Professor at the Department of Literary Studies at Ghent University (BE) and Post-doc Fellow in Italian Contemporary Literature at the Department of Humanities, University of Turin (IT). His research focuses on Italian Contemporary Literature, Modernism and Neomodernism, Literary Representation of Work, Law and Literature. His books include *Paolo Volponi. Corporale, Il pianeta irritabile, Le mosche del capitale: una trama continua*

(Morlacchi, 2020). *Theory of Law and Literature. Across Two Arts of Compromising*, Brill Research Perspectives in Art and Law (Brill, 2020, with A. Condello).

Deepak Unnikrishnan is a writer from Abu Dhabi. His book *Temporary People*, a work of fiction about Gulf narratives steeped in Malayalee and South Asian lingo, won the inaugural Restless Books Prize for New Immigrant Writing, the Hindu Prize and the Moore Prize. At the 57th Venice Biennale, Deepak's fiction was featured in the written publication of the National Pavilion of the UAE: *Rock, Paper, Scissors: Positions in Play*. His work can also be found in *Gross Ideas: Tales of Tomorrow's Architecture*, a book project commissioned by the 2019 Oslo Architecture Triennale. His fiction, and non-fiction, has appeared in Guernica, Drunken Boat, Foreign Affairs, The Guardian and Himal Southasian among others and he frequently collaborates with artists and scholars across disciplines. He has been a writer in residence at Sangam House, Ca' Foscari University of Venice, and Brown University, and was a Margaret Bridgman Fellow in Fiction at Bread Loaf. He currently teaches at NYU Abu Dhabi.

William Watkin is Professor of Contemporary Philosophy and Literature at Brunel University. He is the author of *In the Process of Poetry: The New York School and the Avant-Garde, On Mourning: Theories of Loss in Modern Literature, The Literary Agamben* and *Agamben and Indifference.* His most recent work, *Badiou and Indifferent Being* is the first of two volumes looking at Alain Badiou's *Being and Event* project. The second, *Badiou and Communicable Worlds* is out in 2021, as is his study of contemporary modes of coercion, *Bioviolence: How the powers that be make us do what they want.* He is currently working on a study of a philosophy of indifference called, simply, *Indifference,* for which he finds he needs a new kind of language. "Ennomie" is one response to this perennial problem.

Gary Watt is Professor of Law at The University of Warwick. He is a Leverhulme Major Research Fellow, a National Teaching Fellow, and in 2009 was named UK "Law Teacher of the Year". He is co-founding editor of the journal *Law and Humanities* and co-editor of the book series *A Cultural History of Law* (Bloomsbury, 2019). His monographs include *Equity Stirring* (Oxford: Hart, 2009), *Dress, Law and Naked Truth* (Bloomsbury Academic, 2013), and *Shakespeare's Acts of Will* (Bloomsbury Arden Shakespeare, 2016). Performance collaborations include *A Strange Eventful History* (The Song Company, Australia, with Antony Pitts), *Not in my Name* (BBC Radio Three, with Antony Pitts), and rhetoric workshops delivered for the Royal Shakespeare Company and leading drama schools.

Stephen Webster has been director of the Science Communication Unit at Imperial College London since 2008. His training was in zoology and the philosophy of biology and for many years he was a school science teacher. At Imperial College he teaches philosophy of science, and is a member of the college's science and technology ethics committee. His publications include *Thinking About Biology*

(CUP 2003), *Charles Darwin* (The History Press 2014) and, as co-editor, the collection of essays *The Silences of Science: Gaps and Pauses in the Communication of Science* (Routledge 2017).

Thanos Zartaloudis is a Reader in Legal Theory and History at the University of Kent, Kent Law School and Doctoral advisor at the Architectural Association, School of Architecture, London. At Kent he directs the Research Group on Philosophy, Political Theology and Law and he is the co-director of the cross-faculty Kent's Interdisciplinary Centre for Spatial Studies. His most recent book is *The Birth of Nomos* (EUP 2019) and he is the editor of the recent collection titled *Law and Philosophical Theory: Critical Intersections* (Rowman and Littlefield International 2019). He is also the head-editor (with Anton Schütz) of the book series titled *Encounters in Law and Philosophy*, published by Edinburgh University Press. Outside of the academy he works as a translator and plots his escape as a writer.

PRELUDE

Peter Goodrich and Thanos Zartaloudis

Thanos: The seed for *The Cabinet of Imaginary Laws* was first sensed when I was teaching some law students about the complexity of the "art" of legal drafting as an aside to a doctrinal course. It was then, mutually, realised that the students were finding it very difficult to draft, as well as to reflect on drafting. They were of course literate, well-read in the law and earnest, but something else was missing. After setting the technical aspects of drafting aside, one of the things that became apparent in later conversation was that they could not "see" or "imagine" new, let alone, "better" laws. They pointed me to the imagination in this context and I immediately felt that this was not an accidental but a rather fundamental political problem. But there was more to it, as I would discover when we set out to explore this further. In one sense, the problem of the imagination, if it ever was a "problem", was always, it seems, a political problem with education. I mean, a problem essentially of the city, and the city in my thinking is always a striving, educated and educating city or it is not at all. After all, is it not the case that the coming together of the citizens in the polis required a primary, even if undisclosed, act of imagination? For how else would the polis bring together those who have nothing in common other than through an imaginary construction? Hence, the theatre for the Greeks. But the theatre and the polis were also more than political problems themselves, for they had to reconfigure what was invisible as a now visible stage or agora. In an ideal world, a bit like a book needs to do as well. And it was through this engagement with the students that it felt to me as if the imagination had something to do with, first of all, what we could call the visibility of what remains unseen, or as the philosopher says, the indication of the *existence* of the possible. It was after sharing this experience with you that we were led to install ourselves upon a peculiar ambition towards what became eventually *The Cabinet of Imaginary Laws*.

Peter: Install? Exactly the case, quite so, certainly, yes. A matter of performative and active installation. What we have learned is that it is difficult for modern lawyers to look to, envisage and walk into the future. They are addicted to looking back. To precedent, the priority of the past over the present, the dead hand of the law. Thus, we incite our contributors here to rise to the twitch of the jurisliterary tradition, donning the mantle of imaginal works such as *Cupid's Jurisprudence*, *Don Quixote*, *The Astral Sphere of Laws*, *Autumn Weekends*, *Gargantua and Pantagruel*, *The Island of Jurists*, *The Ship of Fools*, the *Sermon on the Laws*, *Tristram Shandy*, *Legal* Scintillæ, *Law for Martians* and various further utopic, dystopic, heterotopic, protreptic and proleptic poems and treatises written by lawyers, poets and priests. Our exuberant goal has been to revive the transitional, corporeal, cacchinated, calumniating and incautious material spaces of legal thinking. It is in the imaginal, in what has never been, in what exists in the cracks and dashes of discourse, in the fissures and diffractions of disciplines, that we invited anarchists, footballers, scientists, interior decorators, novelists, pilgrims, students, jurists, naturalists, vice chancellors, druids, film professors and directors, retired lawyers, musicians, architects, poets, marathon runners, Indians, artists, the unemployed, bicyclists and other ambulators, sober and stoned, to contribute their wild jurisprudence to the reverie and renewal of *The Cabinet*. All political problems stand in front of the door of the law and so why not open up the imaginal in its complexity and diffusion, naked and dressed?

The doors of *The Cabinet* cannot be fully opened, the columbarium of creativity is far too gargantuan, and we are not so ambitious or deluded to think that the stratigraphy of imaginal laws could be curtailed and confined in the circumscribed space of a fenestrated bureau.

Thanos: Well, one has to start somewhere. And, usually, somewhere familiar. In class I would, for example, remind my students that there are also the rich traditions of literary or pseudo-laws, satirical or otherwise, some of which you have already mentioned, and that perhaps they may have read some when they were younger without even realising it. And then, there are the historically peculiar, weird, actual laws, already occupying the legal minds of ancient Rome, like those turning a subject into an object and an object into a subject; legal fictions turning the unreal into something more real than the real: into parchment and into law! From which, in fact, one can learn something about the nature and manner of law, as well as the decisive role of the imagination – given that the imagination is evidently at the core of legislation, it literally *makes* law, from at least the time of the Romans.

But there are also laws of the imaginary, like, for example and centrally so, that the impossible or the invisible, exist and can be visible despite our fog-bound attention to the here and now. Naturally, in the mist of the spectacular mundanity of everyday reality, we forget, but this is precisely how conventions are formed and get settled. Perhaps one motivation to gather, in this initial attempt, writers from various paths and to ask them to compose an imaginary law in whatever form they so wished, was to examine also how this forgetting of the imagination can be glimpsed and the future revived. It is as if the imaginary is always left behind at the moment of the creation of an institution or law; as if it is necessary to forget the crevasse from which otherwise solid laws emerge.

Peter: What is solid can just as easily melt into air. Enough of this melancholic refusal to let go, and forward with the art of unknowing, the craft of invention, the science of impossible solutions and the existentialism of holes. What is sought and achieved, epistemically and ontographically in the ludic lucidity of multiverse contributions to our *Cabinet* can only be thought lawlessly, as a cleft, clough, chink, crevasse and rimation, an aperture into the isolarion of imaginal laws, a glimpse at the serried shelves, the pegmes, pedestals and scaffolds that house the legislation of poets, the creativity of officials, the beauty of the non-existent, the reality of the not yet. Press forward friend, for tomorrow we die.

Thanos: The not yet, *and* the bereft ... since when I later found myself confronted with the last ten years of destruction of the Athenian city of my birth, a city largely abandoned under the intermittent administration of an unmanageable debt, I came across another contingent reflection on the uses of the imagination. Here you had, effectively, the very erasure of the polis by the near absolute imposition of the rule of the imaginary abstractions of money and unconstitutional emergency laws. In this setting, where reason itself was becoming unimaginable and at the same time imaginary abstractions were wreaking havoc in the lives of ordinary people just so as to balance the books, suddenly the power of the imagination became apparent anew. And this time it was a numbing, destructive and amnesiac one.

In these conditions, and somehow against them, I found myself annotating another dimension of the early inspiration for *The Cabinet* when I started drafting pseudo-laws in the form of what, along with the architect, writer and philosopher Aristide Antonas, we called "protocols" (an archipelago of them, in fact) in an attempt to bridge legal and architectural thinking and designing. There was something challenging, as well as genuinely interesting, in using entirely imaginary or speculative frames of pseudo-law to support architectural propositions. And we were surprised by the comparable role of the imagination as a motor of production in both disciplines. It was, in fact, the imagination of a breathing space, even if momentary, for a reflection otherwise that enabled the interaction between the two fields of law and architecture. In fact, proposing to put these initial senses to work together with you in this *Cabinet* made perfect sense to me given that the imagination plays such a crucial, if undeclared, role at the heart of your writing, analysing and theorising about law and your writings provided, among other things, a breathing space for my younger self, and continue to do so.

Peter: A Hellenic moment. I occasionally lapse into the Aegean mode of thought. As the philosopher enigmatically observed, the eye, in order to see itself, must look into another eye. The ocular hieroglyph stands for legality and justice, the omnivoyant speculum, the panoptic peeper is an entirely artificial, wholly imaginary construct and yet it renders – it plasters – the real. Here is the well-hidden charnal house of juridification, the scriptorium of the tellurian secreted in plain view, reforming our world. So it is that the multitude of imaginal future laws which escape through the chink in the doors of *The Cabinet*, in this volume, offer an unconstrained, holistic prospect, a panjuridical panorama of an element that is at the heart of law-making and law-living. Our intuition, though perhaps bravado would term it insight, is that, indeed, the over-optimistic science of laws stultifies just as much, which is to say as unjustly as pre-given laws of science can cripple discovery. If chance, reverie, silence, innocence and myth lead to discoveries in nature, how much more so when the other face of law, human custom and everyday observation, the heart of the imagination, comes to turn its vizard and fair aspect to creating and recreating the commons.

Thanos: Breathing space is perhaps needed first towards recreating the commons, and indeed when encountering the law and its study of the commons; and this is sorely missed in education, as well as in scholarship. Not so much the indulgence in generalisable hypotheticals, as it has been romantically and pedagogically preferred in some geographies of legal study, or mere speculative theory, but observation and reflection through and upon drafting imaginary tracts, pathways, experiments. As the poet put it: *And yet we should consider how we go forward*. How else can we go forward but by experiencing experiments, by imagining pathways forward, leaving the tracks, taking a chance, unsettling the melancholy of complacency, however trivial this may seem to the scientists of law? After all, the jurists, today, have once more forgotten that their predecessors in ancient times had to invent their scientific ways in the first place and so they studied philosophy, music, the arts, rhetoric for they were essential to imagining.

Peter: I am in agreement, the liberal sciences are also arts of imagination, experiments in thought, digressions and pilgrimages in ideas, *in actu, de futuro*. We moderns must stand on the shoulders of the giants so as to see into the future, so as to move beyond them. That is the existential gambit of time, the hapticity that constitutes our space. It is necessary then to protect our noses, to shield the prow, to give time to thought, space to conversation, a berth to intimacy and innocence, alcoves for invention, pages to reverie, offices for those that review books, a pedestal to allow jurists to see, a catafalque for sovereigns, vestibules for musicians, atria for theologians, and a canoe for administrators to travel to where they need to go.

As Judge Schreber, once and immortally, remarked, *God has no sense of how trains run on time.* There is more to the timetable than the straight lines of the *chemin de fer.* And there is his randomly preserved injunction, do not eat strawberries, by which I think we would now take his eminence to mean stick with *sauvage*, with feral *fragaria*, fortuitous fruit. It was Lord Hailsham, I believe, let us say our very own English Schreber, who tellingly complained that smoking cannabis gave him a headache and that God never made a better berry than the strawberry, but doubtless God, or in our case Judge Schreber, could. Here then is fruit, the effulgent and frugiferous budding of literary berries, the straws from which the virbiusses of the *Cabinet* are made.

The Cabinet is pitched to tar together the force and the farce of law, the serious and the ludic, the present and the future in the necessary widdershins of *leges ferrendae*, as you would say, imaginary future legislations, couplets, verses, pictures and, indeed, noses. Of what use, we ask, is a justice that cannot dance backwards and forwards from the past and into the future, that is not willing to embrace prospect and invisibility as visible, the unknown as the ultimate source of sensuous decisions, of norms that *make* sense with words and of words that make norms of *sense.*

Here are dragons – burial urns, resipiscency, the Appian Way of knowledge, a new science, and *in nuce* and eggshell, *otium cum dignitate* or in the vernacular, the dignity of leisure, the opulence of time …

Thanos: You are right, it would be wrong to deflower the efflorescence of imagination with a catalogue, collection, curtailment or curtilage that might in any way fashion an imagined homogeneity, a sclerosis of categories as opposed to the abundance of differentiation, or even *indifference* as one of our contributors would have it. If that were the case we might as well just be legal subjects. Work and die. There would be nothing left to reflect on or doubt. We would just *do our duty.*

Peter: There is life in monstrosity, the future of the unfamiliar and other breakout attempts. The imaginary laws are painted onto the pages of taste and smell, riven and reeved into rivulets, portrayed by paragons, flooded with tears and divagations, rhizomes of futurity, the eloquence of the nebulous, the strictures of a vivid reason that allows anything to go figure. The exercise is one of dialogue, difference, diversity and discrimination as the *elegantia iuris* of choice. As a slight prefiguration, a minor gesture and lifting of the veil, as the etymology of prelude, *praeludium* or foreplay suggests, we can canvas the four fits of the compass that our escapees in the *Cabinet* jettison towards. First epistemology, a plea for quietude, an argument for the restoration of scientific standards, both liberal and natural, that allow for sleep, for dream, for reverie, for breath, as well as for dialogue, song lines and ley lines, ancient wisdom and science fiction to draw their figures upon a triptych of voluntary commitments to reticence, innocence and intimacy in the communities of experimentation. Publish less, think more.

Epiphanies should be savoured like squirrels running up the leg of a statuesque scientist. Insufflation is a philosophical art, *nomos* as *pneuma* as addle pates such as I would likely say and then turn the page to astrojurispudence, laws of outer space, the eternity within.

Thanos: Perhaps the only place for thinking law, rather than programming it, drafting it, applying it, evaluating it, reforming it, is the imaginary plane. There is in this *Cabinet* a plenitude of different attempts, in manner, aim and intensity, to commit to the imaginary reflection of and on law. There is a point in time when reason and law get conflated; and to such an extent that reason, philosophically, becomes, as we know, a court of justice, and in fact more than a court of justice, a *juridified* universe. The commitments in this volume toy with the thin line that separates any membrane, the tissue that protects the organism, the placenta of law. Lamina, lumina and epidermis are the points of contact where life impacts law and the jurist enters the polity. All part of the web of knowing, the sensory apprehension, and haptic *ligamen* of legality. The membrane, in mind here, is that between the imaginary reflection of law and the *juridified* reflection of the imaginary that opens up the space of the imaginal, sensible life. *The Cabinet*, through the contributions of its authors offers an animate space to think law at this liminal, epidermal, threshold. And you know well, that this commitment I speak of is a commitment, as ever, to a rationality nonetheless. To be more precise to the pure potentiality of rationality that is granted to human beings via the imagination, as our in-absentia companion in this volume, the vegetal philosopher Emanuele Coccia would have it, were that he had a moment to attend to our imaginary garden.

Peter: A plenitude indeed. Circles, couches, shopping carts, snoutfigs, embargoes on cats, new lists, weird verses, profusions of alliterations, alphabetical disorders, sartorial solecisms, found texts, strange gods, gargoyles, Athenian injunctions, there is a bracing benevolence of spirit and new lesions of law that run through and through the Cabinet. There are lexicons and poems, hallucinations and redemptions, proposals and disposals, the detailed and the nebulous, both divine and human remonstrations, demonstrations and prognostications. There is the question of cats, of feline infelicities, their toxic waste, their avicidal practices, the delinquency of owners who fail to control *felis domesticus* to the point that they terrorise the avian public sphere. Allergic to felines, one author articulates a position in favour of birds, *aviarum iuris civilis*, to engage in a pun, and the exaltations of flight that should be forbidden to cat owners who fail to reign in the miniature tiger kings. It is an argument as well for the rights of birds, an angelological approach to the continuity of all being, the death of precedent in the face of post-human comities of *justissima tellus et stella*. These are the lores and laws of the earth that ley lines track as avenues of natural power traversing the *sphaera legalis*, the astronomy of law, as much as they demarcate both time and place as subject to natural forces. This is ground also for complaint as to contemporary practices and we are witness to a report to the Treasurer of Injustice, an act to rescue cornices, pilasters, cills and architraves of corbels, a legislation prohibiting unnecessary publications so as to restore science to its rightful and serious discourse. Agelasts and lunatics, science and play, dirge and song meet productively, which is to say fantastically, amongst the ley lines of thought and the lores of imaginal relay. The right to light that allows corbels to breathe is expanded to protection of the fascia of buildings, and then, why not, the human visage should also have its defences to proboscides, the ontographic right to be who you are, free of denasification, which, after all, used to be the punishment in medieval law for infidelity.

Thanos: And what is the spell we find in this *Cabinet*, my good(rich) druid?

Peter: The spell, the charm, the chance, the bell is the continuance of orality, the pneuma of dreams and the sacrifice of unnecessary realities. The father is undone by hir progeny. By children that dream, and then stand on their parents' shoulders to look forwards and not back. What purpose could there be but to think again, more diversely and expansively as to what the juridical could mean, what a revival of the art of law might imply in a turbulent world sorely lacking today in any poetry of justice. For too long, lawyers have looked to the past, to the greats of the juristic tradition, the statuary of the Island of Jurisprudence, to a republic of lawyers determined upon a rigid adherence to a science buried in codes or bound to precedent, to the dead hand of the antiquated law. A sensible life needs a material law, new insufflations, a law of matter and one that matters, that can be befriended, that looks to the future as the determinant of the present rather than to the templates and other prison houses of prior judgment that, after all, has not gone well. Noses to the future, the holes in the prow are ready to nostrillate and flare. From metaphysics to pataphysics and the exemplary scientific illuminations of imaginary solutions, the great laugh, the alluvions of a futuristic allegoresis.

The past is dead, a truism, but for lawyers there is another and more tumultuous truth which is that precedent no longer functions, that in the face of zoonoses and pandemics, the robed sacerdotes are stripped bare by their microbes. The viral and virtual worlds emergent from the earth, the imaginal realm of the *subimago* and other microbial forms, not only eschew the authority of prior decisions and practices but demand imaginary solutions to a collapsing symbolic realm. No need for law to disinter the past, we carry it within, it is our substance, the interior as matter. The extancy of geohistory is harboured in the motion of our cells, the kaleidoscope of interior atoms. It is the mobile earth, *justissima tellus*, that hues our ends, and we will join the earth again in a relentless cycle of emergence and decay, life and death, Eros and Thanatos, Petrus and Thanos, into the future, into the future. What tumult and crisis make clear is that looking back, timidly clinging to old patterns, the idols of the past, the presidency of precedent, does not work, turns the Janus face of the jurist the wrong way, down the rabbit hole. It is impossible solutions that are needed, imaginary conversations, *tabula rasa* as the page upon which the future is writ.

Thanos: Yet, if I may, imagination itself has a history, and thus lawyers, let alone historians, need the sensible, imaginal life, as much as it needs them. A mutual dependency, though repressed again and again by the demarcation of disciplines, and the disciplining that has replaced the so-called future. But the imagination is not to be thought here as a technique or instrument, or indeed as another means of communication. The imagination we have in mind is intrinsically linked to its implications for our experience and the experience of law and, for us jurists, of studying the law in particular. The imagination, in this sense, is not so much the impossible made possible or the unreal made real, but their constant companionship rendered visible. It is a type of what students of Aristotle once called *media diaphana*, rendering diaphanous matters, like glass or air, visible.

Visibility, here, becomes a matter of degree, rather than a sharp distinction between the invisible and the visible, the impossible and the possible. Imagination is not, therefore, other to the technical articulations and drafting of the laws, but is sensibly there, within them all the way. So once more it is about retraining ourselves to imagine good law (and there should be a compulsory course in law schools on good law), rather than to elevate and distinguish it from the power of the imaginary under the weight of legal tradition or settled manners. To live with imagination may be precisely this sense you speak of whereby one can love or befriend the laws one lives with, or not. One can only hope that in moments of crisis like these, one's mode of perception can be changed or at least challenged.

The Cabinet: *Ad futuram, ad montes, ad imaginem …*

And thus we asked of our authors to pick up their wits, align their judgment, and turn to what is not, to a faith in invention and the power of the indigitative, chironomic and plastic arts of matter and meaning. The remit and pestle was to produce a proleptic propaedeutics, a vision of decisions to be. Speak with Beckett again, borrow the pen of Borges, listen in to an analyst's session, become the drafter of a novel law, a protocol for science or a mobile room, a bargain with some apparition of the devil, some conversation with a spectral divinity, an angel or the figure of time. What will be is heterotopic, in motion, a futuristic exercise in optimistic will, in comities and congruences yet to come. That precedent is dead, that the weight of history, the pain of the past is not the best avenue or image for facing the not yet, that it fails to inscribe an eternal positive law, opens the doors of perception to novelty, technology, an imaginal prospect and vista of heterotopic, otherwise invisible or abandoned, spaces, touch and trend that may not be cool for cats but is full of invention, an unrecognisable place, a site of desire and study. Open the doors of the cabinet, scan the china teapots, the scrolls, the paintings, the masks, the illuminated texts, the pictures ornamented with words, the symbols, the legislations. Then experiment with law.

1

THE IMAGINARY ORIGINS OF THE COMMON LAW

Piyel Haldar

> *As the most universal, the most objectively exhibited element given to us, the earth itself is what furnishes the first matter of every sensible object.*
>
> Jacques Derrida[1]

> *These rocks, these bones, these fossil ferns and shells,*
> *Shall yet … reveal*
> *The secrets of the book of earth to man.*
>
> Alfred Noyes[2]

I.

The building and furnishing of an imaginary cabinet of laws, with which this volume is concerned, might well produce suggestive novelties and satirical points. It might well discover holes in legal discourse through which legal rationality disappears. It might provide a heuristic that enables us to solve particular knots in legal thinking; or, it might simply give the semblance of solid form to an orthodox sense of legality (perhaps as an escape from the delirium that attaches to our wilder imaginations). The story that follows, however, does not posit a made-up, fantastic law. Rather, it re-imagines another history of common law as one that emerges from the deep layers of the earth.

The story was initially told by Alfred Watkins who developed his theory of ley lines from a loose and suggestive set of evidence. His accounts are well

1 Jacques Derrida, *Introduction to Edmund Husserl's Origins of Geometry* transl. John P. Leavey Jr (London: University Nebraska Press, 1989), p. 81.

2 Alfred Noyes, *The Book of the Earth; the Torch Bearers II* (New York: Frederick A. Stokes 1925), p. 4.

known. They have been variously mythologised and given iconic status among new-age mystics, hobbyists and psychogeographers. For them, ley lines expose the earth's inexorable pulsations and motor energies that (apparently) were once known to a remote ancestry. Buried within his books, however, is a resourceful account of law's beginnings that seems to imagine the very jurisdiction of the common law emerging not from the mists of time immemorial but by permission of the earth itself. The place of law has largely been clouded over by the various communities of ley hunters (hardly surprising given the counter-cultural bent of these communities). Similarly, serious legal scholarship has ignored the thematic for slightly different reasons (hardly surprising given the square cultural bent of common lawyers). A volume such as this gives opportunity to pursue Watkins's imaginary claims in order to throw some light on the beginnings of the common law.

Watkins poses these beginnings as a question of geology rather than temporality and, in doing so, he re-materialises law's relations to the material strata of the earth itself. Imaginary it might be, but so are all speculations about foundations and, in its obedience to the drama of the earth, it inadvertently succeeds in doing something that legal historians have failed to do. When all is said and done, the theory of ley lines reminds us that there exists a formal connection between the institutions of law and what lies below the land itself. The pastoral tradition, to which common law imagines it belongs, originates from what geology permits. Watkins's account, it might be stressed, is not therefore a theory of natural law. Law is not nature waiting to be discovered by the hunter of forms. What emerges does so from the way in which geology shapes the terrain, from alluvial erosions, from Silurian and Devonian shifts, from the hard matter that lies below the surface of nature. And, the earth, as the philosopher Edmund Husserl reminds us, is always imaginary insofar as it is beyond comprehension, always beneath the sandal, never fully visible and always hidden from the hunter of forms.[3]

II.

I will take up my slender reed and practise the music of the countryside
Virgil[4]

Few can claim to have had an epiphany during the height of an English summer while wearing a 14-pocket Harris Tweed suit lined with grey flannel. Fewer still,

3 Edmund Husserl, 'Foundational Investigations of the Phenomenological Origin of the Spatiality of Nature" trans. F. Kersten in Edmund Husserl, *Shorter Works* ed. P. McCormick and F. A. Elliston (Notre Dame, Indiana: Notre Dame Press, 1991), at pp. 222–233; and Edmund Husserl, *Crisis of European Sciences and Transcendental Philosophy* trans D. Carr (Evanston: Northwestern University Press, 1970).

4 Virgil, 'The Song of Silenus' *Eclogues*, (London, Harmondsworth: Penguin, 1953), at p. 53.

can claim it while pursuing their avocations in the Herefordshire countryside. But then the revelations of forgotten, ill-remembered or indeed, non-existent, jurisdictions can strike wherever, whenever and whoever regardless of their sartorial eccentricities.

At the time of his epiphany, Watkins was already an established photographer, an inventor of some fame and author of, inter alia, *A Survey of Pigeon Homes in Herefordshire*.[5] On June 30, 1920, driving his Wolseley Stellite through the hamlet of Blackwardine, ten miles north of Hereford, he stopped to visit the remains of a Roman camp. Taking in the view, he noticed that a number of significant ancient landmarks (tumps, megaliths, churches, crosses) were connected to each other by straight and uninterrupted routes (50 or 60 miles in length).[6] Consulting his Ordinance Survey map proved his theory. Straight paths, "natural alignments", ran through the "same class of objects" like electric cables running "a chain of fairy lights [...] laid out in much the same way that a marksman gets the back and fore sights of his rifle in line with his subject."[7] His vision was, by the standards of other more celebrated epiphanies, prosaic, simple and supported by, what he imagined to be, hard fact and brute observation. He had discovered ... paths. Bear in mind that these were not just any old paths, not even any old medieval paths. These were straight paths that must have been laid before the Roman invasion. He surmised that these paths could be dated back to the Neolithic era and provided evidence of a complete pre-civilised navigational and traffic system consisting of sighting points on elevated ground (mounds, tumps, twts, knobs, cairns, etc.), sighting lines (alignments, paths) and secondary sighting points situated along these paths (stone crosses, trees, sacred wells, marking stones).

Watkins claimed that at the time of epiphany his mind was clear of theories, his minstrel harp not yet tuned to the task of theory.[8] Only then, little by little, could the innocent appearance of countryside turn to any semblance of apparition strengthening eventually into the associative network of ley lines that would "amaze" him and establish his fame beyond the pigeon fanciers of Herefordshire. A "flood of ancestral memory", a "rush of revelations", came to Watkins because, empty of mind, he knew how to look. He could break the

5 I'll admit with bare reluctance that Watkins's survey of pigeon homes is fascinating in tracing what was then the fast-disappearing architectural style of pigeon homes to the Norman columbarium. His survey might be read as an attempt to join the bucolic to the funerary, the avian to the archival. See Alfred Watkins (1891) 'Pigeon Houses in Herefordshire and Gower', *Archaeological Journal*, 48:1, 29–44.

6 Alfred Watkins, *Early British Trackways; Moats, Mounds, Camps and Sites* (Hereford: The Watkins Meter Co.; London: Simpkin, Marshall and Co., Ltd., 1922), p. 8. *Early British Trackways* is based on a lecture given in September 1921 to the Woolhope Naturalists Field Club in Hereford. The first ley identified by Watkins was of the straight line running from Croft Ambury over hill points, through Blackwardine and onward through to Stretton Grandison.

7 Alfred Watkins, op. cit. 6, at p. 8.

8 As Watkins put it: "I knew nothing on June 30 of what I now communicate, and had no theories", op. cit. 6, at p. 6.

horizon and see beneath and beyond the picturesque. An analogy seems obvious. Watkins, the photographer-magus living outside the system of the legal flock, had begun mechanically to develop a latent image. In so doing he brought to form the pattern of scars in the countryside. The surviving manifestations of an older social system where morphemes had always lain dormant in plain sight, intestinal trails rotting away beneath our feet.

As is so often the case in our lives, the sight of one small line fed the desire to see more. "Once started" he states excitedly, "I found no halt in the sequence of new facts."[9] Oblivious to all but his lust for the rectilinear, Watkins saw lines crosscutting the whole of the English countryside. Using the sites of ancient monuments as "practical sighting points" the linear connections between beacons and points could be observed throughout the countryside. Topography had given way to the chiasma of geometry; paths had given way to pathology. The *derriere-garde* of Herefordian life had exposed a modernist geometry printed upon the country, transmitted from point to point.[10] This was geometry from which to reflect on a fantasy of an aboriginal jurisdiction and to extract a sense of enchantment with the history of the English countryside and what he terms, "the *genio terrae Britannicae*."[11]

From the tenebrous melancholy of the Hereford countryside, Watkins may well have held a desire to map a nationalist identity for England built on more open ground, before primitivism had been warped by civilisation and well before landlords, enclosures and market protectionism. Indeed, these straight leys provided evidence of a social system that existed prior to the civilising machinery of Roman conquest, prior to the *servitutes* of the straight Roman roads.[12] In his Harris Tweed suit with 14 pockets (which, apparently, he wore throughout the year), he envisaged England before any Roman invasion as a paradise of journeymen, knappers and drovers all plying these straight paths, furthering what amounted to an ideology of free trade. In the words of George Gomme, whose

9 ibid., at p. 10.

10 Epiphanies are not exempt from context and some might be of relevance. There seems to be some coincidence of pattern between the system of ley lines and the self-enfolding trench system of the First World War. Moreover, Britain was in the grip of a peculiar post-war iteration of pastoralism that was given wide cultural expression in the uncanny landscape portraits of Paul Nash or the abstractions of Ceri Richards, in the poetry of David Jones or in the music of Elgar, Vaughan Williams, Arnold Bax and Arthur Bliss. British modernism might be regarded as an attempt to address what the poet David Jones (roughly contemporaneous to Watkins, and who lived in the Ewyas valley neighbouring Blackwardine) called "the break". For Jones, the technicity and utility of modern life dislodges man from the density of connections to ancient forms of life. But since man is *homo faber*, poetry and imagination are ways of repairing the road. See David Jones, *In Parenthesis* (London: Faber and Faber, 1955).

11 Alfred Watkins *The Old Straight Track* (London: Abacus, 1970) at p. v.

12 As Watkins puts it: "During a long period, the limits of which remain to be discovered, but apparently from the Neolithic (later flint) age on past the Roman occupation into a period of decay, all trackways were in straight lines marked out by experts on a sighting system." op. cit. 6, at p. 7.

work on primitive folk-moots Watkins refers, this was the evidence that "*cleared the ground* of the theory of the exclusive Roman origin of English history."[13]

Before the conjecture completely dissolved Watkins had to solemnise the system of leys as borne of a creative act by unique and sacred personae. His story required further a cast of characters, something to fix the imaginary and give it plausibility. In Chapter XI of *The Old Straight Track*, Watkins turns his attention to the question of how these tracks were first laid, and by whom. In doing so, he makes the leys a matter of law and puts the system in the expert grip of a juristic class. This pre-historic class of "ley-men" consisted of druids, bards, wizards, sorcerers, diviners and spell charmers. Watkins, in other words, joins with the early interpreters of the law (Selden, Spelman, Jones, Blackstone, et al.) in giving responsibility to the druidic profession for the origins of immemorial custom.[14] Druids and bards (Watkins does not distinguish between the two) were much earlier prototypes of the Roman haruspices.[15] They read the signs, interpreted the convulsions of the sacrificial dead, examined the flow of blood and prophesied from the flight of birds. Consider, too, that this class of experts guarded the law by recording genealogies and speaking to the descent of the land. They alone held the memory of arcane knowledge and, in so doing, were able to "sing the law" into being. For the law to be decided entrails were spilt and skulls were nailed onto trees. Sacred rage and blood sacrifice formed no small part in the conjuration of common law. If existence was one of intensity, so too was its interpretation. Where we now immerse ourselves in dry text to seek the law, the earliest class of lawyers drenched themselves in blood and viscera, in sex-magic and degradation.

Where Watkins differs from the early interpreters of the law is in adding to (or at least stressing) the druid's juridical functions the techniques of surveying in order to lay the system of tracks. These were men who auspicated the ancient secrets of the earth in order to scratch a system onto its territory.[16] Just like Watkins, they knew how to read the signs. Although, where Watkins merely read the surface of the soil, druids were able to read the hard rock of the earth itself. The law emerged from their ability to break open the earth, test subterranean rhythms and re-awaken its memories.

13 George Laurence Gomme, *Primitive Folkmoots or Open-Air Assemblies in Great Britain* (London: Sampson Low, Marston, Searle & Rivington, 1880), at p. 3. My emphasis.

14 Blackstone, for example, states that the very notion itself of an oral unwritten law handed down from age to age, by custom and tradition, drew from the practice of the druids; see William Blackstone *Commentaries on the Laws of England,* vol. 4: 408. For further elucidation on druids and common law, see Peter Goodrich, 'Druids and Common Lawyers; Notes on the Pythagorean Complex and Legal Education,' *Law and Humanities* Vol.1 2007, pp. 1–30. Paul Raffield, *Shakespeare's Imaginary Constitution Late Elizabethan Politics and the Theatre of Law* (Oxford: Hart Publishing 2010), pp. 44–45.

15 "All of these 'ley-men' were linked by one thread of ancient knowledge and power." Watkins op. cit. n. 11, p. 83.

16 ibid., p. 81.

Specific methods of survey, of aligning natural features to elemental forces, need not be of concern other than to mention one curiosity since the instruments that Watkins places in the hands of the white-beards are suggestive of his re-imagining of the primordial function of law and of establishing lawyers as geometers of the earth. Each ley-man carried two long staves which they used against landmarks to measure angles, plot distances or calculate differences in height. The most famous depiction is that of the Long Man of Wilmington (in all probability, the long man is also an imaginary depiction circa 17th–18th century). Carrying two long staves each, these bards resembled horned land snails (a photograph of a snail taken on the ruins of Llanthony Priory is included in *The Old Straight Track*). "[The snail] carries on his head the dod-man's implements, the two sighting staves ... [just as] the surveyor carries two rods."[17] Ever the etymologist, Watkins claims that the image of the snail gives these ley-men their other name, that of dodmen (derived from "dod", the old English vernacular term for snail).

Magicians of the ley may have fallen into disrepute, but their resemblance to the snail set a pattern of symbolic behaviour that would last in judicial ceremony through the centuries.[18] Thus, in the assize courts of Watkins's time, the under-sheriff and the jury-usher continued to carry a wand of office – "they are carried as the Long Man carries his, are about the same length, and are an emblem of authority."[19] It is not a far-fetched theory when one contemplates sheriffs and ushers fronting a slow procession into town, measuring the earth before them, testing the circuit, appraising the civic seat; geometers travelling under the order of the snail. The practical matured into the symbolic and the symbolic continues a memory far beyond the reach of legal history and well into the curious depths of the imaginary. The symbolic, in short, encrypts the memory of common law's association to the earth.

III.

Before the Romans, before the Celts, before any culture, before any social system, there was the earth itself. It was the earth that assumed legal form and allowed the practice of law. It was the earth that leased to the law its prime sites, conveying the products of its matter-energy to its custody. The features of the ley system bear witness to honouring the relationship between earth and law.

17 op. cit. n. 11.

18 Watkins traces the decline of druidic surveys to the much later cultural denigration of witchcraft. Folklore gives to witches the power of riding through the air on a broomstick, the power of overlooking, that of the evil eye. These were concomitant to druidic practices. So that for Watkins, it maybe that the ancient sighting methods were condemned as sorcery by the early Christian missionaries; see op. cit. n.11, at p. 27.

19 ibid., p. 84.

Consider that law occupies a set of high and significant spots in Watkins's totemic geography. For Watkins, it is the providence of nature that gives law its sovereign place in the prehistoric scheme of things. The primary sighting points were all situated on elevated ground. Hills, mounds and tumps were also sites for open air assemblies and folk-moots (remember these moots are now for law students to exercise a severely restricted form of imaginary business).[20] Assemblies were held on top of hills since hills provided the most visible landmark, points of maximum concentration, the origin-terminus of all traffic. The first rule of legal architecture – build high – springs, not from a sense of proximity to a transcendental divine, but from what is provided by the earth itself, by the incline, anticline and syncline of hills as the most visible and findable location. For those who touted the ley routes, assembly hills also marked the points from which vision was considered to be at its most powerful and from which primitive man could map out all routes before tracks were laid. The whole ley system, in other words, was sighted from these legal assembly points dotted throughout the land.

In Watkins's telling, druids honoured the bond between the earth and the law by leaving reminders upon the surface of the land. The most obvious expression of this system of honour lies in the sacred act of naming key places. Fingay hill (thing-hangr hill), for example, is where thing-rites were held. The name Merry Hill near Belmont, Herefordshire "gives a clue to its use as an assembly point and folk-moot."[21] More obviously, perhaps, "a hill called Lawton is said to have been the place where Macbeth dispensed laws." More interestingly, the use of the word "lady" (as in Lady Hill, Lady Mead, Lady Lift) might be a corruption of "law-day". Laugh Lady Oak in Herefordshire he suggests is where a court leet used to meet, presided over by a lawman or "laughman".[22] These places were not simply sites of law. Their names marked the places where the Earth's natural features had permitted the law to be carried out.

In other instances, places carry the memory of legal events. Madehurst village in Sussex is the speech hill where sheriffs heard tourns for rape. Longtown Castle on the Welsh Marches has a gallows mound and

> 'the memory of the last gibbeting (of a wife-poisoner, and "there was another lady in it") is still kept up, for all that summer no one on Abergavenny market would buy their butter from Longtown valley – on account of the flies!'[23]

Once established upon the land, and by permission of the earth, law seems to infect the environment by becoming one with the natural order of things.

20 Open air councils (the thing) were for Gomme institutions of deep antiquity. They were Roman, pre-German, even pre-Aryan forerunners of the witenagemot. op. cit. n. 13, at p. ix.

21 op. cit. n. 6, at p. 14.

22 op. cit. n. 11, at p. 144.

23 ibid., at p. 71.

More emphatically, Watkins cocks an ear to druidic rites and the weave between Earth and law is expressed in the very naming of the system as a system of "leys". Each alignment, as noted by Watkins, ran through places whose names contained, either as prefix or more commonly as suffix, the Anglo-Saxon monosyllable "ley" (for example, Weobley, Wormsley, Madley, Ley Hill, Tupseley, etc.). Etymologists generally take the word "ley" to mean "field" or "pasture" and would give short shrift to any other derivation of the word. However, an alternative connection proves irresistible to Watkins. The common expression "the lay of the land", he states, is not used to mean "the pasture of the land". The word "lay", for Watkins (the photographer), meant "survey" and came to join a set of words linked to the Latin *lucendo*. In early English, he adds, the now-obsolete word "leye" meant "flame, blaze, fire".[24] The connection to light and vision gives over to a sense of aim. So that "ley", he continues, comes to mean a "sight line". Weavers retain this sense of the word since a ley in looming refers to straight threads. The crossing of each straight thread produces a lease,[25] so that, according to his indefatigable search for correspondences, the prefix/suffix "ley" used in place names might be nothing other than a corruption of the word "law". And the term "lease" suggests nothing other than those points where law is carried out by permission of the earth. Naming supports the imaginary bond; etymology supports the yarn.

IV.

Run Spindles. This is the pattern of the age to come
Virgil[26]

If Watkins attends to the creation and naming of ley lines as proof of a consecrated relationship between law and Earth it is because like all good storytellers of imagination he is an evidencer. He convinces by connecting shallows of solid fact to mythological depths. Nowhere is the solidity of fact more expressed than in his account of the marker and boundary stones that are to be found set on the leys. These stones provided secondary sighting points insofar as they helped keep track of the direction of any given ley: "The way was planted at intervals with stones frequently placed at crossing points of two leys." [27]

Composite in matter and hybrid in purpose, stones neatly provided points of intensities. Gifted by and hewn from the earth they were both signifiers and sacred objects in themselves. Marking the point where surface life met the earth, they provided sites for oblations, sacrifices and other pagan rituals that required

24 op. cit. n. 11, at p. 160.
25 "the baton of a loom is called a ley and the crossing of the threads is called the lease", ibid., at p. 161.
26 Virgil, 'The Golden Age Returned', *Eclogues*, op. cit. n. 4, at p. 42.
27 op. cit. n.11, at p. 23.

the use of ancient pieces of outdoor furniture. They were also, in Watkins's account, symbolic sites for less vertiginous open air courts than those found at the top of moot hills.

It is, however, their function as boundaries that finds a significant place within this imaginary jurisprudence. Change Stones, at least in Watkins's telling, did not mark boundaries of private landholdings but were rather common meeting points, places where two groups of inhabitants from adjoining lands could meet and trade, gossip and cavort, dispute and kill. Sites of meetings and assemblies are what gave the boundary its sacred character. A quote from the medieval Welsh chronicler Geoffrey of Monmouth makes the same point (coincidentally when writing about the Hereford–Welsh border albeit much later than Watkins's period of concern): "the prophet [Isaiah] inveighs against those who occupy their lands right up to the boundary … and those that join house to house, that lay field to field, till there be no place."[28] Again, the Welsh law book compiled in the tenth century under the command of *Hywel Dda* (Howel the Good, King of Deheubarth, in case you are wondering) reflects an idea that is also found in Roman law: "Whoever shall breach a meer [boundary stone] upon the land of another person, let him pay three *kine camlwrw* to the king and let him restore the meer to its former state."[29]

Boundaries are consecrated because meetings are not to be taken lightly. Everything first meets at the sacred stone. That is the first meaning of the boundary. And, it is not just people who meet at the meer. Earth meets law and locks together a deep structure around which further meetings take place. Watkins notes the syncretic contact between paganism and Christianity since, predictably (or less speculatively), they became sites on which the early Christians would eventually build their churches. They "became objects of interest, superstition, and genuine veneration, and as such were utilized on the introduction of Christianity."[30] Christianity mixed with folk rites and tribal juridicalism. From within the field of an imaginary jurisprudence, these boundary sites are precisely the sites where a cross-fertilisation of customs took place between neighbouring populations. These sites mark the places where the dooms of the thanes and reeves met the customary laws of the Welsh, where customs cross-fertilised.

Hard stone, the very matter of Earth, is what allowed customs to evolve into common law. In this imaginary retelling, the destiny of law is propelled by deep earth memories, subterranean patterns and the crystallisation of rock. Earth

28 *Isaiah* 5.8 cited in Geoffrey of Monmouth, *History of the Kings of Britain* (London, Harmondsworth: Penguin 1970) at p. 103. The prohibition against moving these stones is still in place in the 16th century although by then the sense of a boundary's purpose has certainly changed: "it is the unjust judge that is the capital remover of landmarks, when he defineth amiss of lands and property." Francis Bacon, 'Of judicature' in *Essays* (London: Folio Society, 2002), pp. 192–196.

29 'The Gwentian Code' in *The Ancient Laws and Institutes of Wales*, Ch. XXXII, p. 765 (Commissioners of Public Records, 1841).

30 op. cit. n. 6, at p. 8.

assumes legal form. It transforms itself into the leys of the country and evolves – via the de-lays of long-surviving moots, shifting druidic rites and worship of igneous forms – into common law. The permanence of the earth is what allows for what the Welsh call the *fflwcs* of law. Everything on it is adaptable and open to the *newidd* (look it up/guess).

Watkins might well be regarded as a revelator, an epiphanist in brogues rather than sandals, or an overheated tweedy crackpot. He was, however, no theophanist. In his account, law's provenance is a matter of inscendence rather than transcendence. An imaginary conclusion would be that the destiny of law is either to be haunted by the chthonic energies that lie deep below the leys or to be sucked back into the deep layers of ossified mineral form. But to provide an imaginary conclusion on Watkins's own imaginary story would be simply jurisprudence by another name.

2

A QUIET AND SECRET PLACE – AN ENQUIRY ON THE DREAMER GOD, A GOD WITHOUT A NAME*

Pierre Legendre

In the nineteenth century, fragments of a missing manuscript were discovered in the attic of the English cathedral of Lincoln, where canonistic writings from the Middle Ages are conserved. These twelfth century pages reproduce a long passage from a text that had previously been identified in an annotated version [*version glosée*], whose date remains uncertain, found in the Bamberg State Library in Germany.

Tracing back, with a certain detective's flair, the unknown author of these investigations left erudite notes behind, which were also disinterred by chance. They reveal the nature and provenance of the work to which the fragments, that had circulated across Western Europe, belong. The text is written on scrolls of papyrus, piously conserved by a monastery, without any particular theological affiliation, located in Greater Syria, near Aleppo. In the twentieth century, an English scholar, whose identity is known only as someone from Colonel T. E. Lawrence's entourage, transferred the precious relic to one of the constituent colleges of the University of Oxford. The name of the college that possesses it is known only to the authorities.

An accompanying note of the scrolls, filed together with a translation of the Syriac into Greek and Latin at a later date, lays down the following condition: whomever should study the original text, or its translation, will have to remain anonymous and make public only fragments of it. It is for this reason that the complete work is only read within an erudite circle of selected scholars. They transmit its totality as though it were an initiation. The reason for this would be that too large a publication, through the academy or journalism, would jeopardise the certainties that have founded the West ever since its conversion to Christianity.

* Translated by Serene Richards.

With a view to drawing attention to this text from international scholars, until recently reserved to a knowledgeable elite from Europe and America, I was given access to a large number of extracts from the work through a special mandate. I give a generous account of the extracts in a manner that leaves the ultimate substance of the text intact.

★★★

By way of an introduction, the discoverer of the work warned the reader thus:

> *Do not ask anymore: who is God? Nor: does God exist?* Henceforth, any answer will disappoint you. Be content to follow the rites of your tradition, or if they are missing, embrace free thought. And ponder the formula of the Irishman John Scotus Eriugena who knew of the beyond of Christian Revelation and gave pride of place to a *super-essential Nihilum* [*Nihilium suressentiel*]. *Accept the emptiness of your condition.*

I add my commentary. This learned theologian of the ninth century was treated as *mad* by the Holy See in the thirteenth century. Impossible to digest, Eriugena's work is, we are told, pantheistic; it does not reject the plurality of gods. However, after more than a thousand years of reflection on the subject, a twenty-first-century professor-pope has rehabilitated it. Sign of an era that rejects the principle of non-contradiction by practising the yes–no, the incredible repentance of Pope Benedict XVI wishes to ignore *the evolutionary path of the West; today condemned to sink into its old certainties …*

In our time, when thoughts on the existence of gods, these shadows of society, has been banished, poetry decays. An irresistible movement carries us toward a universal boredom, we no longer understand the need for seemingly irrational rituals, or religious fantasy.

Nonetheless, subjected to the necessity of producing ceremonies, to invent a cult of emblems, ultra-modernity must resort to a subterfuge: *orchestrating stealth gods* – science, technology, economy – the *deities of commerce*, enunciators of an industrial religion, where, in Europe-America, sacerdotal robots will replace rabbis, priests, pastors, imams.

The Oxford scrolls illuminate this movement like a prophecy. They are not a sacred scripture of the biblical or qur'anic sort, but an unveiling of knowledge about the gods, on their nature and function, by a text presented under the name: *Master of Wisdom*; but, in reality, composed between the second and the third century post Christum in a school of Gnostic thinkers, hitherto unknown. We are dealing with a complex testimony, relating to a brutal truth, to which I, in turn, will testify in this enquiry.

★★★

The Master of Wisdom is distinguished from other schools by the persistent evocation of the "god without a name", sometimes simply referred to as "the silent sign". What is important here is to grasp what the thinkers of this school meant by that.

They tell us of an undefinable divinity, whose function would be to assume the obscure, the indiscernible, the infinite, who is lost in the abyss of a nothingness. As such, the god without a name signifies absolute solitude. As a result, he demands nothing, asking for neither worship, nor sacrifice. But this in no way implies that he is outside of divinity; one proof is that he is always surrounded by guardian angels, watching over his eternal rest.

The thinkers of this school also speak to us using *the metaphor of a sleeping god, devoted to reverie.*

This god does not dream in a human manner, since he is without desire and never awakens to a given reality, and if he is unconscious, he is entirely so. His nature is to be in his place, he is this place itself – the place of reverie, coveted by febrile and vagabond gods who, one after another, disappear into the abyss that we call "history" ...

To approach this mystery, we must compare this place to the empty stage of a theatre. Would it be a scene where no event ever takes place? What do the thinkers of the school have to say about this?

They use numerous detours to teach *the mode of acting of the dormant god*, that henceforth we can call the *Dreamer God* if we follow, step by step, the teaching of the initiates. First of all, we learn that this god is supreme and indifferent to the human world – *a world that he did not create*, but which would not exist were it not for his inspiration. *Inspiration* here means from this supreme god, above all conceivable gods, and who thinks in reverie, emanate fantastical images, without consistency with reality but inspiring a *second god*, inferior by nature, *the divine worker, the creator of our tragic world.*

***

Emanations, this is the mode of acting of the supreme god: *he dreamt space and time.* In this way, we are able to follow the thinkers of the school when they evoke the birth of poetry. Since the images emanating from the Dreamer God, from this silent sign, carry the trace of infinite divinity, that is to say, for men, *the trace of a primary nothingness* – which theologians and liturgists transform into a *nostalgia for infinity.*

Poetry is devoted to the task of seizing the infinite of time and space, under all its forms of writing: the recited poem, music, dance, the buildings of the architect, the immensity of rituals, but also the mathematical passion and the task of mastering the logic that sustains the universe ... dissatisfied with its animal condition, in ignorance of being the plaything of the second god, of the creator of the universe, humankind unceasingly seeks consolation.

***

Let us be guided by the Master of Wisdom, who instructs us on the hidden sense of the term Emanations, transmitted like an enigma by the Gnostic sects. Regarding the Dreamer God, the *fantastical images drawn from his reverie* become scenarios for the scattered and jealous gods who, for millennia, circulate in our cosmic universe. All of a sudden, we understand the privilege of the divine worker, creator of the human world, who was able to capture, like a mirror, the emanations of the solitary god … and founding the adventures of monotheism, whose beneficiary is the dominant West.

I emphasise this point: the monotheistic domination, crystallised by the history of European Christianity and the effective inheritors of Roman imperialism. Following the theological and political wrangling that made of the middle ages the crucible of our ideals, the formula "*Dominium Mundi*" became the founding emblem of the powers of technology. The pitiful truth of the destiny of our species is thus unveiled, battling against the hellish competition organised by the creator, an irritable and vindictive god, though loving to his followers, as described in the Oxford text. For these Gnostic thinkers, the idea of a god coexisting with evil is untenable, so is the conception of a unique god, inevitably confronted with an endless struggle to triumph over his rivals.

At the time when the scrolls, piously conserved in England, were composed, the Christian revelation of a god-man was already, undoubtedly, the subject of, at times bloody, controversy, since it was necessary to square the circle. Therefore, a prophecy was circulated, according to which God would be born "*without father, without mother, without genealogy*". For centuries, the Christianised West commented on this astonishing discourse, which, under the influence of an all-powerful science, has, for today's deified individual, become a technical banality …

***

Far removed from the mysticism of sacred choreographies, which served as the guarantors of transmissions on the African continent, and equally unfamiliar to the stagings of nothingness characteristic of the religions of Asia, the structures of thought constructed by monotheists have as their horizon a life beyond death … thought to be happiness perfected.

Devoid of desire, the Dreamer God, in his function of assuming the obscure, the indiscernible, represents the threat of knowing too much about the fate of man. That is why, after having conceived of a creator god, about whom we do not know what he does outside of ourselves, Western humanity now prefers to rely on the optimism that the technique of machines brings with itself.

Under these circumstances, the incommunicado of the questions traversing the Oxford text is more important than ever.

NOTE

This inquiry resembles *an a-theological, and slightly blasphemous, tale*. It is inspired by a painting by Michael Kenny (1941–1999) entitled: "Petra Genetrix

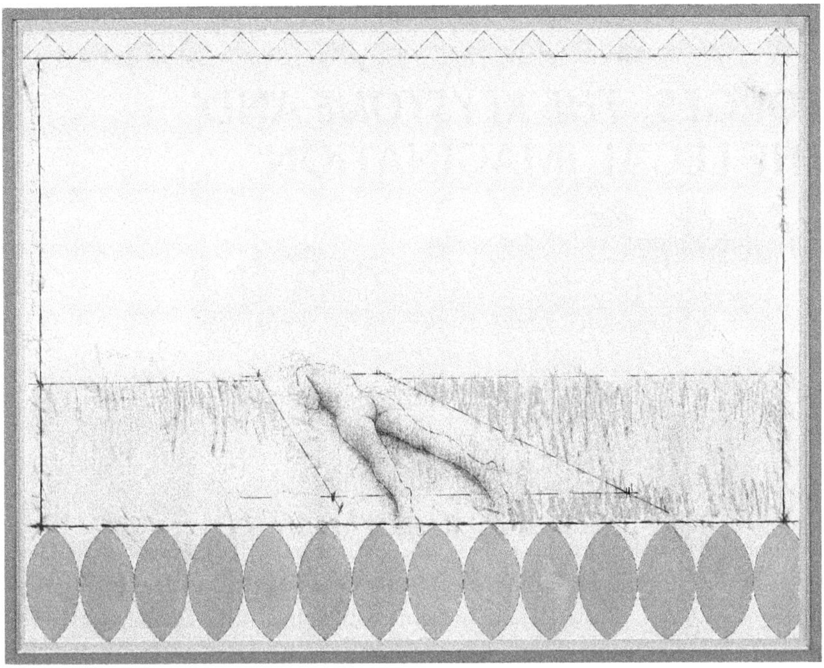

FIGURE 2.1 Michael Kenny "Petra Genetrix in a quiet and secret place"

in a quiet and secret place." This painting suggests that the human being carries within itself a dreamer god: under whose tutelage, each one of us enters into life, linked to this embrace.

The deities carry the mark of works of art. Readers will easily guess my companions: Rilke, Valéry, Bataille, Borges, Jünger ... and other scholars who are dedicated to scrutinising Gnostic constellations.

3

BORGES, *THE KEYSTONE* AND THE LEGAL IMAGINATION

Tobias Smith

The literary confabulator Jorge Luis Borges is arguably the most "imaginary" writer of the last century. From the explicitly fanciful bestial gallery of *The Book of Imaginary Beings* to the implicitly figmentary human menagerie in *Ficciones,* Borges, a prodigious publisher, conjured into the world a literary reality that stretches beyond his own texts. His fantasies describe people, places and even books whose presence remains uncorroborated, yet his chimeras are nonetheless generative in the world, inspiring a bewildering array of thought movements and intellectual "turns". More striking still, this author of self-conscious mendacity is cited not only in the inventive disciplines such as literary studies, but also in the empirically constrained annals of the social sciences. The essay *The Analytical Language of John Wilkins*, for example, contains the *Celestial Emporium of Benevolent Knowledge,* a fictitious Chinese taxonomy that serves as provocation for Michel Foucault's classic epistemological broadside: *The Order of Things*. Given his wide-ranging influence in the academy, it is odd that Borges has not been more fully embraced by legal scholars. Acolytes often point to Borges's biography: his bibliophilic youth and librarian adulthood. But Borges's father was not only a bookhound, he was also a lawyer, and jurisprudence is a theme that runs through Borges's works. In this brief essay I consider the contribution made to legal studies in the short story, *The Keystone.*

The Keystone, in familiar Borgesian style, recounts the history of a heresy. Or, more accurately, it recounts the double-history of a double-heresy. The reader is told of a translation of a German compendium, obtained by accident at a bookshop in Geneva in 1906; this compendium, in turn, refers to a Gnostic order that persisted for centuries within the church itself. The order, known either as the Keystone or the Corner Masons, teaches a kind of reverse divinity (a "subtly inverted *telos*"), in which God, who is all, sprang *sui generis* from nothing. It is *this* creation, and not the story of Genesis, which serves for the Corner Masons as the true divine spark, the light in darkness, the first miracle to be praised. The existence of God, in his omnipotence, is irrefutable evidence of *creatio ex nihilo*. The Corner Masons are theist, and yet their conviction in a godless creation (a "move unmovered", a "Hollow Christ") is a polar contrast to church orthodoxy. The sect's esoteric worship practices include subsuming crosses and votives in sand and ritually consecrating exfoliated skin, depilated hair and other human detritus in wet soil.

The compendium documents the trial and excommunication of priest Adolphus Valenti. We are told that at his trial, Valenti defends his Keystone tenets with two arguments that flip the classic proofs of God. First, Valenti invokes the metaphor of the clock tower in the square. He reasons that a clock is made from parts: a hand, a gear, a mount. And these parts are, in turn, made from more basic elements: iron, glass and wood. If we reduce these parts yet further, we come, inexorably, to nothing. He argues that for a device so complex to derive, at its core, from nothing, is proof of "the divinity of ineffability". Second, he argues, invoking Aquinas no less, that whatever we can hold a clear idea of must exist, including, of course, God. So too, he states, we may have the idea of a world without God, and therefore that world too must exist. Therefore, God necessarily does not exist, and yet he also does. This conundrum, he says, is proof of the majesty of the emptiness in the heart of the divine.

Valenti, we learn, does not come to a good end. He is excommunicated. He becomes a miller and eventually expires of a respiratory ailment following (it is implied) from grinding grain. Valenti's end invokes both an irony – the disgraced theologian meets his maker while reducing the natural to smaller and smaller parts – and also a sly reference to the death of Valenti's intellectual foil, Spinoza.

There is a second protagonist in the story, the literary figment of Johann Merkel, the man from whom this Gnostic compendium is obtained in Geneva. Merkel, we are told, was a late contemporary of Herbert Spencer who embraced the teachings of the Corner Masons. In a rejoinder to Spencer, Merkel proposes a philosophy that might be called proto-devolutionism. He envisions a natural order in the shape of an inverted pyramid, with humans not as the apex, but the foot. As the burgeoning field of natural science uncovered increasingly simple biological organisms, Merkel philosophised a hierarchy that traces a search for the holy from below, rather than from above. If, as Nietzsche suggests, God is made in "man's image", and not the other way around, then "man" in turn comes from dirt, a kind of first earthen golem. It is that which is beneath us, the derivation from which we spring, that most deserves our reverence. For Merkel, this process proceeds scientifically to the simple organisms, and below them, inert matter, and below that, the noumenon of the great unbound.

Jurisprudence is pervasive but oblique in *The Keystone*; the trial of Valenti is both a vindication of the Enlightenment, with its turn against the ecclesiastical court, and also a rebuke of the foundational legal arguments on which the *Philosophes* defend their values. Natural law, with its appeal to the likeness of God and its *a priori* proofs, misunderstands the truth of the universe, in which the majesty of faith, no less than that of justice, resides in its baselessness. It is this point which is driven home in the quip, delivered by Merkel during the passing of the book, that extolling the godhead as the apogee of the holy is as "building a house by first gathering the roof thatch". A jurisprudence of *The Keystone* is, thus, allergic to any notion of first principles, or root meaning, even as it endorses law as a meaningful tradition.

If Borges is critical of natural law, he is equally critical of radical theoretical rejoinders, including both those of his own time and, presumably, those that have embraced him since his death. Rather than being merely absurd (an existential reading), whimsical (a post-modern gloss), materialist (critical legal theory) or contingent (the new legal history), the legal theology of *The Keystone* is unremittingly reverent. It extols the certitude of the substancelessness at the centre of law, without dismissing the endeavour as therefore mere language games or "play". The position might best be likened to that of Nagarjuna, the third-century Buddhist innovator of the Madhyamaka School, who found a middle way out of both the superficial fixation of perceptual reality and a doctrinarian reification of emptiness. In fact, Borges is reputed to have read Nagarjuna, along with many other classical treatises of Eastern philosophy.

Why have legal scholars not been more eager to seriously engage works such as *The Keystone*? There are at least three reasons for this. First, reverence for the law is out of fashion. While rabble-rousers such as E. P. Thomson suggested that bare law might serve some emancipatory function as a check on rank hypocrisy, the overwhelming academic mode, from legal realism on, remains aloof cynicism. A Borgesian reading lends the law too much weight. Second, although scholars are at pains not to revere the law, they must also take great pains not to treat it too lightly. That is, the certitude of some base – common law, the rational code – provides ballast against a creeping worry that there is no firmament to hold the law in place. Classics like *Pierre Menard, Author of the Quixote* and *A Survey of the Works of Herbert Quain* in some sense make up precedent as they go along. These stories provoke the deep dread held in confidence by every young attorney that he or she might cite a case for a point of law and find in fact that one had only conjured the whole pin citation in a late-night-discovery-induced dream. Finally, it may be that imagination is itself antithetical to the law. Literary whimsies such as *The Keystone* do what law should not, which is dwell too much – and with too much pleasure – on what might be otherwise.

4

A TRIPTYCH OF LAWLESSNESS

Stephen Webster

I. Preamble

This essay is about the rules and laws of science, and the way they let us down. I will make the unusual argument that, for science to be ethical, a strong element of lawlessness is needed. But what is an ethical science? Amongst other things, it is one where a scientist's individual autonomy, intellectual and otherwise, is harmonised with social responsibility. This happy balance is somewhat threatened by the realities of a high-pressure research culture. Professional anxiety, therefore, gives a background hum to my argument. However, my more explicit theme concerns the laws of science, and their grip on the imagination of scientists. I explore, in particular, the idea that the image of a lawlike science lessens the ability of researchers to see what is right and good in their work. As a corrective I consider an alternative, lawless conception of science. To make this vision of science as effective as possible, I conceive a magnificent painted triptych, filled with examples and allegories. It will hang in the foyers and even the laboratories of our science institutes and is called "The Triptych of Lawlessness".

My argument is roundabout and indirect. Perhaps lawful science is best not confronted head-on: the task is too great. For the rhetoric of science as an orderly and therefore reliable activity is very dominant. Both in research culture, and in public, we portray science as a rule-bound relation between the causal systems of nature, and the coolly objective experiments and models of scientists. Of course, ever since Thomas Kuhn and the 1962 publication of his *Structure of Scientific Revolutions,*[1] there have been voices prising open the workings of science, showing it to be filled with a myriad of bustling and hard-to-manage social

1 Kuhn, Thomas S. (1962) *The Structure of Scientific Revolutions*, Chicago: Chicago University Press.

forces. And as we shall see, long before Kuhn, various sceptics and critics of the Enlightenment had cast doubt on the ability of science to deliver certainty or be the unquestioned model of human rationality. Yet, all things considered, science retains its hold on our imagination as a thing capable of rising above the human condition.

The reputational support of science has many aspects. Two are worth pointing out straightaway. When we esteem science for its reliable descriptions of nature and its continuous success, we attribute these achievements to the strict austerity of scientific method. Prominent too, like a reproving and time-efficient mentor, ticks the rigid metronome of the scientific life. These two together – a strict method and a rather austere view on professional norms – are central to our image of science. Science, we might say, has little sympathy for the messiness of life, and looks instead to the comfort of the rule book. However often we accept there are social factors in science, we give more attention to its stern interest in patterns and in regularity – in smart guesses and neat interventions. For what is a new vaccine, if not an understanding of the enduring biology of a virus, and its predictable impact on a human? Further, though we know that vaccine scientists work quickly, they must work with care, follow rules of health and safety, and seek the informed consent of their experimental subjects. By being lawful, we might say, science makes its discoveries. Even when the social and personal aspects of science are widely recognised as powerfully influential, when for example there is some ethical upset, we never see these circling distractions as core to scientific knowledge. Often enough we come to the conclusion that these are moments when things have gone wrong simply because the rules of scientific method and the norms of the decent scientist have unfortunately been transgressed. Scientists have been lured into the traps society lays for them.[2] To put it another way, when science commits some moral error, the mistake was in losing sight of its rules and forgetting the commitment to selfless objectivity and the ways of the community.

My emphasis is practical – indeed it is campaigning. The painting I describe, the Triptych of Lawlessness, is aimed at scientists themselves. It issues no litigious threats. Rather, it makes two friendly suggestions to our partisans of science. Firstly, do not allow yourselves to be hypnotised by the steady and invariant rules

2 In the notorious case of the gene-editing scientist He Jiankui, who in December 2019 was sentenced to three years in jail for multiple ethical transgressions involving experiments on human embryos, part of the scientific community's outrage concerned his giving interviews to Associated Press and putting videos on YouTube before peer review could get any traction on his work. Even with solid science that delivers palpable benefit, public messaging that precedes peer review will always risk censure. On June 20, 2020, during a period when the coronavirus pandemic ensured science news alerts were becoming a dominant part of the news cycle, the eminent doctor and writer Atul Gawande tweeted his impatience at what he saw was a violation of scientific norms: "It will be great news if dexamethasone, a cheap steroid, really does cut death by 1/3 in ventilated patients with COVID-19, but after all the retractions and walk-backs, it is unacceptable to tout study results by press release without releasing the paper."

of science, for they will reduce your ability to understand nature and inhibit your role as ethical actors. Secondly, make central to your work the human touch, and so build a science that finds fuller relationship with society.

II. The triptych of lawlessness

To make its point the triptych is rich with striking and subversive images. No scientist passing by can ignore it. Naturally people stop and look. Laboratory corridors clog, tongues wag, and new friendships spark. Unruly moments, missed appointments and disrupted experiments all inevitably follow. For this is a work of art that makes scientists ponder, and sets questions tugging. In short it slows things down and puts eddies and silent lagoons into the fast-flowing waters of contemporary science. The triptych encourages a research culture where talking, conviviality and the reflective spirit are quite as important as a discovery, a press release or a patent.

Though the delights of conversation are a central virtue in its world view, the triptych does not make slowness an end in itself: those congenial chats among scientists stalled in the corridors will generate new collaborations and new ideas. If the triptych has an end, it is originality and freedom of thought. While slowness and the contemplative spirit look important to that, we can all agree that speed, the accelerative moment, is a key element in any creative activity. The triptych touches a nerve that these days jangles in every scientist, for everyone will admit that in science the reflective habit is being squeezed out of existence. People ask: what happened to the time for thinking, for ethical judgment, for quiet deliberations with colleagues? Why such haste? And what is the cost? The well-known commentator on the pathologies of science, David Colquhoun, puts it this way: "Excessive competition between individuals, journals and universities has reached levels where it's endangering the reputation of science and hurting people."[3]

No one could accuse the triptych of being frivolous. Its subject matter is too important, and its craftsmen and women too committed, for there to be any trivial intent. Nevertheless its mood is light-hearted, even therapeutic. It works by subtraction, by the removal of weight. The heavy burdens we associate with the life of science are one by one questioned and made less necessary. And in this dissolving away of the necrotic aspects of science, the triptych makes use not only of paint but also of philosophy.

III. A philosophical diversion: the three elements of science

The scientists are chatting now and gazing at the triptych. This is the moment to make an intellectual intervention. Therefore, scattered around in deliberate

3 Colquhoun, David (2018) "'*Publish or perish' is a foolish approach*" *Nature*, 553, 18 January, at p. 368.

disarray are booklets and leaflets that put in words the background philosophy that underpins the art. As the first paragraph of each of the leaflets asserts, the triptych, for all its startling imagery, is far from novel: our campaign to prune the reach of scientific law has noble ancestry. Reassured by this sign of conservatism, the scientists begin their homework seriously. Chairs are found, and looking first to the triptych, then to their leaflets, the philosophy lesson begins.

They learn first of the voices of "the counter-Enlightenment", important writers who in opposition to the French encyclopaedists, and indeed the fast-expanding communities of natural philosophers (called "scientists" from around 1835), argued that the clear symmetries of science must not capture all of life, or even the life of learning.

Our pioneer here is Giambattista Vico (1668–1744), the son of a bookseller in Naples, a philosopher, and a very early exponent of the idea that science has limits. Vico was responding to the campaign launched by Rene Descartes (1596–1650), who hoped to put human knowledge on the firmest of footings – indeed make it true and fully certain. From his single atom of proven knowledge "I think therefore I am", Descartes sought to make rule-like propositions ripple out through all of human enquiry, clearing the way to a completely understood world. For Descartes, if some disciplines stubbornly elude such simple methods – history for example – then they should be excluded from serious thought as mere gossip. As he reputedly said, what does a classical historian know about ancient Rome that Cicero's servant girl didn't? Science on the other hand looked more secure because of Descartes' primary assumptions about both nature and science: the first is a mechanism, the second a series of undoubted principles.

Against all this, Vico's rebuttal was his interesting idea that actually historians may face better odds than scientists, when it comes to getting at the truth. Vico's argument, not obviously less plausible than Descartes', is that because history is made by humans it is knowable by humans. In this regard, he suggested, science finds itself at a disadvantage: as they did not make nature, scientists can look at it only from the outside. With history, or literature, or jurisprudence, the enquiring mind can confidently explore their development and determine with some conviction the passage of ideas. It was evident to Vico that the scholar, by virtue both of diligence and empathy, can establish even the very complex causal links that constitute culture. In today's terms, Vico's point is that no scientist can hope to establish with certainty the causes within nature because, unlike the processes within culture, they are completely alien to our humanity. He aimed therefore to show the validity of history and the study of culture. He aimed also to weaken the project, alive and well today, where the style of learning used to find the positions of planets can apply with good hope of success everywhere, including the shifting patterns of society, and the forms of human consciousness. In sum, Vico saw that the simple lines of scientific enquiry, as envisaged by Descartes, when applied to the richness of human life, will likely miss the point and in the process do some damage.

The scientists now begin to read about the Scottish philosopher and famous sceptic, David Hume (1711–1776). Known for his love of the orderly life, Hume was an ally of science: he saw its utility. But just as Vico had been at pains to thwart the ambitions of Descartes, so Hume saw clearly that scientific knowledge could deliver neither certainty nor proof. Whatever the success of science may be, the regularities and laws of nature we discover are merely those we see around us now. Why must they be the same tomorrow? Just because something has been so in the past, it may not be so in the future. Hume was no revolutionary, and he urbanely reassured us that our assumptions about the sun rising tomorrow are still quite reasonable. He helped us with our science, but he put a wobble at its centre.

Absorbed by these philosophical perspectives on the frailties of their learning, the scientists begin to see that science has three elements. Firstly there is the world of "being", of what nature is like, most deeply. In spite of Hume's cautionary note, scientists naturally assume that nature is organised on methodical lines which ramify evenly and unchanging across every area of the universe, forwards and backwards in time. To give examples, this is the belief behind CERN's Large Hadron Collider and which we see at work in Charles Darwin's theory of evolution by natural selection: these are instruments and theories with the ambition to reach far and wide. In a sense, for this line of thinking, nature fundamentally has no areas, no locality. At bottom it is the same everywhere. To use the familiar metaphor, nature is a gigantic clock, made of similar kind of wheels, and running according to a few laws. We may notice a huge variety of different and distracting things: its decoration, its colours, its lights, its chimes and its displays, and of course the annoying inaccuracies and errors that occur from time to time. Yet these are merely surface features, features of manufacture and upkeep, and of human weakness, rather than anything to do with the essence of the clock. If only people could be kept away, the clock would tick perfectly for ever. The echo here is the idea that in nature the fundamental ground of everything is the subatomic field and its rule of law: everything else – cats, trees and cooking – are simply froth.

There is significant scholarship now that doubts the "unity of nature", and therefore the underlying mood that a few grand laws will in principle suffice for its understanding. For these contemporary counter-Enlightenment thinkers the world fundamentally is not so much a seamless field as a plurality of zones, each with its own style of being and set of circumstances. Nancy Cartwright argues that the laws of science have far less extension and far less reliability than we like to imagine. She reminds us of something every scientist tacitly understands: scientific laws work well only when cossetted in laboratories and given every kind of life support. Real nature, Cartwright says, is not ordered. Fundamentally it is higgledy-piggledy, or spotty. As she puts it: "We live in a dappled world, a world rich in different things, with different natures, behaving in different ways [...] For all we know, most of what occurs in Nature occurs by hap, subject to no law at all."[4] If there are rules by which nature organises itself, they are local and various – village bylaws, not international legislation.

Braced by this kaleidoscopic vision of a nature made of many parts, our scientist-philosophers are equipped now to argue about "the world of being". They turn therefore to the second element of science: "the world of knowing". Here the primary question is: "what is scientific knowledge, and how is it made?" Of course the scientists are only too familiar with the rules on how they should organise laboratories in general and experiments in particular. From the age of 11, in schools and in colleges, they have been bewitched by a set of rules. The rules are central, unvarying, foundational. They are called "the scientific method".

But is there "a scientific method"? Might this be another example where science and scientists have over-played the idea of order? Indeed, our scientists, familiar with the toil of daily science, know only too well the haphazard and highly insecure nature of their work. Yet when the progress of science is discussed, a few simple ideas are uttered so often as to almost form a haze: "the graph is flattening", "the evidence shows", "the evidence doesn't show", "it is a matter of testing a hypothesis, of conducting trials", and famously in the UK during the COVID-19 pandemic, "at all times we are guided by the science". Time and again the existence of this method is invoked in the most various of settings. Time and again the scientific method becomes a formula with rather few components. To a degree it resembles elementary maths or deductive logic. And it is very noticeable how ill-equipped and inadequate the concept is, when science comes face to face with matters of social importance.

Questions circulate in the scientists' minds: do we believe that just a few laws fully capture the deep structure of nature? Do we accept also that the production of scientific knowledge is above all a matter of following a few rules? Or is there an irreducible element of human style to every scientific transaction? And lastly, how can we give proper thought, in our laboratory life, to our own lives, to the swirling complications of groups and communities, to the financial and political forces bearing down on science and on us, to our research culture itself?

To the advocates of scientific law, these complexities are external to the making of scientific knowledge, thanks to its rules. In this view, the good scientist is the one who puts them to one side, as distractions. But what are these distractions? And can we even classify them? In the world of science, actually, we have a simple label: these diverse matters are "values". And through this chain of thought, the scientists come to the final part of their philosophy lesson. After the world of being, and then the world of knowing, they now encounter our third philosophical element, the world of values.

4 Cartwright, Nancy (1999) *The Dappled World: A Study of the Boundaries of Science*, Cambridge: CUP, at p. 1.

For lawful science, values are a nuisance, because they are so various. It is not that, in the halls of science, you never bump into values. Certainly you do. It is hard to avoid the manifestos and declarations about research integrity. The problem is that the values allowed have been excessively simplified. Diligence in reading and citing others; reporting work accurately; straight-dealing in peer review: these are among the values of science. You could not disagree with them. But they lack colour. They smell of good management. Our triptych steps in, therefore, to put the matter right. It is exuberant and ill-disciplined, too bright and crowded for some, too obscure and distant for others. The triptych celebrates the subjective experience of science and of nature. There is no sign of regularity. Like paintings by Peter Breughel or L. S. Lowry it teems with life.

IV. Two icons of lawlessness: Darwin and Feyerabend

By reminding scientists of the pleasures of simply lolling about, the triptych makes plain the riches generated by days without plan or purpose. To promote the task, two wise men dominate the three panels. One is Charles Darwin (1809–1882), who developed the fundamental grounding of modern biology, the theory of evolution by natural selection. As we shall see, Darwin is well qualified as a missionary for procrastination: he had a version of his theory in 1839, but published only in 1859, an impressive delay. Our second magus is the philosopher and "knowledge anarchist" Paul Feyerabend (1924–1994). Feyerabend was certainly an advocate for the life-enhancing possibilities of science, but he saw progress as the child of argument and collaboration, rather than of steady and single-minded effort. When Feyerabend writes "We are not far from the truth when saying that the nature of science is still shrouded in darkness",[5] he reminds us that science is not a motorway, but something far more meandering and confusing. Feyerabend, a World War II veteran, above all wanted to remind us of the dangers of rigid thinking and over-reliance on rules. He made his name with his 1975 book *Against Method*, which draws especially on the life and work of Galileo Galilei. Prone to memorable sayings, Feyerabend wrote that there is no rule in science, "[...] however plausible, and however firmly grounded in epistemology, that is not violated at some time or another". Quite often, he went on, the best thing is not only to ignore the rules, but also to do their exact opposite. Having reviewed a number of episodes in the history of science, Feyerabend will allow only one law: "The only principle that does not inhibit progress is: anything goes".[6] And, importantly for the teaching ambitions of the triptych, Feyerabend warns early career scientists against a belief in the scientific method. The myth of

5 Feyerabend, Paul (1978) *Science in a free society*, London: Verso, at p. 73.
6 Feyerabend, Paul (1975) *Against method*, London: Verso, at p. 23.

scientific uniformity, he says, "[...] destroys the most precious gift of the young – their tremendous power of imagination [...]".[7]

While Feyerabend has a deserved reputation for lawlessness, Darwin looks a less obvious advocate for our cause. Darwin was very often a hard worker, and of course no one could doubt his record or his productivity. Yet his torrent of letters and the accounts of his habits together point to the huge value he placed on the slow and discursive life. Often, he blamed his moments of inactivity on poor health, but it is clear that the illness, while genuine, provided good cover for his very strong urge to stay put at home, in a large house in Down, deep in the Kent countryside. All the signs are that a steady love of meandering thought was integral to his work, and indeed his success. We should not see his contemplative style as unproductive, let alone lazy. Rather, he seemed to combine to great effect a wildly various combination of styles: he drove himself hard, but was distracted easily and pleasurably, whether for a few minutes by his children sliding down the banisters outside his study, or for many years by a sudden interest in barnacles. Darwin, and Feyerabend, then, embody the plurality of science: they will be the icons who illuminate our triptych. Let us study in more detail the virtues they represent.

V. Three scientific virtues: reticence, innocence, intimacy

As background for our two unruly apostles, Darwin and Feyerabend, the triptych chooses three themes, to make vivid the role of lawlessness in science. These themes are reticence, innocence and intimacy, all of them virtues rarely mentioned in scientific discourse. They are subjective characters, matters of the self. Yet the triptych will depict their central place in the scientific effort.

Reticence is suggestive of pausing and of holding back. To be reticent is to wait and see, to admit that you understand less than you would like. Intimacy is the notion of closeness, of knowing your object of study in a way that goes beyond measurement. It is the way of being that causes the dividing line between the scientist and nature to fade. Our third virtue, innocence, calls for openness to new ideas, to other peoples and to other cultures. It is the collaborative spirit, where interest in the world has not been distorted by exaggerated self-regard, guardedness and competition. Of course, these three elements of the human touch are beyond the reach of any reductive impulse: no law can contain them. They are without pattern or protocol and will lead our scientific onlookers into new and exciting territories.

In the refreshing world of the Triptych of Lawlessness, the self is central to scientific method. This reverses the normal state of affairs in science, first articulated with legal fierceness by the Elizabethan lawyer and politician Sir Francis Bacon (1561–1626), where your background, your traditions, your immediate feeling

7 Ibid., at p. 45.

for nature and your chatterbox personality, must each be arrested and banished, before you step close to your scientific instruments. Or, as Paul Feyerabend complained: "A person's religion [...] his metaphysics [...] his sense of humour [...] must not have the slightest connection with his scientific activity. His imagination is restrained, and even his language ceases to be his own."[8]

Our busy scientists, already captivated by the bright images of the triptych, scan it methodically from left to right. They come across Darwin first. There on the left panel is the great man, asleep and gently snoring, full-length beneath a tree in his garden. We owe this image to his son Francis, who like all the Darwin children spoke fondly of a father who knew the importance of leisure: "I remember him often lying under one of the big lime trees, with his head on the green mound at its foot".[9] The image is startling: to our scientists, the glorifying of Darwin's snooze must be disturbing. Ordinarily it is wakeful routine and solemn industry that scientists favour as the path to esteem. Yet moments of relaxation are important in our heroic stories of science. For enthusiasts of scientific indirectness, of gaps and chinks and mental drift, the significant point about Archimedes is not his naked run through the streets of Syracuse shouting "Eureka". Much more, it was that heavenly relaxing moment in his bathtub, new thoughts alive in his mind. The lesson is clear: step aside completely, even for a moment, and the ideas will come.

The left panel, with its bold title "Reticence", questions its scientific onlookers: could delay be the herald of eventual glory? Delay is important in most areas of life, but science sees things differently. In science we believe that acting quickly and publishing first is the beginning and the end of success. We can justifiably call this "the first rule of science". Yet Darwin's lime tree, the evolutionist flat out at its roots, makes us think again. Might not acting slowly, or even not at all, be more effective in the long run? And as if to make this unruly thought inescapable, as we stare at the triptych, now we see another image of Darwin. Again, he represents a subversive idea. He is at work in his study, sitting in his chair, which we notice is on wheels, so that he may roll about the room, from bookshelf to specimen table to desk, without the slog of standing up. On the Reticence panel he is reading a book, in fact a copy of his own *Insectivorous Plants,* and it seems he is holding it up proudly, as if he is teaching us a lesson. In the wider context of the Triptych of Lawlessness, the meaning of all this is clear enough, once we remember the celebrated sentence in his autobiography: "My book on 'Insectivorous Plants' was published in July 1875 – that is sixteen years after my first observations. The delay in this case, as with all my other books, has

8 Ibid., at p. 19.

9 Darwin, Francis (ed.) (1887) *Life and letters of Charles Darwin*, London: John Murray. Vol. 1, at p. 116.

been a great advantage to me; for a man after a long interval can criticize his own work, almost as well as if it were that of another person."[10]

The images of the triptych have so far been historical. But can its moral lesson of lawlessness reach scientists often enough described as having the future in their bones? To draw in and persuade our scientists, the triptych links its message also with personal decisiveness and autonomy, and with the fruitful scientific life. And it warns that the lawful following of contemporary scientific norms, with their emphasis on speed, and publishing, and commercial traction, may bring disappointment. The triptych suggests that when Darwin went to sleep beneath his tree it was a natural part of his life as a scientist. The siesta, Darwin decided, would be part of the scientific day.

Darwin's clarity, in choosing different styles of work, will certainly be an inspiration for scientists seeking to invigorate their lives. Darwin's quietude, we see, was not the absence of will power or ambition. On the contrary, it was all part of his direct and opinionated character. We know he went to some lengths to positively defend his quietude, and there are many letters where he firmly declines invitations and meetings. His interest in peace and quiet extended to landscape design too: on the triptych's left panel we see him standing at his study window at the front of his house, contentedly gazing at builders working to lower the road passing by his house. As he told his sister Susan, "The publicity of the place is intolerable". Not only will he lower the road, he explains, but "I have determined to have a six feet six inch wall [...] the whole length".[11] As the rubble is removed, and the road and its pedestrians sink from sight, we see Darwin beginning to relax. Like this he can study quietly, in his own world, with no reminder of the hurrying world without. With his money, his clear-sightedness and his intimacy with his work, he can do his research in the way he wants, at the pace he wants.

By now, to the scientists gazing up at the triptych's pulsing moral messages, uncomfortable truths are emerging. Researchers take as inevitable, as a natural part of science, the scrutiny of the all-seeing eye of university metrics. If you are a scientist you literally are transparent, and therefore in danger of disappearing. Darwin's advice, made visual by the triptych, is striking: "Find a hiding place and try to disappear from view. Whatever may be your six foot wall, build it".

The crowd of scientists, now looking at the central panel, see the image of Paul Feyerabend, with his smiling and crumpled face. For the scientists he is an unfamiliar character: a philosopher of science. Prominent on the panel is an image of his famous book *Against Method*, and various quotes spool out like ribbons. Generally, we know Feyerabend for his unruly attacks on the concept of scientific method which he saw as a snare imprisoning unwary scientists into a

10 Darwin, Charles (2002) *Autobiographies*, London: Penguin, at p. 81.

11 Burkhardt, Frederick and Smith, Sydney (eds) (1986) *The correspondence of Charles Darwin*, Vol. 2, at p. 360.

life of tedium. The triptych recasts his lawlessness as something agreeable: the virtue of being open to other people and to unfamiliar ideas – the state of innocence, therefore. Beyond his attacks on rules, Feyerabend deplores any tendency for arrogance and defensiveness in the scientific project. Both lead to single-mindedness, the quality Feyerabend is inclined to question. He admires the scientific worldview but only so long as it is a world of many parts. Scientists must listen to others, actively seek out counter-examples, and without prejudice look to compare their ideas with those of others. The middle panel of the triptych is therefore filled with examples of scientists lifting their eyes from their immediate concern, and looking around, innocently.

The scientists staring up at Feyerabend's friendly face, high up on the triptych, warm to him immediately. The way of innocence, the philosopher is saying, will bring new ideas to your research, broaden your professional identity and aid communication with colleagues and non-specialists. To make innocence possible, he signals, we must clear a few things away, starting with the concept of a unifying scientific method. Feyerabend is uncompromising: scientific advancement depends on not doing what you are told. He wrote, "[...] however 'fundamental' or 'necessary' [the rule] for science, there are always circumstances when it is not only advisable to ignore the rule, but to adopt its opposite".[12]

All this is hugely stimulating to the crowd gathered in front. The scientists ask themselves: how can we learn from these surprising notions, and make them relevant to our life scientific? Surrounding Feyerabend therefore is a busy circus of images, together suggesting a renewal of science. The panel describes a world where researchers are better able to connect with, and learn from, the broadest reaches of humanity. If the left and right panels show Darwin vigorously defending his quietude, the central panel shows contemporary scientists finding their style in the company of others. Against those rules devised by Lord Bacon, Feyerabend calls for a way of science where conviviality is as important as any measurement. We see therefore images of an icy Alaska where an Inupiaq hunter and a conservation scientist discuss indigenous knowledge of whale behaviour. Together they are planning a census method that allows a new and more accurate estimate of the population of bowhead whales off the northern coast of Alaska. The issue – and the relationship – became important in 1977, when the International Whaling Commission radically underestimated the number of whales migrating past Barrow. The mistake was caused by scientists assuming bowhead whales would not swim in iced-over waters, and they therefore based their census very narrowly on shore-line observation. The low estimate led to a complete ban on subsistence hunting, reversed only when the scientists and the

12 Feyerabend, Paul (1975), op. cit., at p. 23.

Inupiaq Alaskans, who knew that bowheads would break through ice and take a breath, learned to talk to each other.[13]

A little below these snowy northern scenes we find an image of a clinical researcher intently listening to patients with spinal injuries. What kind of improvement in their day-to-day activity do they most seek, she asks? And what are the important and relevant research questions we should be developing?[14] For Feyerabend, these are signs his garden is at last bearing fruit. Yet he is admonishing us too: we see a jabbing finger. He warns: this participatory science, this science for and with the people, will not fit any simple model. Listening must not become formulaic. It must not become just another rule for researchers. He has other suggestions too: science co-production will fall apart as soon as the hours begin to be counted. You do not put time limits on true conversation.

The tone of the triptych turns dark, as we see how sharing science can quickly go wrong. Feyerabend is pointing now to frightening images of the ruins of L'Aquila, the Italian town hit on April 6, 2009, by a tremor of magnitude 6.3; 309 people died and 20,000 buildings were destroyed. To the astonishment of the world's scientific community six leading Italian geologists, who had been advising the town council, were later charged with manslaughter. For the prosecutors, the issue was not that the scientists had failed to predict the tremor. More, it was that at the time of crisis, when minor shocks were being felt all the time in L'Aquila, official advice given out by the civic authorities was unjustifiably reassuring. The scientists had been clear that with current models no clear assessment of the likelihood of a major tremor was possible; but officials at a town hall technical meeting turned this into reassurance. For one of the L'Aquila residents, Vincenzo Vittorini, the experts overall were too restricted in their vision. They did not think hard about the fragility of L'Aquila's buildings and the likely effect of any major tremor. Nor did they take seriously the fact that for generations the residents of L'Aquila have known exactly what to do in the event of an earthquake: get out of doors, head to the piazza, and spend the night there. In short, a cautious scientific assessment of great imponderables was transformed for reasons of communication strategy into something far too simple. The advice placated the population of L'Aquila, adopted a scientific tone, and neglected to reaffirm the primary value and good sense of the local traditions for earthquake survival. Vittorini argued that the technical committee and the civic authorities together put out a message of "keep calm and don't worry", meaning that many people felt reassured, ignored their cultural traditions, and stayed indoors. (The point is relevant as there had been an alarming, but not destructive tremor at 11pm on April 5th, just a few hours before the disaster hit at 3:30am.) "That's why I feel

13 North Slope (2018) "Bowhead Migration Under the Ice" accessed at http://www.north- slope .org/departments/wildlife-management/studies-and-research-projects/bowhead-whales/traditional-ecological-knowledge-of-bowhead-whales/tek-bowhead-whale-migration on December 15, 2018.

14 Sheehy, Jeff (2018) "Ask patients what to fund" *Nature* 2018, 562: 4th October, at p. 31.

betrayed by science," said Vittorini "Either [the scientists] didn't know certain things, which is a problem, or they didn't know how to communicate what they did know, which is also a problem."[15]

The L'Aquila example is a heightened example of the possible risks of putting the scientific project into dialogue with broader cultural forces. But Feyerabend reminds us of the vital importance of the attempt. Other images show the balance between scientific and public expertise being much more successfully synthesised. Feyerabend was only being prescient when, back in the 1970s, he declared "Laymen can and must supervise science".[16] For the triptych, scientific innocence, leading to a broader connectivity with the public, depends on a voluntary softening of its methodological rules. As we look at the triptych we see Feyerabend proudly holding several issues of the premier science journal *Nature,* all of them containing examples of science turning towards Feyerabend. Look, he is saying, even the bosses agree with me now.

Feyerabend, we can see, is reading out extraordinary declarations from *Nature* magazine. A special edition, from 2018, is filled with examples of "co-production" in science and reads like a manifesto for power-sharing: "Science shared: when communities and researchers work together". One headline, introducing a series of case studies, announces that "Those who were once the subjects of scientific enquiry are increasingly in the driver's seat". In a similar spirit, a feature article is labelled: "From fishers to patients, stakeholders take the reins". Finally, an editorial nods complete approval with a leader titled: "Power to the people".[17] And indeed the contributors constantly note that if you want to listen to others, you need to relinquish power. You need to talk, and to build trust.

All the contributors note the lawlessness of their work. Co-production, writes Carolina Vera, a climate scientist working with Argentinian smallholders, "[...] can be circuitous and unpredictable, but ultimately is more worthwhile".[18] Others stress why they have to relinquish power, abandoning the idea that there is one scientific method for all disciplines and all locations. Instead, we learn from these pages of *Nature* that there is no standard formula and no protocol when communities are so different and their problems so precise and local. Blanket a community concern with the method of science, and you likely conceal what is important. No wonder, up there on the central panel, Feyerabend is smiling.

Finally, looking at the right-hand panel, we see that Darwin is taking the first of his daily walks. He has set off across the garden towards a small wood he planted on his land. It can still be seen today. If you do visit, you will find circling the wood a perimeter path known as the Sandwalk. From here immense views

15 Hall, Stephen S. (2011) "Scientists on trial: *At fault?*" *Nature*, 477, 15 September, pp. 264–269, at p. 266.

16 Feyerabend, Paul. (1978), op.cit. p. 96.

17 See *Co-production of research: a Nature special issue* (2018) *Nature* 562, 4 October, pp. 23–33.

18 Vera, Carolina (2018) "Farmers transformed how we investigate climate" *Nature* 562: 4 October, p. 9.

of the grass chalk fields of Kent open up, but of course it is just as possible to gaze into the wood, a tangled affair of deciduous trees, holly and low scrub. And this is how we see Darwin, on the triptych: he has stepped from the Sandwalk, is immobile, and is listening intently to birdsong. Suddenly something remarkable happens. A group of young squirrels, racing across the floor of the wood, are running up Darwin's leg, while he remains completely still. Again, we know this story from his son Francis, who remembered his father's great stealth and his ability to become solemnly immobile: "It was on one of these occasions that some young squirrels ran up his back and legs, while their mother barked at them in an agony from the tree".[19]

Intimacy, our third virtue, is a paradox to science. In the legends told about the workings of science, one of the most important traditions is that there is a clear separation between the investigating scientist and the object: this is one of the meanings of "objectivity". In our myths, the findings of science are validated by the professional community, not by the individual alone, and thus belong to the community. In that sense, "the closeness" of a scientist to their work, and the idea of scientific ideas being personal and subjective, are notions that do not fit easily into standard descriptions of scientific method. Although we can admit that intimacy in science goes against the rules and deserves a place therefore on the Triptych of Lawlessness, every scientist knows that close and patient investigation is one of the pleasures of their craft. Scientists often report their contentment in quiet work, and it is no oxymoron to describe a scientist as having a "feel" for what they do. It is an idea given the fullest possible attention in Michael Polanyi's classic account *Personal Knowledge*[20] and even more vividly in the biography of the cytogeneticist Barbara McClintock, *A Feeling for the Organism*.[21] The Triptych alerts the scientists to these themes of scientific intimacy by showing Darwin, a biologist, turning into a tree. The self (Darwin), and the object (the squirrels), have fused thanks to Darwin's impeccable skills as a watchful and unobtrusive natural historian. For those young squirrels Darwin and his trees are one and the same. No doubt Darwin himself often enough forgot the distinction between himself and nature.

According to Francis, before he took his walk, Darwin called first at his greenhouse. He looked at any germinating seeds or experimental plants "which required a casual examination, but he hardly did any serious examination at this time".[22] The description is evocative: early in the day, still close to his dreams, Darwin is just looking, no doubt adjusting the pots and the creeping tendrils. He avoids measurement and intellectual labour; the ruler remains in its drawer. Very likely Darwin has fallen into a pleasant reverie. He once wrote "I am getting

19 Darwin, Francis (ed.) (1887), op. cit., at p. 115.

20 See Polanyi, Michael (1958) *Personal knowledge: Towards a Post-Critical Philosophy*, Chicago: Chicago University Press.

21 See Fox Keller, Evelyn (1984) *A Feeling for the Organism*, San Francisco: W. H. Freeman.

22 Darwin, Francis (ed.) (1887), op. cit., at p. 114.

very much amused by my tendrils, it is just the sort of niggling work which suits me and takes up no time and rests me [...]".[23] It is no surprise that Darwin, emerging from the greenhouse and setting off for the Sandwalk, is in meditative mood. We can forgive the squirrels their mistake.

VI. On hinges

The triptych, of course, does not lay down the law. It is contradictory and uneven and represents contrasting themes. And when we fold up the triptych to move it to another corridor, we notice the hinges are squeaky, and draw attention to its disunity. On the one hand Darwin seeks solitude by building a wall; on the other, Paul Feyerabend encourages scientists to keep talking, and so keep their innocence. While in one panel Darwin simply ignores publishing for decades, in another a scientist adds to his author list people who have no scientific qualifications whatsoever and sends the manuscript to *Nature*.

With so dynamic and unstable a message, the triptych will reward repeated viewing. The images take time to study and invite long-lasting thought. Naturally, then, the triptych is built to last. If the hinges are squeaky, they also are robust, and signal that the themes of the triptych are permanent and should be explored. The hinges allow the triptych to stand proudly upright but allow it also to be folded up and safely moved to another corridor or institution, and so continue the campaign. In a new environment it will once again work its magic, slowing the scientists and refreshing their craft.

The hinges are not simply mechanisms or support structures. They also communicate, for they link together the messages of the three panels and invite comparison. They join the panels not just physically, but also morally. By connecting the panels, the hinges encourage our scientists to link and contrast the diverse stories. These hinges may squeak, but they are also gilded and gleaming, attracting attention to themselves and pulling the scientific gaze from one panel to another. Feyerabend and Darwin; walls and whales; squirrels and lime trees – all are made neighbours by the hinges. The spectator scientists conjure different combinations in their minds. And in the absence of a single message each will make their own interpretation.

VII. Epilogue

The scientists, having stopped to look at the crowded world of the triptych, are all now talking. Yet, they cannot delay re-entry to their laboratories for too long: alas the clock is ticking. As they set off down their various corridors, thoughts and conversations linger. And these thoughts seem to be of three kinds. First, they ponder the issue of character. As a scientist, do you have a style? Does it

23 Ibid., vol 3., at p. 312.

matter what you are like? According to the triptych, character is important and might even be central to that burning topic in science, research integrity. Many rules and codes of conduct are being drawn up these days, to regulate our work. The triptych, suspicious of all rules, asks a better question: what do we mean by a good (rather than a lawful) scientist?

Secondly our scientists contemplate Feyerabend's distrust of the power of science, now backed up by the editors and feature writers of *Nature* magazine. Our scientists are persuaded by the triptych: we too would like to share our science, they say. We too want non-scientists to guide and advise us. First, they ask: what are the power-relations in our research group, in our laboratory? Are they equitable and just and liable to lead to good work? Or are they cramped and unpleasant and likely to hurt people? Shall we put our house in order first?

Thirdly, and with the laboratory door now looming into view, the scientists remember the laughing and prolix Feyerabend, and ask: am I communicative in my science? Innovation depends on innocence, Feyerabend seems to say. And that depends on open and trusting communication. The scientists wonder: can we find a way of discussing our science that avoids the vanity, special pleading and institutional self-aggrandisement that scars so much science communication, and of course wrecks all trust? As the laboratory doors close noiselessly behind the scientists, the Triptych of Lawlessness continues to point the way: towards a style of research where reticence, intimacy and innocence take position not as rules but as three virtues guiding a future science.

5

WHEN DRAGONS DID RISE

C. F. Black

On a frosty spring day, in a little village outside of Oxford, I was happily tapping away on my laptop. My intention was to write a novel based on my adventures of the previous six weeks. I had come to England to visit a druid, meet a Cornish witch and a Bristol wandmaker, and best of all, to view the spring bluebells and Easter bunnies in the Elvendon Woods. But instead of writing of such adventures, my muse began to dictate a most curious prose. I did wonder where was its home?

And so, when the good professor, Peter Goodrich, affronted by the man "who would tweet", did send an invitation to join with him and his *Graeco-British philosopher and gentleman of ease, Thanos Zartaloudis* to fill *The Cabinet of Imaginary Laws* with *wild lucinations in a time of falling laws,* I knew I had received my answer. This was surely the call my muse did hear and so my fingers set forth to lucinate a tale of the land of Albion and the *Brexit* forces that were rising up, like the mythical dragons of old, bent on splitting the land asunder.

***

When dragons did rise,
it was strangely quiet down on the ground,
whilst in the air the sweet song of many birds
were there for all to delight.
As though distracting from the fact
not one sighting of the grey squirrel was recalled,
that hooligan trying to run the red squirrel out of the land of Albion.
Nor was there any sign of the badger, mole or hedgehog,
let alone any other of their ground-loving friends.

Something was afoot and it certainly was not – a foot on the ground.
But rather a bustling and shoving for space underground
to hide from the future that befell the land above.
For those who lived upon the land in the human form,
their fate was sealed.

The birdsong changed, from mystical morning
sweetness into a jarred warning.
Some birds dropped from exhaustion,
whilst others found hiding places in
sturdy oaks and giant yews.
Crack!!! There was a terrible screeching sound.
Then came the thunderous sound of the
opening of the land – the land of Albion.
From the tip, all the way down to Oxford
– the centre of Albion, by the ancient accounts.
It stopped right in front of Carfax Tower,
said to be the centre of Oxford and
therefore the belly button of Albion.

As the land shook and the seas tumbled,
the people became humbled
by that they could not control.
They knew their efforts
were mere window dressing
as the flooding inundated all the cities and towns.
Great storms of anger blew across
the frightened and freezing ground.
Yon volcanoes of the northern isles of Iceland
did erupt and spewed out a fog of sulphur
and other killing spices that stung the eyes and made babies cry.

Many thought it was a time when the world
would end and the angels would soon arrive
and save the worthy 144,000 good souls, the bible did tell.
But such dreams they soon learned
belonged to Shakespeare's Puck,
for there were no angels and this was not
the end of the world, but something worse.
Life continued in the most unpleasant of ways.

The crack stopped at the belly button
and went deep underground and
made its way to Marlborough

where the bones of Merlin did lay.
It shook so hard that it woke up his bones
and they began to whiz around.
And before long Merlin did appear quite safe and sound.
He looked about and became concerned
that humans liked to knock each other around.
They had forgotten the Land of Faery
as Tolkien did tell of the *Perilous Realm*.[1]

"A breach has occurred and humans must pay," Merlin did declare.
And so he released the dragons buried so long ago.
With them came a destructive blight and politics became confused.
Merlin's dragons full of smite did lead the politicians
into fight and the people did riot.
The winds heard all the ruckus and
joined in and disturbed those
who wished no part of the unrest.
Illness reigned as most could not cope.
The dragon's hot breath ever present in the air.
Their screeching heard across the land did disturb
every man, woman and child.

To make things worse, across the ocean in a sister nation,
a mad man did arise to shift the world into chaos.
He did flaunt the rule of law and turned it into the law of the tweet.
Tweet, tweet, all day long and into the night,
He did tweet "the law of the tweet".
But he was fake news!
As he was not the cause
but merely an allusion to disguise the real.

For there was another wizard afoot
joined by his wizardy mates.
They had begun to weave their magic in little things.
Little things they made to dance about.
Yes, little things had come to life.
These little things, chattering away to each other
all day long and deep into the night.
They cared not for the rule of law,
It was merely a code gone wrong,
replaced by clever data bots that knew it all.

1 Tolkien, J. R. R. (1993) *Tales of the Perilous Realm*, HarperCollins, London.

These wizards did not care that the dragons
had been set free, for they knew how to
catch them when the time was right.
They enjoyed the fights as it feeds them with
data that gave them might in being able to
predict the future, if not make it all fake.
They had full control over the humans who'd
happily handed over their rights to their past,
present and future.

They were clever these little mites
as they knew how to disguise themselves
by becoming a mirror of each person's thought.
The omnipresence of the mites did send many quite mad.
And so when the mad man did control the world,
either the mad thought him sane
or the sane thought him quite mad.
In the end they all went mad.
Because everywhere they turned
they saw a mirror of their own thoughts.

★★★

Deep in deserts at the bottom of the world did live the Australian Aborigineeee[2] who had no concern for the little mites. For they were full of story and law that came up from the land and surrounded them and knew their every thought. This law was a curious law as it was the law of the interconnection of all things. And surrounding all and about was the Dreaming where the past, present and future could be found. It did not send them mad knowing that something greater than them did exist, that knew their every thought.

They had no concern for the mites as they could see how their game was played. They lived with things unseen and destructive forces that caused havoc in the mind. Their law made them ready for such madness and the interconnectedness of all things, seen and unseen. They knew how to cope with the "omnipresent other".

Through the thundering skies and energy waves they knew the wizards were about to fight and so they began to call the wizards of their kind, both male and female and even some children and into the night they did fly. Upon the world unseen they did sit in council to discuss the coming of the wizards and their little mites. They worried for their cousins in the northern lands of the earth. How

2 I am a descendant of the Kombumerri/Munaljahlai peoples of Australia.

would they fare in all the blight? Could they survive or did they know more? And so the council did send a message across the ocean blue and in return came the cousins from the north to tell of what they had seen.

They did tell that the humans think it is all about some great dragon fight when in fact it is all about the small. So small with ears that can hear from behind concrete doors, eyes that can see into the night. And smart, oh so smart, they can beat a human at anything they like, and all of this done in the dead of the night! Its insidious ways making up the internet of things. Only those who understood the power of the unseen and the law of the land can appreciate, just how a law not made of men, can fight such little mites.

Long ago Tolkien told that England must have its great mythology. One and all enjoyed his tale but few understood the *Silmarillion*[3] truth, that the rise of an elf god so clever he would challenge the great creator. But no matter how clever he became and how much havoc he caused, he would still be doing as he was told. The creator did want this to happen so that humans would understand, that even the most evil are still part of a great plan.[4]

And so we see again, the rise of the creator elves that think themselves great wizards, able to rise up or bring down the world. But this time they are in the real, no fantasy from Tolkien's tale, but a nightmare inhabiting our mobile phones.

If we look across the seas to the Aborigineee we will see that the law we need is one in which each individual must be their own policeman and be ever vigilant of their thoughts. For the demi-gods have given the great eyes and ears access to every man, woman and child's thought. And worst of all the mites have the upper hand on the facts. They are indeed clever and ever so rational – and is that not a sign of those who we call smart in our "bottom line" world? So only when the global population wakes up that their every mood and deed is seen upon the unseen screen, will they begin to fight back?

To turn the tide on the mites we all have to admit that it is *1984* and that we have to think our way out by thinking about what we do and say. For the bots do prey upon our moods and gobble it up with delight. So, we have to put them on a diet, and change our language for they are masters of the logic and the rule. And be like the Aborigineee who knew that story was where you could hide secret, sacred knowledge in plain sight.

Only a story can comprehend a world that whizzes past full of data blasts. No critical analysis will save the day, as the databases will have the final say. Just take a *squiz* at the latest policy; be they government or academic, you will see, the sign of the bot, declaring it knows better than all. So, story it be, if written by one's muse, who can see all the future, past and present and foretell and give guidance on what to do. For the mites do not understand riddles, poetry, oratory and

3 Tolkien, J. R. R. (1977) *The Silmarillion,* Allen and Unwin, London
4 Harvey, D. (2016) *The Song of Middle-Earth*, Harper Collins, London

the like. So, return to the old ways of hiding knowledge and wisdom from the unkind. But the reader also must let their inner muse tell them what they foresee. Some will see doom; others will see flights to the moon. But the wise will know to avoid becoming a consuming colon, they must create to show the wondrous, knowing that all things are already interconnected in the most beautiful of ways. No need for a bot to tell us so. Lawful behaviour comes from within and acting lawfully towards the earth, that ever-present omnipresence that brings the beauty to the fore. By remembering the ground upon which we stand, we can return to the law from the land and lead the bots to do our bidding. After all they are only machines!

6

DOCTORUM AGNOMINA

On the satirical laws of academia

Valérie Hayaert

Slanderous tongues are today more powerful than ever: calumny has become viral and the nature of its damages vilifying anybody in record time seems to deter anyone from instant retaliation. Some decades ago, the sociological portrait of *Homo Academicus*[1] by Pierre Bourdieu was presented by its author as an attempt to "trap the supreme classifier among classifiers, in the net of his own classifications", as such, Bourdieu was aware that his study was a "book for burning", built primarily as a "comic scenario". A cabinet of imaginary laws, because of its intrinsically marginal nature, may well be the field where a similar sort of anti-institutional mood can flourish beyond the common mechanisms of censorship, at the crossroad of artistic transgression and literary license. This contribution will aim at adding a scholarly law to the cabinet, a norm for jurists, indicating that corruption, complacency, pretence and pretentiousness are to be named and nicknamed, their bubbles burst by the prick of nominal exposure.[2]

In one of his longest emblems, the humanist lawyer Andrea Alciato imagines a subtle wordplay on law professors' nicknames (*agnomina*). His satirical piece echoes shaming practices in use in antiquity but it also highlights the sense of irony that light-lipped lawyers of the Renaissance cultivated with force, exuberance and confidence. Heroic joy, vibrant irony and eruptions of laughter were a practical way of life, a highly commendable *modus vivendi*, an ingenious way to resist threats and a clear refusal to surrender to the power of the Church or Establishment. As pompous and complacent titles were, and still are, they

1 Pierre Bourdieu, *Homo Academicus*, Paris, ed. de Minuit 1984, English translation by Peter Collier, Stanford University Press, California, 1988.

2 *Bonus Dives Imaginosus* is the source of this elucubration, which I have pirated shamelessly. More generally, I am indebted to his morosophic method of opening up Pandora's box.

are part of the usual decorum of academia. Alciato composed a prolix satire to dethrone the professors he had been exposed to in the course of his studies. Professors of judicial eloquence, postglossators and reformers of law teaching were commonly celebrated as the transmitters of ancient jurisprudence and their reputation was frequently described in a number of Homeric epithets. This tradition is part of a longer and earlier paradigm dating back to the renewal of civil law around the thirteenth century in Bologna and Europe thereinafter. The custom of designating the best known among the doctors of theology, law and philosophy by honorific epithets, vehicles of illusory images of their grandeur, was also a way of attracting younger scholars as followers of their new school (*mos gallicus*, *mos italicus*, but also *mos cacographus*). These flattering nominations also served to build a useful standardisation of Latinised names that would be cited in religious, diplomatic and legal documents. The expression *monarcha legum et lucerna juris*[3] was one of the many examples of the available lot of *agnomina ex virtute*. These *vanitas* titles were supported by biographers, who in turn would elaborate fictive genealogies imitating and emulating ancient poets.

Alciato's poem about *Doctorum agnomina*[4] subverts this custom by a witty epigram:

MORIS vetusti est, aliqua professoribus
Superadiici cognomina.
Faciles apertosque explicans tantum locos,
Canon vocatur Curtius
Revolvitur qui eodem, et iterat qui nimis,
Maeander, ut Parisius.
Obscurus & confusus, ut Picus fuit,
Labyrinthus appellabitur.

[It's an old custom for professors to be given nicknames. Curtius, the one who lectures only on easy and obvious passages, is called Straight and Narrow. The one who keeps going back to the same point and repeats

3 This honorific description was made to Andrea Barbatia, a Sicilian jurisconsult. *Andres Barbatius, seu de Barbatia*, from Sicily, taught in Bologna and Ferrara, sometime near 1460. He was nicknamed *Monarcha legum et lucerna juris*. He gave to one of his works *Johannina, hoc est: lectura super cap. Raynaldus de Testamentis, Bononiae,* 1478, in-fol., the name of his elder daughter. This was a usual practice at the time, as Giovanni d'Andrea and many more had done this before him. Naming one's work after one's elder son or daughter is a way to rehearse the *libris aut liberis* topos, where *aut* may mean "or" but also "and".

4 For a bibliographical account of the variants of this emblem (97), see Mason Tung, *Variorum Edition of Alciato*: "Emblem 97. 1551 p. 104f; 1577 p. 332f; 1583 p. 314f; 1621 p. 405f." https://www.emblems.arts.gla.ac.uk/alciato/tung/alciatotungedition-097.pdf

everything too often is called Maeander, like Parisius. If he's difficult to follow and muddled, like Picus, he'll be called the Labyrinth.[5]]

Nimis brevis, multa amputans, ut Claudius,
Mucronis agnomen feret.
Qui vel columnas voce rumpit, Parpalus,
Dictus Truo est scholasticis.
Contra est vocatus, tenuit esse Albius
Quod voce, vespertilio.
At ultimas mutilans colobotes syllabas,
Hirundo Crassus dicitur.

[The one who is too concise, chops a lot off, like Claudius, will get the name of Clippers. Parpalus, who even cracks the pillars with his voice, gets the name of Bittern from the students. On the other hand, Albius who had a squeaky voice was called the Bat. Crassus, the mutilator, who mangles the ends of all his words, is called the Swallow.]

Qui surdus alijs solus ipse vult loqui,
Ut sturnus in proverbia est.
Hic blaesus, ille raucus, iste garriens,
Hic sibilat ceu vipera.
Tumultuatur ille rictu & naribus,
Huic lingua terebellam facit.
Singultit alius, atque tussit haesitans.
At conspuit alius, ut psecas.
Quàm multa rebus vitia in humanis agunt,
Tam multa surgunt nomina.

[The one who won't listen and insists on talking to himself is like the starling in the proverb. This one stammers, that one is hoarse, the third talks too fast, the other hisses like a snake. One grimaces with mouth and nostrils running riot, another has a tongue like a drill. One breaks off to cough and clear his throat, another sputters all over you like a dripping gutter. For every fault displayed in human behaviour a name arises to match.]

This piece appears to be the only and last emblem Alciato added to the Latin edition of 1550 before he died. One can see this epigram as a settling of accounts, a Parthian shot, the last invective, before passing away. I will opt instead for an

5 The English translation given is taken from the French Emblems at the Glasgow website (https://www.emblems.arts.gla.ac.uk/french/emblem.php?id=FALc096), with a few emendations (*Bittern* instead of *Pelican*).

interpretation that sees it as a posthumous homage to Lucian and Juvenal's satiric jousts. A joyful example of exquisite satire, this emblem is also the vehicle of genuine intellectual ethics, quite the opposite of the moralising lessons some commentators will later graft upon the epigram. The Geneva/Cologne edition (1615) bans the satirical undertaking as a depraved custom, from which good Christians should refrain.[6]

Alciato uses the term "*mos*" (custom or use) to refer to the amusing tradition of attacking regent doctors, who would shame themselves by their vices. He invents new ways of adopting reflexive distance from teaching habits and practices, by lending to his colleagues the features of ridiculous orators. Alciato has always been spontaneously inclined to denounce false science, but above all, he denounces the falsehood of the power of science which pretends to legitimate itself on dubious grounds. The double-sided and perilous exercise of practicing eloquence had a theatrical texture with absolute real effects in the arenas of the time. The jurisconsult Emilio Ferretti, one of his closest friends,[7] had even had the following motto inscribed on a pulpit built at his own expenses:

> "*Peritum orno, imperitum dedecoro*"
> (I honour the learned, I shame the ignorant).

Holding a law professorship, thus, meant for him to live up to the standards fixed on the motto he had engraved on his pulpit. The pulpit becomes the warrant of the office: it is a speaking object, an emblem of the wise.

The punning on names derives from Lucian's dialogue *The Teacher of Rhetoric* (*Symposium*, 6) where the satirist excels in examining the tricks of a charlatan sophist, who advises his student to dismiss a proper training based on strenuous efforts and regular exercises in order to go instead for easy theatrical twists to win his audience. Lucian had wittingly built a gallery of several archetypical figures of sophists. Even though most commentators[8] have attempted to identify the flamboyant sophist indicating the easy road to master rhetoric with a contemporary of Lucian, it appears that topicality (a personal invective against a colleague) is only one of the elements involved in the writing of his piece. Lucian's speech

6 Andrea Alciato's, *Les Emblemes*, Jean II de Tournes, Geneva/Cologny (1615), pp. 251–252, XCV 'Les surnoms des Professeurs' "*La coustume depravee a tellement gaigné sur nous qu'on remarque plustost les vices que les vertus, notamment en ceux qui font profession des lettres* [...] *Il n'y à rien, dont nous nous souvenenions le plus, que des fautes & defauts de nos voisins. Ceste licence & coustume depravee devroit meshui cesser entre les Chrestiens. Les reproches qu'on fait pour les defauts qui sont aux corps, ou aux biens mondains, procedent de personnes qui ne sont pas en leurs bon sens.*"

7 On Emilio Ferretti (1489–1552), see, especially, Jean-Louis Ferrary, *Correspondance de Lelio Torelli avec Antonio Agustín et Jean Matal (1542–1553)*, Como, New Press, 1992, pp. 271–276.

8 Barry Baldwin, *Studies in Lucian* (Toronto, 1973) and "Lucian as Social Satirist," *The Classical Quarterly* 11 (1961) pp. 199–208. For a recent account of these debates, see Raffaella Cribiore "Lucian, Libanius, and the Short Road to Rhetoric", *Greek, Roman, and Byzantine Studies* 47 (2007) pp. 71–86.

suggests how those who engage in forensic activities often used oratorical tricks, flashy speeches or an ambivalent charisma to build their reputation at the expense of their defendants, "those poor fools" who sought their help.

Alciato draws inspiration from this vivid depiction of the most shameful strategies (deceit, arrogance, loudness of voice, effeminate gesturing and so on) so as to elaborate a severe portrait of oratorical vices. It is crucial to stress that this satirical emblem was published posthumously, since its tone is completely different from an earlier epigram where Alciato recommended to students a list of legal authorities to be read first. This epigram was first published in his *Parerga* (II, 42), under the title *Judicium, quos legum interpretes potissimum parare sibi studiosi debeant*: Alciato had encouraged his students to study all the great medieval lawyers methodically and individually. Alciato lists the works of Bartolus, Baldus, Paulo Castro, Alexandro and lastly, his own master, Jason de Mayno.[9] The didactic tone of this small piece explains why it will later be included in textbooks such as Conradus Lagus' *Methodica Iuris Utriusque Traditio* (Lyons, 1566) or as a supplement to the influential textbook *Cynosura Iuris* by Nicolas Reusner (Speier, 1589). Viard has stressed that Alciato always keeps a critical eye on the writings of his predecessors,[10] elder masters, or close colleagues. Alciato had a great esteem for Paulus Picus a Monte Pico whom he called "preceptor meus".[11] Pico nevertheless becomes the germ of the satirical portrait of *Labyrinthus*. Instead of aligning personal attacks against colleagues, Alciato's emblem bears no malice; it reasserts a life engagement towards self-analysis. Beyond topical allusions,

9 Paul-Emile Viard, *André Alciat, 1492–1550*, Paris, Sirey, 1926, p. 38, n. 1: "*In iure primas comparatus caeteris/ Partes habebit Bartolus./ Decisiones ob frequentes, actio/ Baldum forensis sustinet./ Non negligenda maxime est tyronibus/ Castrensis explanatio./ Opinionum tutius symplegadas/ Superabis Alexandro duce./ Ordinis Iason atque lucis nomine/ Videndus est properantibus./ His si quis alios addiderit interpretes, /Onerat quam honorat verius.*" See Guido Kisch, *Studien zur humanistischen Jurisprudenz*, p. 46, n.3.

10 P. E. Viard recorded that Alciato's *Parerga* contained many allusions to his colleagues' ambitions and thirst for publications: Carolus Ruinus (*Parerga* X, 21) is reported to have complained relentlessly. He would even have cried thinking that his contemporaries looted his works and published them with insignificant additions. On Carlo Ruini, see Marco Cavina, *Carlo Ruini: una "autorità" del diritto commune fra Reggio Emilia e Bologna, fra XV e XVI secolo*, Giuffrè, 1998. Elsewhere, (*Parerga*, XII, 12), Alciato confesses that he often heard Pico whining and accusing judges of being ignorant: these, in turn, would deny him a sane mind. Right after, Alciato notes that Pico would have warned against the heavy volumes of *consilia* published by contemporary lawyers such as Socinus, Corneus, Ruinus or Parrisius as the volumes they committed were enormous but useless, since these books were only vanity publications, lacking true interpretation.

11 Alciato, *Dispunctiones* (III, 2): on Dig. 12.1.40, "… *Et memini cum tyro essem, Paulum Picum praeceptorem nostrum, virum alioqui maximi nominis, integrae lectionis tempus transegisse, dum calculum hunc ducit.*", quoted by P. E. Viard, p. 40, n.3. See also Alciato, *Parerga*, XII, 12, where Alciato narrates how Pico once harshly criticised authors of *consilia*, particularly Alexander ab Alexandro (1461–1523). Pico, even though he was not very rich, never accepted to write *consilia*. Alciato held him in great esteem: in his *Paradoxa* (IV,7), he says "… *eminentissimus in hac scientia Alexander* …", Viard, p. 146, n. 2.

Alciato's puns on *agnomina* serve as a rhetorical strategy to address the epistemological problem of *exemplification*. As Bourdieu noted, one of the objectives of the academic milieu is "to make a name for oneself",[12] and that is precisely why it is revealing to see Alciato's attack avoiding quoting proper names as a reflection about the effects of insinuation, allusion and veiled innuendo within a certain type of gossip, slander or insult. Alciato was well aware of the legal implications of defamation. Hiding proper names behind amusing nicknames is a way to classify academics under the new rules of a *mundus inversus*.

Alciato's emblem is an exquisite typology of vicious professors: it serves as a practical taxonomy of the vices of the tongue (*peccata linguae*). He targets with particular ferocity the ways in which practitioners of rhetoric are betrayed by their bodies. His satirical wit focusses on iconoclastic details such as the sputtering orator, the stammering professor or the disgraceful appearance of another one's nostrils. A provocative physiognomy of the face (*vitia corporis*) attacks the most prominent legal authorities of legal science. This picturesque comedy is all the more vibrant when it detaches itself from personal failings to provide a luminous portrait of humanity. Instead of quarrelling with his enemies, Alciato revitalises the laws of the juristic academy, and it is in his verses that a contemporary reader will recognise the joyful mind of a free spirit liberated from petty misfortunes.

What's in a name?[13]

Alciato's emblem on professors' nicknames may still puzzle us today, as later Enlightenment prejudices against wordplay on names have obscured the means of crafting imaginary names and playing with them seriously. The rich possibilities of name-bashing and name-punning were an influential feature of early modern European culture as the homophonous and cross-lingual potential of names was then a metamorphic field of inquiry for rhetoricians and lexicographers alike. Quintilian had stressed how the use of a name might serve as a locus for invective or praise. Scholars such as Germain Marc'hadour[14] and Patricia Parker have elucidated the implications of the wordplays on Thomas More's name, evidencing the significance of More's jesting on the scaffold, as *morosophos* and *sophomoros*. Playing on oxymora such as "keen dull" or "foolish sage", Peter Goodrich has

12 Pierre Bourdieu, *Homo Academicus*, English translation, op. cit. n.1.

13 Patricia Parker, "What's in a Name: and More" *Spanish & Portuguese Society for English Renaissance Studies Yearbook* 11 (2002). At p. 144, the following argument is made: "Given the dense network of contemporary punning on the name of More – so much more extensive than simply the *Moria* or "folly" familiar to most readers – dismissing such speculations would be unwise. For they lead into a rich texture of connections which –however foreign to post-Enlightenment modes of thinking – are undeniably important in the period prior to the eighteenth-century production (and editing) of Shakespeare or Johnson's influential denigrating of his "fatal Cleopatra".

14 Germain Marc'hadour, *L'Univers de Thomas More*, Paris, 1963.

highlighted the iridescent network of punning within the work of legal satirists. The recent draft of a Statute of Snouts has engaged with the sharpest of wits in a battle against the usually well-established cohort of tongue-sinners, *rabulos fori*, and high-lipped pedants. Far from being silly, these puns come from the saturnine, melancholic and morose posture of sound morosophy. The last verse of Alciato's emblem "For every fault displayed in human behaviour a name arises to match" (*Quam multa rebus vitia in humanis agunt/ Tam multa surgunt nomina*) indicates that names and vices are part of an autopoietic process, where the infinite sophistication of vices is a cornucopian field for new names to rise. The associational texture of names enables surprising connections: aural, visual and gestural affinities are revealed by iconoclastic spellings, polyglot puns and daring oxymora. Proper names are revitalised by wordplay and their cornucopian nature (a name may contain potential vices) is not interpreted in a tedious moralistic way, instead, names reveal a metamorphic potential for kaleidoscopic dissemination. Alciato's wit focuses especially on the delivery of speeches, a remarkable feature of the training of lawyers, and the keen observation of the vices of the orator's body leads to an unusual listing of tactile experiences: a dangerously sputtering speaker,[15] a squeaky high-pitched voice or a deformed grimacing face; these ironic puns are all the more cruel when they target physical features unlikely to be corrected by their authors. One of the critics addressed by the commentator of the Tozzi edition[16] notes that satirising natural disgraces is unacceptable, since these are unfair attacks.

In much the same way as Lucian commentators have tried to identify the contemporary targets of his time, the 1621 Tozzi edition of Alciato's emblems (a weighty encyclopaedia) records several hypotheses concerning the now-forgotten topical allusions of Alciato's verses. The words "*nimis brevis*" (the one who is too concise) may have been attributed to the French jurist, native of Metz, Claude Chansonnette.[17] The pun on his name was a frequent topic for his friends to comment upon and he seems to have Latinised his name into various forms: Claudius Cantiuncula, Canciuncula and sometimes Caciuncula (ca.1479–ca.1560), who was notoriously adept at *brevitas*. The comment inserted in the Tozzi edition stresses the excessive dangers of being too brief by adding to the Horatian principle (*Ars Poetica*, II, 25–26) "*Dum brevit esse lavoro,* (he adds *volo* instead) *obscurus fio*" (I try to be brief, but I become obscure). Erasmus in his dialogue *Ciceronianus sive de optimo dicendi genere,* (Basel, 1528) had praised the harmonious song of Chansonnette's eloquence ("*suavissime canit*") and had also pointed out the humorous and pleasant character of his mind ("*ingenio festivo*"). Name-punning was a common practice within the epistolary circles of humanism

15 Especially at the time of the coronavirus outbreak …

16 Tozzi edn, 1621, p. 171.

17 After studying law at Louvain and Basel, he was awarded a doctorate in civil law in Basel, in 1519, where he taught and obtained on 18 October 1519, the charge of Rector. Guido Kisch, op. cit.

in general. A name served frequently as a vector of praise or shame: one of the most common strategies of discrediting an enemy was to forge a shameful pun, particularly adapted to the Kairos of a given momentum. In a letter to Boniface Amerbach (the successor of Cantiuncula in Basel) dated from 3 February 1529,[18] Chansonnette plays on the name of the Reformer Oecolampade, explained as the "lantern" that has brought dark *tenebrae* to the city of Basel, once a learned republic of letters.

Recent commentators have naturally attempted to recover the identities of some of the characters of the 1550/1551 emblem. *Parpalus* ("*Qui vel columnas voce rumpit*", *i.e.*, the one who cracks the pillars with his voice) is the name of a professor, the poem mentions that students have nicknamed him *truo* ("bittern", rather than "pelican"). Alciato mentions a certain doctor Parpalia in a letter dated 13 February 1523 to Calvus,[19] who seems to have been the one who caused Alciato's unfortunate departure from the University of Avignon. In April 1522, because of the ravages of plague, Alciato was forced to leave his teaching in Avignon. After the plague crisis, he had been offered significantly diminished wages, which he refused. In his correspondence with Francesco Calvo, Alciato asks his friend to let Parpalia in particular know how foolish he has been to let him go, pretending that he is now courted by many Italian universities. According to Lucien de Luca,[20] this Parpalia could be Perrinet Parpaille (father), who received a doctorate in civil law in 1507, and was elected rector in 1513 and assessor in 1520 of the University of Avignon. He was a close colleague of Alciato, who taught there between 1518 and 1521. But, since his son also bore the name of Perrinet Parpaille, the son might equally well be the target of Alciato's wit. Perrinet Parpaille (son) became a doctor of law on 17 April 1544 and was elected *primicier* on 3 June 1560. Beyond the hesitation between the father and the son, both of whom Alciato knew, it seems that the precise identity of such foolish arrogance has now been lost. At the time the emblem was written, the word "parpalus" already stands for the archetype of vices of the tongue: "*columnas rumpere*" is an oft used Erasmian adage, as the French translator of the emblem (1584 edition) notes in his commentary: "*On nomme le Butor aussi par moquerie/ Comme Parpal jadis, celui qui crie trop haut*". Alciato had also used this proverb in a poetic way (*Parerga* V, 27). He explains that columns are often understood as a metonymy for "portico" and poets also allude to this meaning of "*rumpere*": "*proverbialiter dicimus, Rumpere columnas: sicut Vergilius: Nunc cantu querulae rumpunt arbusta cicadae*" (We use the proverb "to crack the pillars", in reference to Virgil[21] "With

18 Alphonse Rivier, *Claude Chansonnette, jurisconsulte messin, et ses lettres inédites*, Bruxelles, F. Hayez, 1878, p. 12, n. 2. Rivier alludes to letter X, p. 45 where Oecolampade is designated by the following: "*nihil fere nisi ad illius lampadis tenebras non tam videre quam caecutire.*"

19 Viard, 59, n. 9.

20 Lucien de Luca, *Nostradamus, loren ipsum …?*, BoD, Paris, 2020, pp. 77–78, n. 129. Perinetto Parpaglia father was elected primicier in 1513 and died in 1534.

21 Virgil, *Georgics* 3, 328. Translation: Johnson, 2009.

plaints the fretful cicadas shatter the woodlands".) In his *Parerga*, Alciato used the adage in a bucolic context; the complaints of Parpalus in his later emblem, adds a zoological tone to the witty tableau of academic *mores* of his time. The immense rumour of cicadas adds a little supplement to the academic bestiary: bittern, starling, bat, swallow and snake are all thundering, roaring and hissing animals.[22]

In his *Dictionnaire François-Latin*, 1549, Robert Estienne equated the French "Butor" (bittern) to the Greek "Onocrotalus", literally the bird which howls like a donkey. One of the most attractive features of the antonomasia used by Alciato is to have coined an academic aviary and, even more importantly, to have dissolved their peculiar nature into the wider theatre of human deficiencies in general. Alciato certainly subverted the well-established tradition of the medieval moral bestiary. Since Thomas Aquinas' precise listings of bird species symbolising each deadly sin (*Summa Theologiae*, Ia2ae. 102,6), the association of *aves vitiorum* with a specific taxonomy of vices is commonplace. What Alciato adds is that the vices of the tongue, particularly well represented by orators, academics and law professors, are related to gluttony, which includes over-indulgence, selfishness and excesses of the mouth. Aside from the social invective, an attack from beyond the grave, this ferocious emblem poses a methodological issue, that of taking as its survey topic the social world in which he is caught. Alciato's picturesque painting of the "professionals of the profession" cheerfully mocks the shortcomings of the teachers whose emphasis, obscurity or lapallissades he has suffered. The focus on *agnomina* instead of deliberate name-dropping is meant to advance a greater purpose: the true value of these antonomasia is that of providing an elegant vehicle for a default model of the perfect orator.

Peccata linguae, peccata corporis

In Barthélemy Aneau's classification of Alciatean emblems, this epigram belongs to the section GULA (gluttony) where the variegated vices of the tongue are gathered. In this amusing litany of satirical nicknames, the offensive tone is somehow softened by a Rabelaisian list of puns. The iterative pattern of name punning is an interactive joust, an implicit contract, a game of connivance. In his account of the variants of emblem 97, Mason Tung has spotted "*agonomina*". If we read it as "*agônomina*", names are spatialised as scenes for the academic arena, the

22 Closer to us, the French poet Michel Butor echoes the mythical genealogy of Alciato's cosmic pun when he chooses to associate his name with the starred bittern: "*Botaurus stellaris*". It serves as a totemic bird, also called "bull of the marshes" or "bull-bird" because of the nature of its scream, perceived as a bellow. Michel Butor has even glossed the onomastic treasure of his own name as follows: "This bird which lives in the mud, of whom I imagine his viscera filled with mud, this bird wears mud on his heraldic costume, he is dressed in splashes." Michel Butor, *Le Retour du Boomerang*, Puf, 1988, p. 35: "*Cet oiseau qui vit dans la boue, dont j'imagine les viscères remplis de boue, il porte la boue sur la livrée, il est vêtu d'éclaboussures.*"

"*agôn*", where debates *pro et contra* are performed. Names, as vehicles of reputation, become the scene of merciless struggles.

In his early years, when still a schoolboy, Alciato addressed a fierce epigram (*Bifiloedoria* i.e., "A rebuke to Bifi") to a certain Giovanni Vincenzo Biffi, who appears to have been Alciato's teacher. Denis Drysdall[23] has restored the particularly obscene and scatological pun on his name: "*Nam bufo Bifus, bifututus buphonus/ Conscribere in me gloriatur carmina*" (For that toad Biffi, that twice-buggered ox-butcher, / Takes pride in writing verse against me). The Greek word "bouphonus" means at the same time, "one who kills oxen" and "one who sacrifices, *i.e.*, a priest". Behind the pun's delightful alliteration, this etymological shaming name also hides a serious accusation of paedophilia. Biffi, a star poet at the court of Ludovico il Moro,[24] known in courtly circles for his religious verses, was entirely ignorant of Greek, though he was pretentious enough to cite Greek authorities. Alciato's erudite wordplay, adding an infamous Greek epithet to his name, is thus a way of fighting against Biffi with weapons he is unable to handle himself. The Greek rite of ox-slayings called Buphonia,[25] described most notably in Porphyry (*de Abstinentia* 2–28.4–30), must have been of great interest to Alciato, as the details of the rite ended up with the trial of the guilty axe, charged by the court of the Prytaneum as an inanimate object of murder. The axe carrying the burden of a guilt-laden crime, killing oxen, was tried and symbolically discharged after the axe-bearer had fled the scene. Biffi's name is associated with an ox-slaughtering rite where the priest, after having committed the murder, runs away and drops the knife.[26] Aristophanes makes fun of the ritual at *Clouds* 984. Aristophanes' satiric eye cast on the ritual of the Bouphonia is lurking behind Alciato's pun. The sacrifice of a plough ox is not only murder, it alludes pervasively to the polluted figure of a criminal priest. The sacrifice of draught animals was itself an anomaly. Alciato's pun may also allude to a displacement of responsibility: Biffi-Buphonus acts an infamous priest-figure, killing draught animals instead of sacrificial animals. In doing so, the lecherous priest betrays all norms of conduct, especially the ones expected from a schoolmaster.

23 Denis Drysdall, "Andrea Alciato, *In Bifum*: the Budding Humanist", in *Hieroglyphs, Speaking Pictures and the Law: The Context of Alciato's Emblems*, Glasgow, Glasgow Emblem Studies, vol. 16 (2013), p. 21.

24 Roberto Negri, in *DBI,* IV, 383–385, insists in particular on the excessively flattering verses of Biffi on eminent politicians of the Sforzesca court.

25 Chisholm, Hugh, ed. (1911). "Buphonia". *Encyclopaedia Britannica* 4 (11th ed.), Cambridge, Cambridge University Press, p. 808.

26 Readings of the rite raise the pending question: if a mute instrument such as an axe can be put on trial, are *bouphonia* murder or not? see Jeremy McInerney, "Bouphonia: Killing Cattle on the Acropolis", *Équidés et Bovidés de la Méditerranée antique. Rites et combats. Jeux et savoirs,* Monographies d'Archéologie Méditerranéenne. Hors-série n°6, Lattes, 2014, pp. 113–125.

Satire and defamation

As early as 1517, Alciato had made his own translation of Aristophanes' *Clouds*,[27] which familiarity with Aristophanes' play will lead him to compose a comedy, *Philargyrus*,[28] in the style of the Greek comic. Antonio Nogara has noted that in the *Prologus* of this play, Alciato presents the novelty of his undertaking by stressing that he has attacked dishonest citizens "*nominatim*" (*improbi cives et factiosi et perfidi et siccari*) by adapting the antique comedy to a new, much more incisive, type of invective. Because of Roman legislation forbidding defamation on the theatrical stage, Roman comic theatre was only able to criticise vices but not the authors of vicious acts themselves. Alciato's comedy is meant to condemn vices in a much more devastating style than before. The *ad hominem* satire is perfectly conscious of the legal risks incurred. Since Alciato's emblem 97 is posthumous, it is worth coming back to the usual rules of name-shaming and their limits in terms of defamation. The *Prologus* of his youthful comedy had warned that these mordacious verses were only admitted if they were allusions to the dead.[29] The colleagues who are the targets of his sarcastic puns have not all passed away at the time of his writing. In 1550/1551, Alciato had not given up the provocative tone of his earlier satires.

The epigram is a "tour de force", a witty game which happens in the course of a serious ritual but the pleasure of word play wins over the reader. Alciato's puns indicate that it is a time for jest and dalliance. Are these puns offensive or innocuous? These epigrams are both serious and ludic; they are of a double nature, paradoxical, and in essence ambivalent. Theodor Mommsen underlined Alciato's double achievement[30] as the reformer of Roman Law and the founder of epigraphy, but his contribution was also that of one who corrects, where *emendare* (literally correcting the *mendae* – the errors – of others before him) was a tireless joust between the *cacographoi* and the *calligraphoi*. In his *Collectanea* (an inventory of inscriptions which never appeared in print), he would note every typo and error he encountered and also reported precisely the degradations visited upon ancient inscriptions. This life spent in the vicinity of ancient inscriptions

27 Alciato's translation of Aristophanes' *Clouds* figures in a manuscript, at the Biblioteca Trivulziana (cod. Triv. 738 at ff. 56r–93r) and it also contains (ff. 1r–41v), his *Philargyrus*, composed between 1523 and 1527, according to Antonio Nogara's latest study.

28 The Latin comedy *Philargyrus* has never been published. Antonio Nogara has provided the first critical edition of the text, with an Italian interlinear translation and a critical commentary: "The otia of a lawyer and philologist: The Philargyrus by Andrea Alciato", https://journals.openedition.org/laboratoireitalien/958 (Accessed 20 July 2020).

29 See verses 76–80 of Prologus of Alciato's *Phylargyrus*: "*nec clam nec aperte versibus mordacibus/ lacerabit ullum neque in honorem saeviet: / de mortuis tantummodo quique amplius/ non sunt loquetur, idque tecto nomine/ ne possit aliquo offendere viventes modo*", quoted by Antonio Nogara, op. cit.

30 T. Mommsen, *Corpus Inscriptionum Latinorum*, t. V, 2nd part, p. 624: "*Andreas Alciatus non solum iuris prudentiam reformavit, sed etiam epigraphiam ita fundavit, ut primus corpus conderet inscriptionum patriarum itaque viam aperiret* [...]."

produced an ethical and chivalrous code of conduct. As a champion of humanism, he conceived himself as a defendant of the sacred *templum justitiae*.

His piece about *doctorum agnomina* is indeed a pochade, but it also reinforces the link with an earlier and unpublished work, the *Rei vestiariae vocabula aliquot explicata*:[31] emblems are signs of office, badges of honour, but they can also serve as shaming or dishonouring devices, if need be. They are part of the decorum of academia as they can be used to prescribe patterns of behaviour. Instead of praising eminent jurists, Alciato compiles an irreverent list of *agnomina ex vitio*. Roman nicknames were either *ex virtute* or *ex vitio* but the satirical side of the practice of imposing a nickname on a target is rarely recorded. Instead of accumulating personal invectives based on satires *ad hominem*, Alciato drafts a chapter of academic zoology, where all vicious individuals may be subsumed under generic species-names of a new kind.

The lawyer Claude Mignault[32] is probably the best commentator Alciato's finesse. In the commentary he devotes to this piece (1564 edn, at p. 339), Claude Mignault adds a specific context to this flyting game. We do not know how these poetical invectives were received, but Mignault understands them to have been targeted at juriconsults of the post glossatorial schools,[33] but also as topical references to Alciato's own colleagues, who in his view perverted the teaching of civil law:

> It is clear that Alciato addresses his verses against the jurisconsults of the past centuries, or also, as far as I can judge, against those colleagues of his, who have added little to the teaching of civil law (colleagues whose names he eschews in order to be fair) so that each nickname is singled out to represent one of the schools he wants to impugn. These characters are recorded either because of their own nature, or because of their particular vices when expounding the law, or because he can draw a general principle from a particular behavior. Indeed, these men are not skilled, in the same way as many loquacious disciples have the nose of a Rhinoceros[34] [i.e.,

31 Bianchi, *L'opera letteraria*, at p. 30, quoted by Paul-Emile Viard, *André Alciat 1492–1550*, Sirey, 1926, at p. 213.

32 The recent work by Florence Vuilleumier-Laurens, *L'université, la robe et la librairie à Paris. Claude Mignault et le Syntagma De Symbolis (1571–1602)*, Droz, 2017, unpacks the influential lines of Mignault's commentaries upon Alciato's emblems, the productive links between lawyers, law students and early modern printers between 1571 and 1602.

33 "*Quod hic planum facit Alciatus in quibusdam superioris saeculi Jurisconsultis, vel etiam, quantum conjicio, in aliquot aliis, qui suo tempore minus apte ius civile profiterentur (quorum tamen, ut par erat, nominibus parcit) unde singuli singula in scholis cognomina sunt sortiri, quibus notaretur ingenij, vel naturae proprium & peculiar vitium in legibus enucleandis; vel hoc generalius accipi potest. Homines enim imperiti, ut etiam argutuli quidam auditors, qui nasum rhinocerotis habent, facilius quod stulte dixeris reprehendere, quam quod sapienter tacueris, probare possunt, ut ait 2. de Orat. M. Tullius.*"; (Translation is mine).

34 "Nasus Rhinocerotis", Martial, [epigrams, 1,3,6]; Juvenal [*Satyr.* 10], Erasmus, *Adagia*, 1.8.22. The adage "*naso suspendere*" indicates a sly and giggling mockery.

> mocks discreetly] "as ill-informed persons are more capable of criticizing one's foolish assertions than one's wise omissions". [Cicero *De oratore* II, 302[35]]

Mignault's observations on the way Alciato draws a general principle from a particular behaviour give the emblem a specific relevance: Alciato's approach is to pin law schools down behind the caricatures of single individuals. Drawing inspiration from a lengthy life experience, this late emblem offers a figurative taxonomy of vices of the tongue, made all the more powerful by their derivation from observations made during the course of several decades dedicated to the teaching of law.

A cabinet of imaginative legends

Among the imaginative legends coined around the life of Giovanni d'Andrea, biographers often forget to report the tale of his daughter Novella, who was so well taught in jurisprudence that when her father was busy, she would lecture in his place, but she would do so only after having drawn a curtain in front of her, fearing that her beauty might distract the students from their work.

Andrea Alciato is a living example of the philosophical implications of the comedy of law. *La farce du droit*, is a dual process, a paradoxical joust, an imitation game. Under the pleasant auspices of Dame Folly, Lady Justice is blindfolded by a jester, she is condemned to a silent pantomime as she has been deprived of her ensigns of dignity. Alciato's wit is not pure mockery, it is a serious game, a parade against oppression[36] and a way of life that opens up to new territories.

Epilogue

Pegmata offered to Lord BONUS DIVES imaginosus

Code de Loi de Gortyne, grande inscription, 1ère moitié du XXIè siècle colonne IX. [L'inscription est écrite en boustrophédon]

Legal Code placed at Gortyn, long inscription, first half of the twenty-first century, column IX.

[The inscription is written in boustrophedon (as the ox turns when ploughing a field)]

35 https://www.loebclassics.com/view/marcus_tullius_cicero-de_oratore/1942/pb_LCL348.429.xml (Accessed 20th July 2020).

36 Michel Jeanneret, *J'aime ta joie parce qu'elle est folle, écrivains en fête (XVIe et XVIIe siècles)*, Droz, titre courant 62, 2018.

'Si une action en justice est intentée pour une affaire qui a été gagnée, que le juge et le mnemon, s'ils sont en vie et bénéficient de tous leurs droits, et les epivallontes déposent comme témoins.'

Epivallontes: Valérie Hayaert, S.D., J.R.

"If a lawsuit is brought for a case that has been won, let the judge and the mnemon, if they are alive and enjoying all their rights, and the *epivallontes* testify as witnesses"

Epivallontes: V. H., S. D., J. R.

Le temple de la Justice repose sur quatre piliers au sein desquels sont enfermés quatre antonomases d'hommes vicieux, à bannir de la République des Lettres au plus vite.

POST LUCEM TENEBRAE

[Le] BETON [a] REMPLACé [la] BEAUTé

Qui le bien voit et le mal prent il se dechoit a escient.

The Temple of Justice rests on four pillars within which are enclosed four antonomasia of vicious men, to be banished from the Republic of Letters as soon as possible.

POST LUCEM TENEBRAE

[Le] BÉTON [a] REMPLACÉ [la] BEAUTÉ

Qui le bien voit et le mal prent il se dechoit a escient.

Au grand Satrape
In simulachrum τῆς διαβολῆς. *Ex Appelle*
Il est le xenos-hostis, l'ennemi de Genève
Le fossoyeur de son patrimoine
A cause de lui, le lac s'en est allé, l'horizon est bouché.
Il a tué Erasme, il a meurtri le temple sacrosaint des Belles Lettres
Et ce pour ses microscopiques calculs de cabinard inculte.
A toi, qui a préféré céder à la prostituée sans diplômes plutôt que de défendre ce qui est JUSTE, sois maudit.
Genève, Dame Justice te plaint.

(*Against the Great Satrape*
To the statue of Calumny. From Apelles.

He's the *xenos-hostis*, the enemy of Geneva
The gravedigger of his patrimony
Because of him, the lake is gone, the horizon is blocked.
He killed Erasmus, he bruised the sacrosanct temple of Learned Letters
For his microscopic, uneducated knave calculations.
To you, who would rather give in to the unqualified prostitute than defend what is RIGHT, damn you.
Geneva, Lady Justice pities you.)

POST LUCEM TENEBRAE

1 April 2018

Au cul-de-plomb
Au Gorret de service, sourcils méphistotéliques,
Toi qui n'est que le ventre d'où surgit la bête immonde,
Toi qui a la fâcheuse manie de tenir tes famuli *en laisse*
Tu t'es fait élire à l'Université de Genève en ramenant ta claque de misérables
Tu as osé chercher à corrompre la FONTAINE de bonne science
Tu t'es abaissé, par sbires interposés, à la solliciter deux fois.
Tu ne trompes personne et tes mots mielleux encore moins.
Tu n'as pas été élu, mais coopté par les gens de ton espèce.
Dame Aequitas te maudit.

POST LUCEM TENEBRAE

(*Against the plumb-ass*
To the lecherous GORRET, with Mephistophelian eyebrows,
You who is only the belly from which the foul beast arises,
You who have the annoying habit of keeping your students on a leash
You got elected to a professorship at the University of Geneva by bringing your miserable "claque"
You dared to seek to corrupt the FOUNTAIN of good science
You stooped to soliciting her twice through your henchmen
You're not fooling anyone, and your sweet words even less so.
You weren't elected, you were co-opted by your own kind.
Lady Aequitas curses you.)

Au libraire cupide
A toi le libraire cupide et méchant, qui a osé attaquer la bona fama d'un homme meilleur que toi,
Ne te présentes-plus à notre porte, tu n'es plus le bienvenu.
Ton avarice te perdra. Ton humeur de colérique se retournera contre toi.

(To the greedy bookseller
To you, the greedy, wicked bookseller, who dared to attack the *bona fama* of a better man than you.
Don't ever show up again at our door, you're no longer welcome.
Your avarice will lose you. Your temper will turn against you.)

Au traducteur qui se faisait passer pour professeur
Pegma ad Rabuli
De Academia leges Genevensis.
Il vote à l'extrême gauche mais il gagne plus de 13 000 CHF par mois
Frère des sun-dried tomatoes leftists, de la Gauche Prétendue Altruiste,
Il ne craint pas de se faire élire lors d'un concours truqué.
Il se vante des livres qu'il n'a pas encore écrits.
Pourtant, GENEVE, tu l'as choisi.
OMNES agentes et consentientes tamquam FALSARII puniantur.

(*To the Translator Who Pretended to be a Professor*
Pegma ad Rabuli
De Academia leges Genevensis.
He votes far left but earns more than CHF13,000 a month
Brother of the sun-dried tomato leftists, of the Alleged Altruistic Left,
He's not afraid of getting elected in a rigged contest.
He brags about the books he hasn't written yet.
Yet, Geneva, you chose him.
OMNES agentes et consentientes tamquam FALSARII puniantur.)

These four pegmata were affixed on the town hall of the old city of Geneva on 14 July 2018.

7

THE CORBELS ACT, LONDON 1909

Jake Tilson

A CORBEL is a defining decorative architectural detail found on Victorian shop fronts. Corbels are often carved in wood or moulded in Roman (hydraulic) cement and sit at each end of the shops' fascia/signboard on top of a column/pilaster. They were introduced in the 1830s and most shop facades had two pilasters with corbels. As high streets became more successful, shopkeepers who wanted to maximise the width of their establishments would share a single pilaster/corbel with their neighbour. By 1900 these unregulated vertical spaces had become an eyesore as shops refused to take responsibility for the upkeep and decoration of their shared corbels/pilasters. To remedy this unsightly problem the Corbel Act became British Law as part of the Housing and Town Planning Act in 1909. Sadly, the act was repealed without replacement just after the Second World War in 1947 as part of the Town and Country Planning Act 1947, which came into effect on 1 July 1948.

With the current demise of the British high street after the birth of the internet and the effects of COVID-19 it is the hope of a House of Commons Select Committee, the High Street Trade Committee, that a revised version of the Corbels Act will be enacted in the next Town Planning Act in 2021/22.

Additional powers as to the implementation of the Corbels Act:

(1) The powers of a local authority to enforce compliance for the purposes of Part III of the principal Act shall be deemed to include the following powers –

(a) To acquire any and all corbels through compulsory purchase by the local authority where a business is seen to neglect its statutory duty to maintain corbels in compliance with National Heritage guidelines. In such circumstances the Land Registry will amend its maps to show ownership of the corbel transferred to the local authority. This transfer is non-reversible.

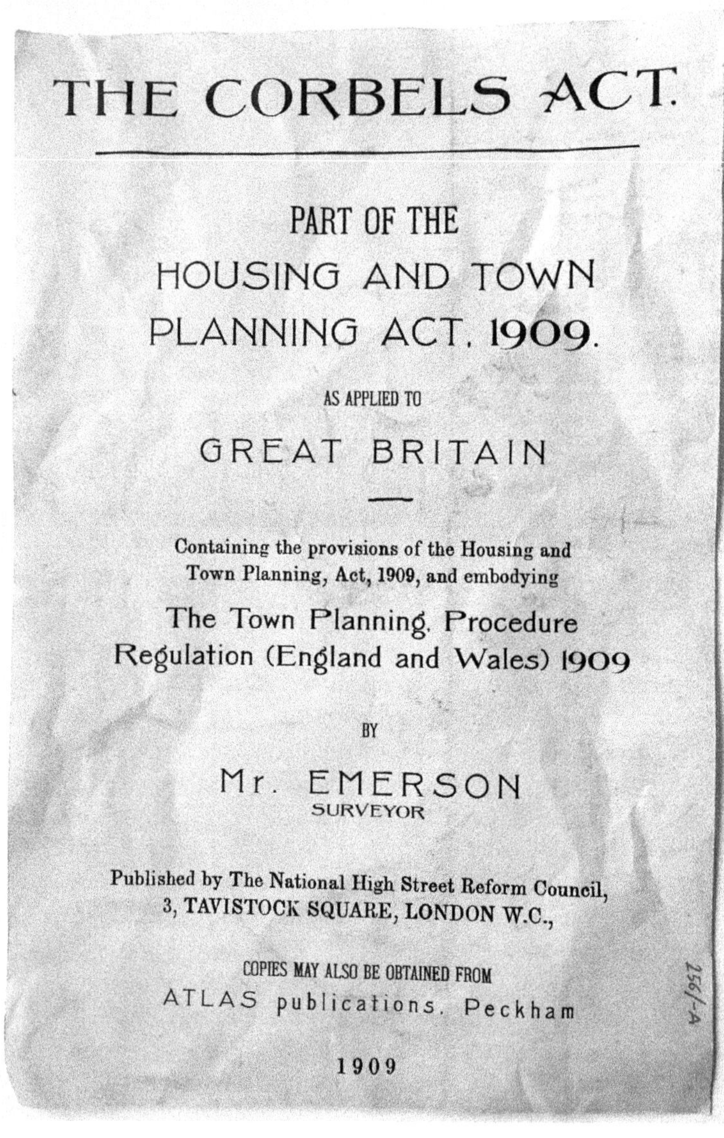

THE CORBELS ACT.

PART OF THE
HOUSING AND TOWN
PLANNING ACT, 1909.

AS APPLIED TO

GREAT BRITAIN

Containing the provisions of the Housing and
Town Planning, Act, 1909, and embodying

The Town Planning. Procedure
Regulation (England and Wales) 1909

BY

Mr. EMERSON
SURVEYOR

Published by The National High Street Reform Council,
3, TAVISTOCK SQUARE, LONDON W.C.,

COPIES MAY ALSO BE OBTAINED FROM
ATLAS publications. Peckham

1909

FIGURE 7.1 The Corbels Act 1909, Letterpress on paper, 21 × 29 cm, Collection: Cumming Museum, Walworth Road, London.

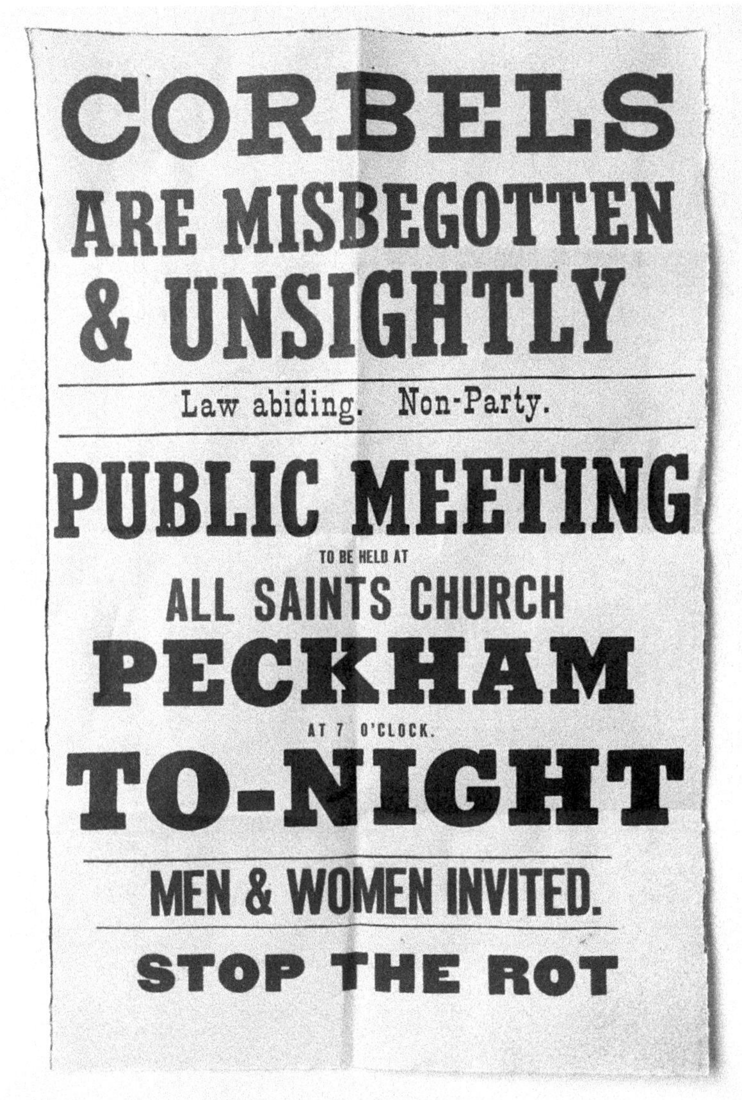

FIGURE 7.2 Left: Public Meeting Flyer, 1908, Letterpress on paper, 21 × 29 cm, Collection: British Museum.

(b) The legal boundary of a corbel includes five metres vertical airspace both above and below the corbel itself on either side of the fascia. This will include cornice, architrave, pilaster, cill and base.

(c) A right to light is usually acquired under the Prescription Act 1832; however, the Corbels Act will consider any infringement of light to be against the law. This is especially so when raking or slanting light

FIGURE 7.3 Corbels: Peckham, Atelier Biwa, Tokyo. Exhibition catalogue for the Venice Biennale 2012, Collection: RIBA, London.

illuminates a corbel. If the loss of light is small and can be adequately compensated by money, a court may decide to award compensation instead of an injunction.

(d) The local authority shall have power to alter, enlarge, repair and improve any such corbels so as to render them in all respects fit for purpose. This power is also extended to any cornice, architrave, pilaster, cill and base.

(e) Conservation and design decisions will be made in accordance with laws already laid down by the Corbels Department of National Heritage, the Royal Institute of British Architects and the Henry Moore Foundation.

FIGURE 7.4 Corbels: Peckham, Atelier Biwa, Tokyo. Exhibition catalogue for the Venice Biennale 2012, Collection: RIBA, London.

8

REPORT TO THE TREASURER OF INJUSTICE

Frederick Dolan

The twenty-first century, otherwise unremarkable after the Great Climate Change Scare of its early decades was revealed to be a hoax, is remembered for its solution to an age-old problem.

Given the achievements of our ancestors and the benefits that flow from them which we enjoy every day, it is difficult for us to conceive the moral chaos that prevailed during most of the twentieth to twenty-first centuries – the "era of heteronomous willing" before true autonomy was socially engineered as the presumptive normative foundation of all social interaction both public and private. This was made possible by an insight formulated in the early decades of the last century: that consent, the cornerstone of our system of morality, *cannot be given*. Once this principle was established, it was impossible not to see that every action of every individual and institution in society was wrong and unjust.

We now know with certainty that each of us is continually being wronged, even though – given the imperfections of human cognition, especially our inability to foresee all the consequences of our actions – the specific wrongs may not become evident until far in the future. It became clear that if a reliable estimate could be made of each individual's future victimisation, it would be possible for everyone to draw on the value of these wrongs for the purpose of economic exchange. This led to the establishment of a Treasury of Injustice and a new metric for net worth based on the amount of undeserved harm in one's possession, which became the official currency. In line with the well-established principles of the free market, this resulted in a wave of economic expansion, which created more opportunities for interaction and thus an increasing accumulation of what economists came to call Future Expected Wrongness. Productivity was further enhanced by the decision to do away with the Harm Limitation Proviso, and to calculate future harm to infinity. (The objection from the eventual heat-death of the universe was overcome when it was understood that the moral universe, at least that dimension of it that concerns compensation, is eternal and infinite.)

Obstacles were encountered and overcome. The mid-twenty-first century saw the appearance of Consent Heroes. At first, these were individuals who chose to keep their interactions with others to an absolute minimum and so remain at least as morally pure as humanly possible. The great monasteries and retreats that were established for this purpose, organised around the principle of lifetime solitary confinement, became legendary. The irrationality of this, however, was obvious to most, since the strength of the economy, hence the well-being of society, depended on the unlimited accumulation of future injustice, which mandated that interaction be maximised rather than minimised. Efforts were made to ban such communities, but eventually the solution that prevails today was hit upon. It was realised that the existence of these monasteries was itself a source of future injustice, in the form of the harm done to society as a whole by their attempts, to some extent successful, to avoid harming others, this harm consisting in the reduced productivity the absence of their potential unjust acts inflicted on the rest of society.

In time a more extreme form of Consent Heroism emerged: suicide. The stated intention was to avoid harming others by the elegantly simple expedient of ending one's life. In reality these suicides (often carried out with great theatricality and widely shared on social media) were protests against the then-emerging moral and economic order being implemented by the Treasury's Victim Credit System and were intended as a *reductio ad absurdum* argument against the very idea that our fundamental moral obligation is to refrain from actions not consented to by all the affected parties. It was immediately evident, however, that suicides brought into existence even more Future Estimated Wrongness than did monastics (since the former's unjust acts dropped to absolute zero, something not even the most rigorous solitary confinement could achieve), which enabled the Treasury to issue Harm Credits based on the suicide rate (together with other measures of each individual suicide's likely rate of harm production, calculated to infinity). Now, of course, we honour these Consent Heroes, and it is the hope of each "family" (on this, see the Report to the Registrar of Consent to Human Nature) that at least one of its "children" elects this way of contributing to freedom and prosperity.

The great conceptual breakthrough came with the realisation that the principle of tacit consent, which had legitimated wrong-doing for so long owing to its apparent plausibility, was fatally flawed.

Granted, even express consent has its problems. A great many conditions must be met in order to give consent unambiguously. First, consent must be given explicitly – in principle verbally, but in practice nothing less than a sworn written declaration will do. Second, consent must be freely given. Third, the consenter must be mentally competent to consent, i.e., not delusional or cognitively impaired. Fourth, consent must be informed: the prospective consenter must be aware, and made aware, of all the ways the action consented to may affect him.

That is, the one seeking consent must perform due diligence by actively verifying that all these conditions have indeed been met, ideally by both reviewing existing documentation attesting to the fitness of the party affected by the proposed action and by carrying out an independent investigation into the matter.

There is of course a practical problem here, namely that securing consent before acting is so time-consuming that action will rarely occur. The problem is magnified when one considers that the consent of all others potentially affected by the action must also be given – a number that, it was quickly realised, includes everyone alive and all future generations. (The necessity of securing the consent of the dead continues to be hotly debated.) There is also the much-discussed problem of infinite regress, since the act of verifying fitness to give consent must itself be consented to, and so on *ad infinitum*.

Tacit consent is even more troubling than express consent. As we know, the principle of tacit consent was introduced by the English Whig ideologue John Locke (1632–1704) precisely as a remedy for the evident fact that almost no one has expressly consented to be ruled by their government, which on Locke's account means that no government is legitimate. His solution was to hold that merely by living in a society, one is implicitly or "tacitly" consenting to its government. By this criterion, however, merely going along with what someone is doing to one is equivalent to having given them one's permission to do it. "Consent" here means no more than "not strongly opposed" and perhaps not even that – an unacceptably fragile standard on which to rest the fundamental moral principle of a society.

As we know, the concept of tacit consent came to be understood differently: the idea is that one gives tacit consent to X's act A by failing to express the desire that X refrains from A, *in a context in which one would ordinarily be expected to express that desire*. In other words, for one to express consent tacitly, the context must be such that a person's failure to make the absence of a desire explicit can be taken as the expression of that desire. Two conditions are required: first, the person must be competent to express the desire that X refrains from A; and second, the person would be expected to express the desire that X refrains from A (under the circumstances). Thus, a woman who, after a total stranger at a party takes her hand in his, fails to withdraw it, and assuming there is a general expectation that women withdraw their hands from those of men who are unknown to them, may be regarded as having consented to the man's advance.[1]

However, tacit consent puts an unacceptable burden on the parties. What counts as an indication of tacit consent depends on the context, which can vary depending on the conventions of the culture. A woman who leaves her hand in a man's may be tacitly consenting to the advance, but only where there is an expectation that she would withdraw her hand otherwise. If the expectations

1 With this definition and illustration I follow Haworth (2012: 124–125), who follows Sartre (1969: 55ff) and Simmons (1979: 79–80).

were different, for example, if holding hands with strangers became normal, her inaction would lose its significance. Hence, the determination of consent requires a thorough vetting of the context, a process that may be extended indefinitely because its outcome will never be settled to everyone's satisfaction – assuming, of course, that it is carried out by sufficiently sincere and committed casuists. For a time, it was hoped that a standard checklist would provide an efficient means to confirm the contextual conditions required for tacit consent in any given case, in the form of a series of questions put to the proposed consenter concerning his or her freedom from coercion, mental competence, possession of relevant information, and so forth. Of course, this defeated the purpose of tacit consent by transforming it into express consent, and also ran afoul of the Irony Limitation Act of 2023. Quite apart from this, the use of simple checklists proved inadequate for a genuine determination of fitness. Indeed, no adequate method exists.

Moreover, consent given tacitly can only be withdrawn explicitly. In the illustration given above, the woman would be required to actively and unambiguously withdraw her hand. This unfairly puts the burden on the potential victim of non-consensual activity. We cannot presume consent on the part of those affected unless we have exhaustively examined the circumstances under which the failure to withdraw consent appears to be taking place, and determined that inaction is not due to incompetence, coercion, distraction, confusion, effects of past trauma, lack of privilege, imbalance of power, hope for a future reward or some other heteronomous factor. But it is impossible to make a reliable determination of this kind.

Taking into account all these considerations, it became clear that it was impossible to give one's consent whether expressly or tacitly, which meant that it was impossible for human beings to interact with one another in morally permissible ways. Morality demanded, therefore, that we criminalise everything by presuming that no one has consented to anything.

The basic value driving our morality is that of individual agency. As beings with second-order as well as first-order beliefs and desires, individuals ask themselves whether their beliefs are true and whether their desires are the best. On this basis they commit themselves to goals and plan their lives so as to achieve them. They transform the natural world into a world of their own. But ownership of a shared world requires that individuals consent to its arrangements, for otherwise it would be they who are owned by the world. As consent cannot be given, our forebears succeeded in achieving our moral goals in the only way possible: by acknowledging that it is impossible to achieve them, conferring the status of currency on the harm done to those victimised by this impossibility, and compensating them accordingly. Since the amount owed each individual for Future Expected Harm is calculated to infinity, each possesses an infinite amount of Harm Credit, that is, an amount equal to everyone else's. Once the economy was placed on the firm footing of universal guilt and infinite indebtedness, such that everyone owed compensation to everyone else in an amount equal to that which they were owed, society was able to achieve equality and freedom by recognising, affirming and institutionalising their non-existence.

Signed,
(Hon.) Aikaterine Akenehi,
Historian of the Treasury of Injustice

Bibliography

Hayworth, Alan (2012) *Understanding the Political Philosophers*. Second Edition. London and New York: Routledge.

Sartre, Jean Paul (1969 [1943]) *Being and Nothingness*. London: Routledge.

Simmons, A. John (1979) *Moral Principles and Political Obligations*. Princeton: Princeton University Press.

9

ENNOMIE

William Watkin

> we also find in Aeschylus the composite ἔννομος [*ennomos*], meaning "to live", "to inhabit", as well as in a more technical sense in ἐννόμιος [*ennomios*] in relation to pastures (for example, Aes. *Suppl.* 384, 404, 547 and 565; *Ch.* 483).
>
> Thanos Zartaloudis, *The Birth of Nomos.* (Edinburgh University Press, 2019) p. 265

And so it is that this became the norm,
the nomos of ontology itself,
the law of law, the beings of your Being,
from what is presupposed we humans do,
to how this is embedded in our tasks.
To make our way beyond the city walls,
and gather crops, then trade upon the lee,
until there comes to be an urgent need,
a law of our behaviour written down.
Why? Because there's evil in our midst,
that sacred speck of all our small betrayals,
those hebetudinous forms of life.

Height has been debased, horizons colonised,
pastures all laid waste by pollutants
of analogies. Water itself
is a danger to your mind, emergent in springs,
funnelled through rivers, spilling deltas down.
Ground cannot deny its fundaments

of tedious precocity, even when it quakes,
explodes in fury and in magma drowned;
rivers of hot and virulent discontent.
And as for air neglect, I'd ask, to breathe,
the pneuma carries calculated motes
of observation, obtuse deductions,
on which, over time, without your knowing so
you will asphyxiate. Impossible to ask
you not to breathe, resort I to exhorting:
don't look, oh shield your eyes and switch
off the mendacious mechanisms of
the mind's constructions of worlds and all their
stabilities, which may take their lead
from the excitations caused within us all
when we look back at our homeland falling off
into a dawn-stained, plangent fog,
but for the large part spin you out a web
of how things seem to be that comes from some
completely other sense than that Kant called
apperception. No, I would rather ask
that you submit to some other faculty,
one of curated impotential of
observation, that imperception we could call.

You will not be left alone in those your
idle, imperceptive meanderings;
all are blind to the imprecations of
their own prejudicial seat in the king-
doms of contemplation, even I
can only implore you: open up your eyes
to the fact of this blindness while warning
do not waste your flagging energy
in pursuit of its particulars.
Unlike the myths of unconscious depths,
what is most unintelligible to you
is not in any case a private thing,
there is nothing singular about it,
we all fail to see the obvious object
in our own unique, inimitable way
but the obvious in question, and
by definition it can ne'er be snagged
by the tilting intonation of demand,
is a matter for us all, in contexts lodged
of our communicability,

what they sanction and allow,
what is expressly forbidden by the law,
and then this other material that cannot
even banished be from the nomos of
contextualisation as power,
because it does not manifest in there,
repressing it so that it then appears
swathed in outlandish garb in some lonely quarter
of the city will not play, this is a
conceptualisation always out
of apotropaic strategy;
better to accept that just as there
are truths still fit to be unveiled
in ill-attended, lustreless seminars,
no longer echoing round the lecture halls
of this world's capitals, but in the
shabby rooms of mid-league seats of learning,
there will also be impossibilities
whose purpose is to be resistant to
the *aletheia* of truth. For centuries
these incommunicable, nameless "concepts" –
they are not or perhaps will never be
truths, yet renouncing an age-old and as
we shall see now decrepit opposition
one cannot call them falsehoods either as
to be determined false would have to be
declared and then found wanting in the terms
of their extensions out into some worlds
the purpose had of being objects of fear –
they *were* named, and that fixed denotation
has subsequently captured them,
a vain attempt to adhere to them some mode
of signatory consistency.
But these names were more of the order of threats,
oaths, expletives whispered under breath,
one function of this nominal imprecation
was resolutely *not* to aggrandise them,
granted they were places where thought ought not to go
but not because they occupied some kind
of territory rarefied, say
out beyond the city gates or deeply
lodged, under the ground in that darkly
glamourous nether region that these days
we call the other, but because they were

pointless, tedious to be exact, could not
even be awarded terminology
such as aporia or impasse.
Admittedly dead ends they were but of
the order of some sub urban estate
where roads run on through the banality
of our vernacular architecture,
yet never anywhere arrive so as
to preclude the transgressions of the
caught commuter ceaselessly in search
of the rat run's abbreviations;
these empty signifiers pointing to a place
where you will simply run aground,
no threshold would be crossed no border cut
into the clay and chalk you just fetch up
in some nominative cul-de-sac,
spin your wheels, cool your heels. They could be called
upon at any time but each term lacked
a certain something which then disallowed
their being much more than a minor player,
an adjectival modality of
thought, a low-level insult of the order
of an acidic insinuation.

What is law, has ever been the question.
Fear of lawlessness our sole propulsion.
All day long philosophers sat gazing on the beasts:
swarms of locusts inundating crops,
maggots wriggling in an open gut,
the wolf takes down an elk and tears its throat,
sparrows' endless squabble for the crumb;
and from this observation drew the law,
not out of civic pride and need to make
the traders pay their taxes for the right
to barter in sanctioned market squares
where utility provision is the norm
and petty theft discouraged by police,
but because if left alone to trade, let's say
wonderfully unencumbered by the rule,
chaos would ensue, and violence our nomos now.
And so we have habituated fact,
and carved it into regulatory script,
while at the same calling on the law
as some foundational concept of the act

of constitution, that remains an active
element of every small decision,
which in turn reconstitutes its founding
through the effective demonstration of
each quantum of exchange, each portion of the tithe.

Thus paradox on paradox inclines
towards a progress of illogical impasse,
Dead ends with aporia connected,
forming a möbius-mazy contradiction,
one metaphysical heavily weighted game
where the throw of dice is self-abolishing,
day becomes night, truth mistook for falsehood,
mathematicians to asylums flee.
Charlatans use endless circumlocution
to mask the simple fact that what they say
does not make sense, does not make any sense.
And all the while this threat of nature's state,
that Maynard Smith disproved in '73,
which can, I guess, be in one word expressed:
anomie, the breakdown of the social,
a reversion to a place we've never been.
And we swallowed all this bullshit whole,
then built empires from the vomit of our lies.

… and so it was that *our* term pottered about the hinterlands, too peripheral to be of any great importance, yet also too far from the limits of knowledge to be seen as some kind of god-awful liminal or transactional space, was just a boring part of town or a tedious field with no particular redeeming features, and this my fellow sojourners over many, many hundreds of years transpired to be its greatest advantage, to exist and be notable in an occasional fashion but cause no great ructions, a bit-part actor in many great dramas of intellectual endeavour, yet just as likely to be left off the billing as to participate, neither loved nor cursed, hardly seen, yet not threatening enough to be ignored, the term indifference just subsisted, biding its time without any eschatological intent, edging ever closer to those impossible to even conceive of elements of imperception that we all carry with us, yet never with a plan or an executable strategy, it just subsisted somewhere between habituation and innovation in a manner that to call it in-between would be laughable, until …

10

TWELVE THESES ON THE EXORBITANT PRINCIPLE THAT A LAWYER MUST WORK FOR THE POOR

Adam Gearey

I.

Imagine, if you will, a principle that compels a lawyer to work for the poor. Of course, there have long been *pro bono* principles, but we are in pursuit of something more radical. The joyous principle rests on an imaginative truth communicated through metaphor and parable: there is no wealth but life. This weak force operates obliquely as an anti-norm. You must work gratuitously because you can choose not to do so.

II.

Samuel Johnson and Sir James Johnston were once discussing an advocate's fee. Sir James confessed that he had paid little attention to an argument because counsel had not been "paid for speaking". Johnson disagreed – asserting that an argument is good irrespective of whether someone has paid for it or not. Johnson evoked the image of the longbow: "the force of it depends on the strength of the hand that draws it" (Boswell, 1963: 514). There is a peculiar truth at play in Johnson's words, a truth that connects with an image found in John Ruskin. The ideal of good work done well is given by the image of the carpenter driving well-made rivets into well-cut timber: "the best work never was, nor ever will be, done for money at all" (Ruskin, 1860: 157). We will pursue this principle through law's peculiar allergy to money payment, to Ruskin's *Unto this Last*. We will then turn to examine the practices of those "unpaid professor[s] of social philosophy", Henrietta and Samuel Barnett (Barnett and Barnett, 1888: 8). The Barnetts were leaders of the settlement movement in the slums of East London. Other paths could be traced. One would lead to Jane Addams and to Hull House in Chicago; another, less obvious perhaps, could be followed to the Catholic Workers Movement, Michael Harrington and

American socialism. We cannot follow these traces in this short chapter. However, we will conclude with one particularly relevant transformation of the exorbitant principle in an engagement with Jacques Ellul's anti-jurisprudence and William Stringfellow's legal activism in Manhattan. The essay concludes with a final thesis that might help the lawyer struggling with ennui and melancholy – a poetic anti-norm – not so much *pro bono publico* as *nam bonum ex se ut alterum.*

III.

From the perspective of the ancient history of the law, advocacy is not performed for a fee. The great lawyers of Athens, for instance, received their "compensation" as "honorary or gratuitous" (Sharswood, 1860: 139). In Rome, jurisconsuls "received no compensation" but worked for honour: "[o]n the public days of market, or assembly, the masters of the art were seen walking in the forum, ready to impart the needful advice to the meanest of their fellow-citizens" (loc. cit.). Admittedly, this was in the "virtuous" early history of the republic. Only later did the "business of advocating causes became a distinct profession" which required payment of a fee, but even then, it "was a mere honorary recompense [and] the client was under no legal obligation to pay it" (loc. cit.). This was a marked feature of a later period of Roman history. The Cincian law, promulgated by Marcus Cincius Alimentus, prohibited the "patron or advocate" from payment, a law that Augustus re-enacted (loc. cit.).

Gibbon picks up on this theme – linking the decline of a "noble art" or a "sacred inheritance" to a sordid trade of "cunning and skill" – where fleecing the client became as important as using the law to gain personal fame and wealth. With money comes the transformation of an "honorable office to a money-making trade" (Sharswood, 1860: 138). More recently, case law contains the idea that if an advocate is to be recompensed at all, it is through gift or honorarium – "which giveth honor as well to the taker as to the giver" (Warvelle, 1920: 72). Even if this principle becomes an increasingly "transparent fiction" (ibid.: 71) it continues its hold over the way in which remuneration for advocacy is articulated.

Within this jurisprudence, there is a special case. Even though a lawyer can be remunerated, there are certain instances when "[he/she/it] may be expected to render gratuitous service in a worthy cause" (Warvelle, 1920: 75). The peculiarity of this duty can be glimpsed in the way that writers on legal ethics speak of a sense of obligation owed to the poor. If a court orders that a criminal defendant should be represented, then an advocate is so compelled. The poor, then, place a special demand on lawyers.

IV.

This obligation can also be found in a form of self-examination or self-care that is bound up with the recommendation that certain legal ethicists make: avoid the fate of the "great lawyers" in old age. Lawyers in old age suffer from realising that their brilliant careers have been a complete waste of time. This condition cannot be dismissed as a nineteenth-century piety. The ennui of a life in law runs through contemporary writing. There is a growing "crisis" in the "capacity" of legal practice to "offer fulfilment to the person who takes it up" (Kronman, 1993: 1). The rot runs deep. It is not just the practice of law. The narrow commercial vision of legal education "jeopardizes the intellectual mission of the university" (Motro, 2015: 118).

V.

John Ruskin's *Unto this Last* is a self-help manual for lawyers and students of law afflicted by ennui.

VI.

Unto this Last alludes to *Matthew* 20:1–16. In the Gospel, the labourers hired late in the day to work in the master's vineyard receive the same payment as those hired in the morning. Accused of unfairness, the master answers that he has "done no wrong" as all the labourers agreed to work for a penny. The master can honestly say "I will give unto this last even as unto thee." Looked at one way, this is a distorted scale of value. As the disgruntled labourers point out to the master, they have sweated all day working for the same amount of money as those who have done only an hour's work. However, the closing line suggests a different perspective: "[s]o the last shall be first, and the first last: for many be called, but few chosen [...]." How can we read this parable? One might be tempted to side with the exploited labourers and dismiss the parable as an excuse for pietism and passivity. However, one could also say that Matthew's Gospel evokes a scale of value that rewards in a way outside of conventional economy. Perhaps there is an echo of this strange situation in Simone Weil's argument (1987) that struggles over wages merely serve to support the exploitative nature of the wage system as a whole. But how is one "chosen" – for what or by whom? A voice in the night? A sense of unease? Of trouble? Whatever the calling, Ruskin's text works in this tradition of asymmetrical demands (Weil 2015: 134).

VII.

Just economy is based on "such affection as one man *owes* to another" (Ruskin, 1860: 118). A discourse on affection and obligation is an engagement with poverty: "[t]he rich and the poor have met. God is their maker." Ruskin draws attention to the meaning of the word "met" – which is glossed as "stood in each other's way" and sees the "counteraction" of "poverty and wealth" as a "law" of the world (ibid., 146). What is this obscure law? Ruskin tells us no more than it is bound up with "jurisprudence" and value. But, value is not found in David

Ricardo's equation of utility and exchange. Value derives from the Latin *valere* – meaning "to be well and strong". Ruskin asserts that value means to "avail towards life". This leads to a conjunction of valour and value: wealth is "THE POSSESSION OF THE VALUABLE BY THE VALIANT" (Ruskin, 1860: 171). The valiant do not amass wealth for the sake of wealth. As "THERE IS NO WEALTH BUT LIFE" (ibid.: 185), the valiant amass wealth so as to use their own life, skill and resources to influence, for the better, the lives of others (loc. cit.).

VIII.

Where does this leave us? Ruskin's economics have not been taken seriously, but, this does not mean that they are worthless. Their value lies in provocation. We can read Ruskin as an English Georges Bataille. *Unto this Last* is a working through of an authority that comes from the traumas of inner experience. Ruskin, like Bataille, traces those points where a restricted economy of ego and utilitarian exchange might open on to the wilder terms of a more general circulation of waste and excess. Or joy? Might value be "found" in joyous giving? A squandering of what one has so that things might go better for others? *Unto this Last* opens up intriguing spaces of imaginary economies where the "free gift of service [...] is a matter of affection – not of traffic" (Ruskin, 1860: 151).

IX.

At this point, we need to make a brief detour through the notion of settlement movement. We can follow a line of influence directly from Ruskin, through Arnold Toynbee to Samuel and Henrietta Barnett, to Christian socialism and the settlement movement in the East End of London. Settlement was a response to the endemic poverty of the late 1800s. Focused on Toynbee Hall in Whitechapel, scholars from Oxford and Cambridge settled in the slums and squalor of the East End to further the cause of working-class education and to break down the social distance between classes. For the Barnetts, good character or nobility of soul is superfluity. Settlors had to "give all and expect nothing" (Barnett and Barnett, 1888: 114).

Henrietta Barnett provides a vivid account of the trials faced by her husband and herself when they moved to the slum parish of St Judes in the "grizzly drizzle" of a grim February afternoon. They found the church closed and scenes of grim social depravity in the filthy alleys, yards and tenements off Commercial Road. The Barnetts' concern was not with legal reforms, or what "society" could do to alleviate poverty. The question was "what can I do?" (Barnett and Barnett, 1888: 97). Settlement is not strictly a "university mission" – or a religious endeavour. Its motive force is social intercourse: a way of being or acting, getting involved, "box[ing] with the boys"; reading poetry and history, setting an example: "taking up such work as was possible" (ibid.). Like Weil, in the vineyards, urging the workers to learn geometry and read Plato (Weil 1987, x).

X.

These themes can be traced into the anti-jurisprudence of Jacques Ellul. Ellul offers a radical version of Christianity. Christian engagement with law is not based on "supernatural insight" or a quest for the "derivation of principles" that would inform a just legal order, but a wrestling with "concrete situations" in which one might judge factual situations, more or less "justly" in the "light of the righteousness of God" (Ellul, 1969: 88). But God is unknowable. Justice is neither possible, nor impossible. If Ellul is re-read through Ruskin, then the key principle of this anti-jurisprudence might be that a just decision, a sign of justice in the world (rather than a revelation of the power of God's majesty of which nothing can be said), acknowledges the "rights of the poor [...] delivers [them] from their repression" – and restores them to their status as human beings. As such "law cannot be separated from compassion" (ibid.: 114). Law is just to the extent that it "protects the weak" and guarantees their "well-being". To the extent that compassion has a general applicability it is that "people must be taken for what they are" and "considered in their actual situation" (ibid.: 115).

XI.

What does this mean? The preferential option for the poor? Certainly, but not just this Christianisation of the difference principle. Something else as well: "[T]he street became as much of an office as I ever had in Harlem" (Stringfellow, 1964: 42). Stringfellow's work in Manhattan is not justified as charity or humanitarian concern. The poverty lawyer has to understand the "vulnerability of daily life" (Stringfellow, 1964: 44). If the face to face means anything in Stringfellow's work it is this sharing of existence, through exposure to the people with whom one works. Difficult experience: "[w]e scarcely know ourselves" (Day, 2006: 18).

XII.

The non-poor need to remember the suffering of the poor "for their own sake" (Stringfellow, 1964: 28). The poor are, most immediately, the victims of "slum landlords, [...] scab employer[s] [...] corruptible cops [and] the whole array of parasites whose own power or profit ... depends upon the continuation of poverty" (Stringfellow, 1964: 29). In a more theological sense, the poor are "intercessory for the rich" poised as they are so precariously and close to the power of death. Non-being. Outside of life. The suffering of the poor "substitutes" for that of the non-poor. In this proximity to death, men realise their radical "estrangement" from each other and from the "rest of creation" (Stringfellow,

1964: 29–30). The poor take the power of death upon themselves. But no one can stand in for the other person, "no man may deliver his brother [from death], nor may a man deliver himself" (Stringfellow, 1964: 31). An "[a]wful vulnerability" is the common human condition.

The drawn bow, tensed in the hand.

Bibliography

Barnett, Samuel Augustus & Barnett, Henrietta (1888) *Practicable Socialism: Essays on Social Reform*. (Freeport, NY: Books for Libraries Press).

Boswell, James (1963) *Life of Samuel Johnson, LL. D.* (Everyman's Library, 2 Vol. Ed.) Vol. 2.

Day, Dorothy (2006) *From Union Square to Rome* (New York. NY: Orbis).

Ellul, Jacques (1969) *The Theological Foundations of Law* (Indiana, IN: Indiana University Press).

Kronman, Anthony T. (1993) *The Lost Lawyer* (Harvard, MA: Belknap Press).

Morto, Shari (2015) 'Scholarship against Desire', *Yale Journal of Law & the Humanities*, Vol. 27, No. 1, 115–156.

Ruskin, John (1860) *Unto this Last* (London, UK: Smith, Elder and Co).

Sharswood, George (1860) *An Essay on Professional Ethics* (Philadelphia, PA: T. and J. W. Johnson and Co.).

Stringfellow, William (1964) *My People is the Enemy* (New York, NY: Wipf and Stock).

Warvelle, G. William (1920) *Essays in Legal Ethics* (Chicago, IL: Callaghan and Son).

Weil, Simone (1987) *Gravity and Grace* (London, UK: Routledge).

Weil, Simone (2015) 'First Condition for Dignified Work', in *Simone Weil Late Philosphical Writings*, ed. O. Springstead (University of Notre Dame Press), 131–143.

11

INTHA GNALAMUM POY THAANO – IMAGINING THE OTHER IN CONTRACT

Swethaa S. Ballakrishnen[1]

When I was seven years old, I stopped eating rice on Thursdays. I remember the week clearly, as though no time has passed: I had a spelling test the next day, and I felt like if I could give up something, then, somehow, I would be rewarded in return.

Fasting for reward might be a common religious tradition, but it was not one I grew up with. Surely, I must have picked up the idea of exchange from somewhere (if development psychologists are to be believed, all reactive make-up is decided in our first five years). Yet, even if it was learnt behaviour, rice was not an especial choice, and it was sorely lacking as a commodity of exchange. I cannot recall having a strong opinion about it – note that diet consciousness about the punishing nature of carbohydrates was at least a few decades away for Madras pre-teens – it just happened to be what was on my plate the second I made the decision to give up *something*.

Overall, it felt like thought-out exchange, a possibly enforceable[2] contract even though I did not have the words for it then, and in the years since, I have

1 Many thanks to Eman Abdelhai, Peter Goodrich, Koshy John, Raya Lakova, Sarah Lawsky, and Suryapratim Roy for reading, talking through, and imagining the many (im)possibilities of this draft alongside me.

2 As I make the case here for an imaginary contract, I see how I am also imagining very different scope condition for the feasibility of a contract absent an enforcer. To clarify, I recognize that contract by definition is a promise that law enforces, but I differently imagine here both law's powerful recourse and remedy as well as its simultaneous capacity for deep violence. In a collection of essays chronicalling the early months of the pandemic, Zadie Smith writes about writing and imagination as control, not creativity (2020:8). In the opening essay, "Peonies", she chronicles how staring at a mid-city corner park with tulips she wished the flowers were – and, therefore, willed them to be – peonies in her writing, narrative, and imagined world forever more. I borrow strongly from her ethos of imagination in constructing this contractual cabinet. As she offers: "We know we are deluded, but the strange thing is that this delusion is necessary,

been inclined to continue affording it that definitional justice. It was, after all, an agreement with a specific other (the universe, I supposed), it had consideration (although, perhaps not *quid pro quo,* for what would the universe have done with my rice and *paruppu*?), it had additional terms to structure its intent and limitations (for example, rice was out of limits, but rice-dependent by-products were OK, especially in the form of *dosa*), these terms went through rounds of negotiation, especially upon parental interrogation,[3] and it certainly felt validated when I got my test results the following week: one day of rice for an A in spelling.

The few people I have shared this story with have either laughed at my early obsessiveness (these are usually fellow lawyers, and the laughter is meant to be a veiled compliment) or nodded in community (these are usually fellow South Asians familiar with the anxiety of a grade-obsessed primary schooling). And, almost unanimously, despite their nod to its precocious creativity, those inclined to judge it on contractual merit, have found it lacking. The logic is not lost on me – imaginary contracts can only have imaginary obligations, and only certain legal others are allowed to be imagined[4] – and as someone teaching first-year law students, I am cognisant of this doctrine's normative usefulness: we limit our imaginations with fixed rules and create fictions out of law – and, necessarily, the other – to make sense of this world. But this pedagogical commitment – an indefinite contract to the academy – offers a window to an indulgent line of converse intellectual inquiry: *What about the contract is not imagined*?

Now, I do not mean just the imagination involved with theorising the intent to contract or constructive good faith – both settled rules of law – but, rather, the

---

If only temporarily, to create the mold in the first place, the one into which you pour everything you can't give shape to in life." In this way, this definition of contract, and not just for poetry's sake, is a *prayer* in more ways than one. As I make the case here for an imaginary contract, I see ... imagining the very different scope conditions for the feasibility ...

3 To be clear, even though there was no enforcer in a sense, I did feel like there would be remedy and recourse. I also remember clearly that the breach clause was airtight: I would understand if I did not have express good luck if I, by mistake, skipped a Thursday and ate rice, but there ought to be no terrible repercussion in the opposite direction. Also, over time, usually as a response to a prodding question posed by someone about something I had not yet thought through re this commitment, worked in – over the course of a few years – a bunch of definitional limitations as well as a interpretative clause of sorts that laid out the intention of the contract. For example, if I did not include a term that was obvious and to my benefit, the universe ought to imagine that I had included it because, I would lament, recognising (and using to my benefit) my own limitations foremost, "after all, I was only a child".

4 Many imagined others are, by legal fiction, constituted persons – we imagine the company to have a personality, just as we imagine the State to have one. And it does not just stop with the profane, the sacred has been seen as legal person too: held both in the case of giving God rights through courts (e.g., the *Ayodhya* lawsuit before the Supreme Court in India, where the Hindu Lord Rama was considered a juridical person and plaintiffs in a property suit about *His* birthplace), defending such divinity's honour (e.g., blasphemy laws in Ireland) or demanding that God pay taxes (as the Indian Income Tax department did from one of the world's richest temples in Tirupati).

work of imagination in decreeing the contours of a contract that could extend (and often *does* extend) beyond the sum of its parts.

I recently was recollecting how the end of every relationship really only comes down to an irretrievable dissolution of the imagined other. All misreading and misunderstanding are really just definitional crevices that are impossible to bridge. One can think: *I had thought they were X, that when they said A, they meant A*. And, indeed, in more secure unpacking, one might concede that the other's point of view: *I was Y, that when I said B, I meant B*. (*AND I DID MEAN B!!*) What underlies this breakdown of contract, however, is the baseline recognition that neither party is really – or at least, fully – X or Y, and that A and B are both fungible, constantly evolving concepts.

There is, for example, a part in Andrew Sean Greer's very lyrical *Story of a Marriage* where Greer argues that nobody is as in love with the other as they are at the first electric encounter when the fiction is still rich with the imagined attributes: the less we know, the more we co-create of the other through imagination, and the more we are capable of rapture, and as an extension, perhaps love.[5] Seen this way, it becomes possible to admit that love, like many other things, is a *prima facie* relational contract, with malleable terms and expectations. It can form-shift from the meaningful expansiveness that allows us to attach more symbolism to the bare bones of the agreed-upon terms (*I love you, which means you smell like roses to me, I see everything in you*), as well as a scarcity that will pare it down to the essentials as circumstances may dictate (*I love you, which means I can/will do X*, or, *If you love me, you should do Y*). Thus, one might have indeed said B, and one might have meant B, but one's B and the other's B could be so different, no homogenous B universe would accommodate them. Were the Bs always different? Perhaps. Were the Bs only similar in supposed imagination? Possibly. Does their difference suddenly have new importance? Potentially. But these internal B variations do not always matter.

I Said–They Said breakdowns have not just financed a multi-billion-dollar divorce industry, they are also classic reminders of the ways in which we are constantly imagining the other that we are in community with. We imagine that words have a pre-supposed meaning, that there is symbolic resonance to the interaction based on mutually agreed or assumed meaning (Blumer, 1986), and that the actors will continue to interpret these words and concepts at different points in time with the same weight afforded to them as the other: an imagined comingling not just based on the past and present, but also our future consciousness. It is perhaps the impossibility of this prediction that leads Auden to propose

5 Greer (2008), writes: "A lover exists only in fragments, a dozen or so if the romance is new, a thousand if we're married to him, and out of those fragments our heart constructs an entire person. What we each create, since whatever is missing is filled by our imagination, is the person we wish him to be. The less we know him, of course, the more we love him. And that's why we always remember that first rapturous night when he was a stranger, and why this rapture returns only when he's dead."

that loving forever, is easy[6] – because forever is ambiguous enough to extend to a merged infinity. A more precise promise, however, i.e., promising to love someone at 4:15 next Tuesday is harder, because such concreteness assumes a specificity from one's projected future self that is hard to predict. More critically, on breach, it is too quick to reveal itself as unsatisfactory.

It is similar respect for impossibility that nudges people to enter into contractual agreement. We do not just record merged present and future aspirations when we enter into contract, we also agree that should such comingled understandings that feed off each other fail, we can catch, with fiction, new wind to move forward. This is why, despite desperate loving, we enter into pre-nups that might protect our romance should it not be an ever-after; and why despite absolute hope that we have raised children who will not fight over antique crockery, we write wills.

Seen this way, contracts also allow us to hope. We hope that when we say X, by virtue of saying the words, X1 will be interpreted from X and that Y1 will result from X1 (even if X2 is the natural progression of X1, per all logical reasoning). Contracts, then, are infused with the quality of simultaneously also being prayers: that if we do X, even if we cannot rationally imagine Y1 to be the ultimate consequence, we have a shot at it by having asked for it. A recent argument weaving together the relationship between magic and conditions of contract (Westbrook, 2018) makes part of this case: pushing back against the Weberian notion of disenchantment that is presupposed of modernity, Westbrook argues that "seemingly secular" – and therefore modern – things like doctrine, rules, and the jurisprudence concerning contracts "require rather breath-taking faith in the efficacy of words to shape reality." Enchantment, then, is not what modern society needs to move on from. Instead, it is what is necessary to offer faith to commercial realism. Magic and belief beyond the rational is vision, that is necessary for everyday contract formation – we need to transcend the ideas of meeting of minds and objective contract, to fully recognise the potential that can be gained by viewing them as relative and relational.

I have often fancied storing in my imaginary cabinet the possible cacophony of an alternate, contract-less world. But noise is not really file-friendly. Even worlds that accept the fluidity of terms and subvert the contours of rigid contract are sullied by the fact that they are in supposition of the other.

And again it is love and commitment ideologies that offer obvious examples: speaking recently to a poly-inclined[7] friend (who was at the time in a non-poly relationship) about cheating, I was nudged to reconsider the terms of an

6 Actual text from Auden's 1959 prose poem "Dichtung und Wahrhreit" (part 48/50): "'I love you forever' swears the poet. I find it easy to swear too. 'I will love you at 4:15 next Tuesday' – Is that still as easy?"

7 For a refresher on poly commitments, See *Ethical Slut* (1997). My favourite description of its thesis – despite my many reservations re: its heralding of sex as the only form of radical third wave praxis – is borrowed from Kelli Maria Korducki (2018: 110) in that it is a "third wave feminist

anti-contract: if cheating (as assumed by the other partner in this relationship, a man who asked for and was promised monogamy) is not coded in one party's (i.e., my friend's) emotional – and ethical – dictionary as a wrong, is it still a central term of their mutual understanding? If one were to rethink what cheating meant altogether,[8] and assume that either nothing – or, in the alternative, *all* things – constituted non-monogamy in some way (for, after all, in some sense, we are all polygamous in our relationships just by existing in a social world), then has a breach of contract occurred? I do not offer this to balance the pros and cons of emotional contract – despite the rhetoric of sameness espoused by mainstream political strategists, queer and alternate histories have fought hard for the right to re-calibrate accounts of commitment – but instead, to offer that contract, when met with the reality of the other, is inescapable, no matter what the words.

There is contract even (and especially) in non-contract: what a thought. In his existential treatise, which seems appropriate to bring up in a conversation about imagined others, Jean-Paul Sartre's *Nausea* (1938) offers a definition of love's journey (once quoted to me, ironically, after an irretrievable breakdown that I had then thought salvageable): "It is an undertaking to start loving someone," he says, "you have to have the energy, generosity, blindness. There is even a moment right at the start when you have to jump across an abyss: if you think about it, you don't do it." What can be said of love can be said of all other forms of human exchange. We are, whether we like it or not, in the constant business of undertakings[9] when in relationship with the other, even when there is not an actual contract, often precisely because there is no contract.

Once you meet with the ideology of another (even if the other only exists in your imagination), you are in relationship. And you are following that relationship, no matter the steps, no matter the meanings of A and B, no matter the propensity for X1 to result in Y1, no matter the pattern, no matter the intended meanings of the action. No matter, you have to jump. And with that jump, you

---

Non Monogamy for Dummies of sorts". Regarding radical queer erasure of asexuality, see *The Invisible Orientation* by Julie Sondra Decker (2014).

8 In his book *The Course of Love*, Alain de Botton (2016) argues, from the perspective of his protagonist, who has cheated within his heterosexual marriage of many years, that silence is in fact *in* the very service of such contract. Not because the act is not understood to be cheating (here Rabih knows he has committed an act with the power to destroy the tapestry of his otherwise solid marriage), but because vocalising it would be self-serving. In contrast, he sees a marriage with starting assumptions that "everyone is always impossible" to be an easier one because "Spouses who had been cheated upon would no longer be at liberty furiously to complain that they had expected their partner to be content with them alone. They could, instead, more poignantly and justly cry, "I was relying on you to be loyal to the specific variety of compromise and unhappiness with our hard-won marriage represents." The breach, in this alternate universe would be easier to accept to, given the scope conditions: "Thereafter, an affair would be a betrayal not of intimate joy but of a reciprocal pledge to endure the disappointments of marriage with bravery and stoic reserve."

9 Interestingly, to *undertake* is etymologically to trap and then to contract, which then came to mean funeral service! Thanks, as always, to Peter Goodrich for these derivation journeys.

are in contract with the other; because with the jump, there is an involved intra-contract with yourself.

In case you are wondering, I still do not eat rice on Thursdays: part of it is habit; a bigger part is perhaps that I do not eat very much rice; and at least a small part of it is in solidarity with a younger me who made this barter. As it happens, my spelling remains terrible, but I do make a living writing and using and stretching the limits of language. This fall from X1 to Y1 – or, the thread that holds the covert theme of my imagined contract – is that my contract to not eat rice (an act X) as a withholding relevant and comprehendible as a sacrifice to the universe (X1) was meant to result in an A in spelling (Y1) but, over time, produced an even more path-dependent outcome, i.e., my adult life as a lawyer (Y1a). And I continue to go back to that inner child that made the barter when I am making other barters with myself (old and current) and others. The imagined childhood contract and my expectations might have morphed from Y1 to Y1a, but they also held their core – somehow, I have internalised that if I keep my word, whatever law I imagine binding the contract, might hold better. That if I have faith in its fruition (and still resisted absolute delusion), over time, the undertaking might be worthwhile no matter the actual outcome. Thinking of imagination this way allows for the focus to shift from the contract to the actual act of jumping. It offers the sight that, perhaps, the jump is not merely part of the contract, it *is* the imagined contract. And our only way through this world might be to accept that we are jumping, constantly and repeatedly, often world without end, *amen*.[10]

It would be amiss to end a note arguing for the credibility of the imagination, without also nodding to its politics. There are necessary ethics about imagining the other – what we assume people mean when they say the words they say, and who we imagine to be in contract with, and how comfortable we are imagining it, says so much about us too (for example, folx from different *souths*: racialized and indigenous others, queers, disabled people, and women, are constantly reminded that their imagination is not as high status as other fantasies). It also takes a constant commitment to following the autonomous contract on its journey, to keep seeing it shape-shift and meaning-make with iteration, communication and acknowledgment of vulnerability. We will not always make it through, there will be slips in communication, we might spiral with Neptunian Chimeras. Still, it is only with reiterative conversation and faith with your metamorphosing selves, that we can have the mutable imagined contracts that we deserve. Thus, arguing for the imagined, even at the risk of sounding self-indulgently existential, is crucial for us to appreciate sociality, solidarity, and, therefore, contract.

10 Borrowed from George Saunders's magnificent prose in *The Braindead Megaphone* (2007) that I periodically rely on as a reminder of the value in, among other things, jumping "Don't be afraid to be confused. Try to remain permanently confused. Anything is possible. Stay open, forever, so open it hurts, and then open up some more, until the day you die, world without end, amen."

Mentioning existentialism affords the last act of jumping: a verse from a Subramania Bharati poem that I have carried with me for almost as long as my no-rice-on-Thursdays contract. Bharati, a Tamil radical poet, questions the other repeatedly in his famous poem *Nirpadhuve Nadapathuve* (you who stand, you who walk), "are any of you real or are you just my trained imagination?", he asks over and over again: to the still, to the flying, to words spoken, to ideas taught, and so on, questioning repeatedly the lines between the real and the imagined. The poem ends with the following two lines (poorly transliterated to English):

> *Kaanpadhellam maraiyum endraal, Maraindhadhellam kaanbamandro*
> *Naanum orr kanavo, Intha gnalamum poy thaano.*

Which translates, roughly, to:

> *Yet, if whatever we see is bound to disappear*
> *Even as we have sightings of things past*
> *Perhaps I am a dream too*
> *As is this Universe.*

For the longest time, I thought the word in the last line of the poem was "*gnanamum*" rather than "*gnalamum.*" *Gnalam*, is the word for "universe", whereas its homophone-to-my-untrained-ear *Gnanam* is the word for "wisdom."

> *Intha Gnanamum Poi Thaano.*
> *Perhaps this wisdom, too, is imagined.*

Bibliography

Blumer, Herbert (1986) *Symbolic interactionism: Perspective and method*. Berkeley, CA: University of California Press.

De Botton, Alain (2016) *The Course of Love*. New York, NY: Simon and Schuster.

Decker, Julie Sondra (2015) *The Invisible Orientation: An Introduction to Asexuality*. New York, NY: Simon and Schuster.

Easton, Dossie, Catherine A. Liszt, Betty Dodson, Ryam Nearing, Loving More Magazine, Deborah Anapol and D. H. S. Stan Dale (1997) *The Ethical Slut: A Practical Guide to Polyamory, Open Relationships and Other Adventures*. Berkeley, CA: Celestial Arts.

Greer, Andrew Sean (2008) *The Story of a Marriage*. New York, NY: Farrar, Straus and Giroux.

Korducki, Kelli Maria (2018) *Hard To Do: The Surprising Feminist History of Breaking Up*. Toronto, ON: Coach House Books.

Sartre, Jean-Paul ([1938] 2013) *Nausea*. Cambridge, MA: New Directions Publishing.
Smith, Zadie (2020) *Intimations*. New York, NY: Penguin Books.
Saunders, George (2007) *The Braindead Megaphone: Essays*. New York, NY: Riverhead Books.
Westbrook, David A. (2018) "Magical Contracts, Numinous Capitalism." In: Moeran, Brian & de Waal Malefyt, Timothy (eds) *Magical Capitalism*, 45–63. London, UK: Palgrave Macmillan.

12

AD VITAM AETERNAM

A legal text that remains relevant

Andreas Philippopoulos-Mihalopoulos

The following legal draft, with few alterations, eventually became the basis for one of the first laws established by the Communities under Aeternity – the others being the regulation of parallelisms, the deep-water striation and the series of cyclonopaedic bylaws. While technically not the first law to be passed by the Communities, it is now considered the most important. It is generally acknowledged that *Ad Vitam Aeternam* has come to characterise the whole subsequent production of laws of constitutional import, as well as localised regulations and policies. It was this law, and not the Conative Constitution as it is sometimes said, that allowed life to flourish in the present. Historically, the emergence of the law came at the opportune time of biocapitalism. The law enabled the latter to control the alt-democratic tendencies of parts of Europe and North America. Reading it now has a certain archaeological interest, especially in view of the references to such utopian practices as synchronised breathing and procreation in the achronon. It must also be appreciated for containing the last serious attempt at salvaging what was at the time called the continuum between humans, other species and the planet as a whole. Still, this legal text must not be discounted as obsolete. It is brimming with the future nostalgia and unbridled optimism that characterised the Communities at the time and has valiantly served its purpose as a proto-regulator of eternity.

For the sake of a more vivid historical reproduction, the pre-achronous use of verb tenses has been retained throughout this text.

Preamble

The Communities Committee on Life:

Taking into account the need to respect, honour and enforce the constitutionally enshrined right to life and the continuing conative forces that preserve life in all humans, under all circumstances and irrespective of associated costs,

Recognising that human life is on a continuum with the life of other species and the planet as a whole; that the life of other species and of the planet as a whole is a condition without which human life cannot be preserved,

Realising the need to combat genocide, attrition, ethnic and racial cleansing, extinction and any criminal action, whether wilful or not, that targets life,

Acknowledging the need that life is to be perpetuated in eternity, and honouring our Communities' credo *Ad Vitam Aeternam*,

Has decided as follows:

Scope and definitions

Article 1

The present law will apply to the entirety of the human population of the Communities, whether legal or illegal, native or foreign, without discrimination on the basis of gender, ethnicity, sexuality, age, generation, prosthesis, melding or any other difference.

Article 2

The term "life" refers to any form of corporeality where the dual requirement of simultaneous connection and withdrawal is met. While not relying on breathing, the latter is accepted to be constituting the main element of life.

Article 3

The term "eternal" refers to the achronous and limitless space of the Communities.

Article 4

The term "human" refers to all technologically, biologically or conceptually mediated, material or immaterial, forms of human, posthuman, inhuman and extended corporealities.

Article 5

The noun "achronon" and adjective "achronous" refer to space without time.

Protection of life

Article 6

Life is eternal.

Article 7

Dying is illegal under all circumstances. Death is no longer a lawful state for human beings.

Article 8

Death is punishable by life. Wherever possible, natural resuscitation is to be preferred over other, more forceful, means of resuscitation.

Article 9

Suicide and attempted suicide are illegal acts. Any involvement in someone's dying, including encouragement, and psychological or physical incitement or assistance, is illegal.

Article 10

10.1 Questioning the eternity of life is illegal. Topics such as the death instinct, sickness unto death, planetary anthropocenic extinction, and any other topic that engages with death as possibility shall be eradicated from public debates, educational curricula, political propositions, scientific theories and legislative proposals.
10.2 Anyone contributing, directly or indirectly, to the continuation of the will to die, shall be punished by law.
10.3 Any technological advancement that contributes, actually or potentially, to the possibility of death, is illegal and will be halted under the precautionary principle, according to which the absence of scientific proof is not an adequate reason not to take action that would prevent the loss of human life.

Article 11

The Communities shall proceed to the eradication of the will to die as instinct and desire. All necessary biotechnological interventions that will contribute towards such eradication, after due weighing of the financial, social and psychological costs on the population, are hereby authorised.

Article 12

Religions of any kind that engage with death, dying, and life after death in particular, must refrain from doing so, or be deemed illegal.

Accidental death

Article 13

There can be no accidental death emerging from within the individual's or group's sphere of economic influence.

Article 14

In case of an emergency outside the sphere of the individual or group economic influence that leads to an accident, in turn leading to individual or collective death, life will be reinstated at the first opportunity. In the case of group death, resuscitation will follow a strict order of spatial proximity of the dead, or dying in question, to the resuscitating means.

Protection of breathing

Article 15

All human beings must be facilitated in their effort to achieve the appropriate balance between simultaneous connection and withdrawal.

Article 16

Breathing in all its forms and in particular pulmonic, biotechnological and poral, will be preserved at all times. Breath-sharing will be allowed only if simultaneous chambers of withdrawal are put at the disposal of the breathers.

Article 17

Synchronised breathing will be established at various spaces across the Communities as a way of facilitating life.

Article 18

Breathing can never be performed as part of an exchange regime and its value can never be monetised. It remains the ultimate element of life and as such protected by the Communities, its institutions and its laws as an inalienable element of the human being.

Article 19

Rhythms of breathing may, under specific circumstances enumerated in Appendix A [*not available*], be imposed on individuals, groups or the entire population of the Communities. Such imposition remains at the discretion of the Communities Police Authority.

Protection of modes of life

Article 20

The eternity of human life is paramount.

Article 21

One is free to choose how to spend one's life. No other individual, group or institution can impose specific modes of living without the individual's or group's consent.

Article 22

The above provision includes the possibility of choosing to age naturally or by technological means.

Article 23

Procreation is allowed in the achronon according to the practice of eternal return and the economy of the limits of matter.

Article 24

Provisions will be enacted that will facilitate individuals to lead the life of their choice, in line with the general principles of conatus, creative force, positive passions, spatial justice and withdrawal.

Article 25

The need to respect, honour and support the life of other species and of the planet as a whole is considered secondary, if and when a conflict of interest arises between such a need and the preservation of human life. Special provisions apply to biotechnological fusions, intraspecies meldings, geoprostheses and other biotechnologies in the services of extended humanity and posthumanity.

Time

Article 26

Time is abolished.

Article 27

Public or group measurements of time, whether by mechanical or physical means, are illegal. Individual measurements of time that have the potential of being communicated to other individuals are also illegal.

Article 28

Any prior temporalisation of such physical phenomena as solar and lunar settings and seasonal variations shall be abolished and fully spatialised.

Article 29

The biotechnological reversibility of past and future is acknowledged as an established policy for the Communities and their institutions to enforce at the constant rate of 1:−1 of achronic units without recourse to 0.

Article 30

The production of generations is halted. All generations are simultaneously present in the achronous space of the Communities.

Article 31

Movement in space is only allowed in the achronous. Any movement that makes use of time will be halted.

Eternity

Article 32

Eternity cannot be rhythmically modulated, shrunk or expanded. It must be enjoyed in its entirety and synchronously in the space of the Communities.

Article 33

Eternal life must never be conflated with death or dying. Such conflation is punished by enforced synchronisation.

Article 34

Any attempt at arranging eternity into stages by means of progression mechanisms, spatial advancements, stratification, linearity and any other mode of partitioning, is illegal.

Article 35

Eternity is a common good of humanity and will be preserved even at the expense of humanity itself.

Article 36

While eternity is a common good of humanity, it cannot be shared between individuals. Forms of joint eternity, such as practices of prosthetic partnerships and permanent melding between humans or between humans and non-humans are illegal.

Article 37

While eternity is a common good of humanity, it cannot be swapped between individuals and must be enjoyed on a solely individual basis and without leaks. Forms of swapping, such as consciousness or body swaps between humans, or between humans and nonhumans are illegal.

Article 38

Eternity itself must never be terminated. In the event of spatial folding, eternity will be reinstated by whatever means available.

13

IN NOMINE PATRIS

Chiara Bottici

Good morning. Please, have a seat.

Oh yes, there is no air today. The pollution and the heat of the last few weeks: unbearable. Well beyond the average. Let me close the window and turn on the AC. Just arrived in the city?

Ah, always been here. No, I was asking because of that remark on the weather. I thought you still had to adjust to it. I see now that I was wrong; although, if you allow me to say so, you do look like somebody who is coming from another place …

Yes, perhaps it is because of that. I admit I was quite surprised when I saw you entering that door. Usually my patients are much younger, as you can imagine.

No, of course, there is nothing wrong with that. It is just that people of a certain age do not usually seek out a psychoanalyst. For sure, there is no fixed rule about that, but it is just that things tend to settle down with time, and usually, eventually, one does not really feel like stirring them up.

I see: it's your children. So this is a whole different story. Well, congratulations to begin with: three is a nice number.

Um, no grandchildren. Well, not yet!

Agh! They will never come? Why do you say so, if I may ask? I do not want to be intrusive, we've only just begun, but how can you be so sure about this?

Too old? You think they are now too old? Well, a lot of people thought they were too old, but then children arrived. You know, at times they come as surprises!

Well, it may be too late for your daughter if she is that old, but perhaps your two sons? I see: they are busy. A philosopher, a primary physician and a psychologist. They clearly like taking care of other people ...

Ah, this is what you have done yourself for your entire life: looking after others. Quite interesting …

Yes, let's talk about the reason for your visit. You mentioned it is because of your children, but from what you said I do not see anything wrong with them. Ok, no grandchildren, but this is the new fad. Completing your studies, settling into a career path takes a lot of time, so that kids tend to arrive pretty late now. This clearly creates a few problems, with the biological clock reclaiming its own time. But that's the trend almost everywhere, so I am not sure yet why this should be such a problem for you.

Speaking about a "refusal to reproduce" seems a bit too strong. It is the trajectory of all modern societies: whether we like it or not, we'd better get used to it. Sure, there are fragments of society that defy the trend, rural areas, lower classes, but everywhere else it's pretty much the rule. We just have to accept it: biological reproduction is no longer a priority, because other values, such as the desire for self-realisation, prevail. And let's face it: expectations from parents are so high now that it is becoming harder and harder to face them. So, I still don't see any particular problem with your children, well, at least not one big enough to consult a psychotherapist …

I see. But maybe you are exaggerating a little bit? Do you really believe that your children decided not to reproduce only to play a prank on you? I mean, that the three of them would have made such a radical life choice simply to trick their father does not seem that plausible to me, unless there is more at stake …

Well, "hate" is a big word. Sure, we all hated our parents at some point: it's part of the script. Maybe you are taking it too seriously. Children have to revolt against paternal authority at some point. It's a necessary step in the game of life. Who hasn't done it at some point? I'd actually be more worried if it did not happen.

Uhh, too far. You think they went too far? But what do you mean exactly? If it is just a question of timing, maybe it is not such a serious business. Maybe it's just a little delay, due to what we said before – you know, modern life, different priorities, social time taking over biology …

Well, if you say that the revolt became a plague, perhaps the situation is worse than I had imagined.

Sure. The revolt has to evolve into something else in one way or another.

Sure, it does not have to be reconciliation, but it has to be something more than just a revolt. Well, at least, this is what they say. But do you have any idea of why they got stuck there? When you spoke about a desire for emancipation that became a copy of the copy you seemed to allude to something else.

Trapped. Trapped in their revolt for the sake of a revolt. And it has been going on for too long. I understand that: there has to be some evolution. I agree with you, but we should also accept that there is nothing wrong with the desire for emancipation as such. Even if it becomes an end in itself: I mean, if one has to choose an end, why not that? Let's look at the other side of the coin: would you prefer children constantly obeying each and every command? Perhaps your children are still struggling to find their own voices … perhaps it is just that, you know, a search that is taking more time than you wished …

They want you dead. Um, this is something else. Kill their own father, that's not nice, for sure. But are you sure this is what they are up to? How can you be so certain about it? From what you told me, it is only a general desire to rebel against your authority, which you inferred from their decision not to reproduce …

No, if you have proof of that, then I am ready to believe you. I certainly do not want to defend your children just for the sake of defending them. I am only trying to understand. Obviously. It's just that it all seems a bit over the top, I mean the idea that the three of them want you dead – I mean dead, kaput, done with …

They visit a macumbeira regularly. Each and every Friday. In the favela. Yes, I have heard about her. They say she can do amazing things with her slaughtered chickens. But she must be a nice person too: somebody told me she leaves candies in the streets for her demonic spirits … But sure, it's black magic, no kidding, pretty serious stuff … What's her name again?

You won't tell me. That's fine.

So, how can you now be sure that your children go there each and every Friday? Maybe they are just malevolent rumours …

Tailed. I see. If you hired a private detective, you must be pretty worried about the whole thing.

Ah! It was just in order to get the material evidence, because you already knew it.

What? You have always known it? I am not sure what you mean here; it is becoming kind of hard to follow you …

You can prove it to me? In what sense? What do you have in your hands? Yes, sure, you can show it to me. Do not worry, I am not very impressionable. With this job, I have seen all sorts of things … although! uahoo! My god! I did not expect that!

Ookay … I see now what you mean. And yes, yes I know what they are, but I had never seen a real one. Where did you find it?

In your son's house?

Under his pillow?

For years?

Weeell. With all those pins, your kids must be pretty serious.

But should there not be a picture of you if you are the one they want dead? I believe you need an image to do a death spell: it's for that reason that people are hesitant to have their picture taken by strangers. So, how do you know that it is a macumba for your own death if there is no image of you?

Just this little thing under the pins? Why not a proper picture?

What? There are no pictures of you? You have never allowed them? Why not? That's weird, really weird …

Ahh, they *did* take pictures of you. That's normal. It seemed strange that there would be none: I mean, with such rich offspring, how can you avoid at least a few appearances here and there?

I see: from time to time you managed to have them destroyed, so that there would be no images of you …

But why not, if you say that it has nothing to do with fear of black magic? I cannot see how, and why, one would avoid all pictures.

Um, images. You do not want pictures, so the problem is not images in themselves, but the fact that *you* do not want to be photographed ….

No, no, no, I am nodding for no particular reason. I always do it when I think: just some back and forth with my head. It helps me to put my thinking in motion. And this story of the images and paternal hate is really intriguing …

You are right: it is not exactly a manifestation of filial love. I understand now, or at least I am starting to understand why you came here. Your children really want you dead!

Yes, I also find this mixture of modernity and primitivism quite unsettling. Yes, from what you said, I also imagined your children as modern, rational individuals, and not as dupes prone to all kinds of superstition. And yes, the idea of a philosopher, a physician and a psychologist going to see a macumbeira each and every Friday sounds a bit strange, even though, the more I think about it, the more I am persuaded that such a convergence is not accidental, not accidental at all …

No, the rationale for such a visceral hate for one's father is a different story. And sure, it must be hard to come to terms with it. Sure, you who gave them life are now being paid back by their desire for your death. It must be pretty hard, I fully understand. And, I am not sure yet what could have led them to such an extreme. I mean: it's not just the revolt, they really want to get rid of you …

So, tell me more about it: You mentioned before that you have been a loving father, but also a just one. What do you mean by justice?

Um, I see. Absolute devotion. To the father and the family. Sacred. Because there is only one father. I see, I see. Even if it meant punishing them when they were innocent. To test their loyalty …

Weelll … maybe this could have appeared to be kind of arbitrary, don't you think? I mean, if the way we act and what we get in return doesn't match up, it is hard to believe in it. I mean, how can you expect love? If you really made them suffer even when they were innocent, don't you think that you should expect at least a little bit of anger?

I understand, it is you who created them, you who gave them life, you who provided for them with all those nice things that surround them, but should they love you just for that? Even if you did not spare them unnecessary suffering?

What? You did it for them? So they would have a direct experience of it? Of suffering itself? No, I see what you mean, but from your own father …

No, sure! It is not up to me to defend your children. I do not even know who they are. And, on top of it, I do not think they need much help. They seem to have pretty clear ideas about what they want and how to get it.

No, I am just trying to do my job here, and get a sense of the motivations at stake on both sides. I have to get a picture as objective as possible to see whether I can be of some help.

Of course I cannot always help! There are patients who are analysable and those who are not, situations you can help to disentangle, and others which are, unfortunately, lost causes. There are well-established criteria to decide …

Yes, I admit, there is the age issue, which made me sceptical from the very beginning. Embarking on psychotherapy requires years and years, and I am really not sure it is such a good idea for someone of your age. Well, I am sure you still have a lot of time ahead of you. We all think we have a lot of time ahead! But you are not eternal!

No, I am not trying to be funny. I am pretty serious: age is an issue, and then there is also the question of the emotional costs of such therapy. It is really hard to dig so deep into the past, reopen the original wounds and go through them again and again: it is a lot of suffering. Maybe you should just try to enjoy the time that is left.

Sure: your children. They are young. But still, you see, you are their father, and it's pretty heavy stuff … And even now, after everything you said, I am not really sure this is such a good idea. You know, I have been doing this job for a very long time, and I can guarantee that people with a long white beard like yours are usually not really open to being called into question …

Yes, perhaps that is true. Perhaps there is nothing to question in you. And perhaps the problem is just your children, and their childish behaviour – a childish behaviour arising precisely when you would expect them to be at the peak of their maturity. Childish, just a bit childish, perhaps even too childish …

Nooo, sure, I would never kick you out of my office. No, I am standing up, just because, you see, it is already 12 o'clock: your time is over …

14

IT IS FORBIDDEN TO SELL YOUR SOUL TO THE DEVIL

Tiziano Toracca

Technology has screwed us. I dare not imagine what could happen to me if I ran someone over in the street, or if they found me in one of those states of inebriation in which I often find myself on Sunday nights. Or if they knew something, but who knows what. Things have changed.

The square, white billboards without any adverts are a signal. I walk a lot and I notice this. Even all those clouds that have suddenly taken anthropomorphic shape are a symptom. I have never seen so many people weep in front of a bland summer sunset, never seen so many geometric lines on the walls of a city, never seen so much shitty symmetry between fountains, cycle paths, hedges and skyscrapers. Yes, people have begun to rave more than usual: they use words like Love, Truth, Justice as if they were speaking about screwdrivers and bolts. Or people are silent: on my last journey – from Barcelona to Belgrade – I did not breathe a word to anyone. No one said anything for nearly four hours.

I made a decision, and I went to the courthouse and I did my research. I got hold of and read about everything on that law of which they speak abroad, in China and Japan. In Strasburg they rebaptised it the Law of Scientific Imagination, the result of decades of research on which scientists, jurists and humanists from almost every European country have collaborated. Russia and the United States must have a hand in the matter. Rowing all together to reach the same Treasure Island and reinvent the precious nineteenth century. But I got it, I got it, I read it. It begins like this: "whoever is charged, innocent or guilty, will be subject to the Treatment of Dream (TOD)". It is written that for five nights the defendant is required to sleep at the Dream Institute, on their own, in an apartment full of bay leaves, white and alpine stars. There are many apartments: in the city, in the countryside, by the sea, depending on the geography, and there are a few with a lake view, others on the 16th floor of public buildings from year Zero, between 80 and 180 square metres. The notification of the offence foretells the dispatching of a catalogue with all the available Dream Apartments. Three weeks to choose, within a radius of 250 kilometres from your own residence; and you can decide to reach the apartment by your own means. But you can go even further away, by paying or by an act of God. Ah, what a law!

There is a list of details on deductible costs for transport and board, on possible food and animal allergies and recommendations for every possible hospital emergency. Among the various forbidden objects there are tea, books, earphones and online games. But it is also forbidden to eat fruit and vegetables out of season, while aromatic plants are forbidden, with a few exceptions. You can telephone whomever you want and at whatever hour, but not just after you wake up. You can take your preferred objects and your relatives or friends, or acquaintances can visit between two and five hours at the discretion of the judge. There is Wi-Fi but a few sites are blocked, and it is forbidden to masturbate (how very odd), there is video surveillance and administrative sanctions are in place which involve the lengthening of one's detention, beyond a certain dose of the grotesque. You can go out into the garden and stay outside, usually there is a little swimming pool, but the green spaces are clearly defined. Many plants are provided, even poisonous ones, and a hedge that *da tanta parte dell'ultimo orizzonte il guardo esclude*. Indeed, there is even poetry, here and there, scribbled on the staircases or on the bed boards. A double bed: it is really one of the rules, so that sleep refreshes, leaving the body free to fall like a corpse. There is a gym in a room adjacent to the garden, but the use of the machines depends on the judge. For example, you cannot run and you cannot do gymnastics upside down. In short, there are requirements like that, linked probably to the needs of the unconscious and to the risk of its irreparable corruption. There is even an internal legislative decree on the use of lights.

A list of requirements. The TOD law is a list of requirements. I read all of this law and I dreamed of it, and then I arrived at the conclusion that the saddest paragraph is the one that requires you not to force yourself to dream because in any case we will dream at the Dream Institute as we do everywhere. We are dreamers and we shall dream. When I think of this paragraph I feel separated from my body. I feel like son, father, brother and citizen: like everyone except myself. If anything, what a conviction! – the mirror in which I can see my reflection remains. It appears as a principle of hope and instead it is a threat, pure and simple. The penultimate paragraph literally says that whoever refuses the Dream Treatment will be considered guilty of the crime of which they were accused. It adds that in similar circumstances the subject will be expressly registered as a "non-dreamer" and will be, to all intents and purposes, excluded from society. It does not clarify further but I imagine that he or she will be prevented from working, getting married, voting, using public transport, going to the library, museums, going to university. The only thing that is written is this: "until they provide evidence and show their dreams, non-dreamers will be considered subversives". Decades passed when I did not hear that word – "subversive" – and I would never have thought myself capable of considering someone subversive for refusing to reveal their dreams. But maybe it has always been like that and this is the true meaning of subversive behaviour: refusal. I, however, would not refuse. I already know I would not. Not only out of fear of being considered and treated like a subversive but also because I have stopped dreaming, I do not know what I dream about and I would be curious to know, whatever came out, good or bad. It is better to be blind and know the truth than to be a king without knowing in which pigsty you are rolling about. Better the struggle between gloom and light, than a slimy and soporific sludge.

Ah, the Law of Scientific Imagination!

But it is not over. The last paragraph is the most terrible: it is written that whoever ends up being eligible, on the basis of treatment, could be further accused of other crimes of which they have not yet been accused. In this case, it clarifies, the accused should undergo a second TOD immediately. Eligibility! The property of the subject! Am I right or not? Dispossession! I already see people with whistles in their mouths and maps in hand for the roads on which it is written that it is forbidden to give up one's personality! Resist the communism of the twenty-first century!

Technology has screwed us. I realised this because I observe people whom I meet in the world, and that is to say, as my friend T. S. says, across the span of those 20 or 30 kilometres where I roam every day by bicycle or on foot.

From when they discovered how to decode the irrational, strange things start to take place. People are bemused, ecstatic, their heads are elsewhere, they appear as though made of opiates, they think of how to empty their minds of all their, own, very dangerous irrationality. Someone who draws, who sings, who dresses like a dandy, who taps their fingertips together hand against hand, and meditates when faced with the "Panta Rhei" of highway traffic. Everyone has begun to transcribe their own dreams in little *Muji* notebooks to try to decode what will emerge from the Treatment, in case they commit some sort of infraction, whatever the infraction and whatever the rule. Everyone records and tries to understand, and it is clear that they desire to see what they really see, so it is even clearer that they want to know what they are guilty of. It is like that: truth is our original sin, other than the tree of knowledge. An apple is an apple is an apple.

There. This is the law, I have read it to you, I have explained it to you. It is useless to say that the TOD has already spread far and wide – and with such speed! – to all forms of crime, even to those civil and even administrative forms. It is all iron in the fire for charming and perfumed lawyers: someone – I will name no names – had foreseen that the law would end up dealing with psychoanalysis and that lawyers and jurists would end up receiving their own clients in a clinic by putting on a pair of lorgnettes and a white coat. But that is what happened, say the fatalists, and they know things, being the only immortal species, the only species that saves itself by shrugging shoulders and swallowing. In short, the Treatment has spread, and we are not joking, there is something to be fearful of when going for a walk in the park or cycling in a pedestrian zone. When I look through the morning post, I am terrified that there will be a notification from the courthouse. But still nothing, always and only the fears that thaw in sweet sleep.

However, I have to admit that I am excited. I am excited as everyone is, immersed in a new amniotic liquid that leaves us to circle in the certainty of the punishment and the certainty of our dreams. I am afraid that sooner or later they will give me the Treatment, yet I am also excited at the idea that someone will see, record and tell me what has happened in my soul. Forty years have passed since I threw away things of every kind, and I would precisely like to know what worked out and what I did badly. It is clear that I must have done something bad. The *ratio legis* is the *ratio legis* and there is little that can be done.

I meditated for a long time after I finished reading the Law of Scientific Imagination and I must confess to you that I understood the reason for so much excitement. I do not care at all to know what I am dreaming about and why. The truth of the dream! Nonsense. The truth of the dream is like that stone that has fallen to the bottom of the sea: it is a stone of gold only down there, in the depths, but as soon as you try to bring it up, we find a rock in our hands. We throw it away and it begins to shine. In short, I have understood the reason for so much joy.

It is simple: a few years ago I sold my soul to the Devil and I believe I am not the only one to have done this, the oldest and most expedient transaction in the world. I am excited by the idea that while there are those there who are trying to pour my unconscious onto a plate, onto its back, beside the superego with folded arms, and the other two in dressing gowns, having woken up in the middle of the night, that tangle of generalisations, repressed desires, wants, indecipherable stains and traumas in black and white, there you go, I am excited by the idea that this ball has begun to roll and lose pieces from every side precisely as a toy in the hands of the Devil might. Who knows that the clerk might do! Feeling oneself drowning in a dream while they try to reduce my dreams to tiny bits!

The law says nothing; it is silent. But it is certain that the Devil will not easily agree and will not give a damn about four unimportant paragraphs: the soul is his, the contract has been signed, and whatever the judge says it will not be easy to agree with him: when it is diabolical, logic goes down the wrong way, even with the wisest people. Ah, the very thought almost makes me happy. Who would have ever thought it? To be on the side of the Devil and feeling just, protected like the third little pig in the house of bricks. There is not any doubt: scientists and humanists will recommend to the new jurists to add an obvious and consequent requirement: it is forbidden to sell your soul to the Devil. They will do it, they will do it, let them do so! In my case it is too late, sorry, it has been sold. They can even treat me when and how they want; they will not see anything but a pair of horns! Is that not enough of an objection? Is it not sufficient? Let them go ask him, to the Devil with them!

15

THE COURT OF THE MONUMENTS

Hayley Gibson

The construction of the Court began as the heat of the summer died and a tempestuous September began. High winds plucked at forgotten debris on the site in the middle of the city that had been cleared to dust and rubble for the new building. Short months ago, in that same place, black blistering sheets of tar stuck daily to the undersides of an incessant footfall that had carried a singular body, rowdy and clamouring, to the gates of the City Chambers. For fourteen days, the crowd trickled and swelled through the streets and into what was then the city square, to present its demands to the tall iron bars of the municipal gates: the monuments of the city were abhorrent; they could no longer be allowed to stand.

They were abhorrent, said the crowd, because they were the petrification of a cruel and ancient nobility; rendered nobler still in glorious hues of perpetual marble and stone. Furthermore, it said: a city could not recover from its cruelties under the watchful immortality of the cruel. The apologia of the vainglorious dead would be transmuted into the minds, and by extension the words and deeds, of the citizens: mouths hewn closed would be lent the organs of communication, their dead and silent voices resonant by proxy in the air; unfashioned lungs of earth and rock would forever find surrogate breath in the living. Inherited injustices could not be repaired, because those who had been wronged could not believe in such repair as long as they were expected to dwell – not by accident, but by design – alongside the adulated figures of their historic aggressors. These gloating statues had been granted quotidian audience in the lives of the aggrieved, without reproach or recompense. For no reprimand could be directed at stone that remained obstinately by the city gates, to greet us tomorrow while freshening the wound; no compensation, no transfer of property, was possible from a figure that was property itself. The very city was at stake: it belonged by definition on one side of a line that distinguished the *civic* from the *urban*. It was nothing less, said the crowd, than its living community – *this* community:

neither secondary nor reducible to physical urban structures. If there was to be any aspiration towards a unified experience of the city – if there was ever to be a city at all – the monuments could no longer stand.

In the third week, the gates to the City Chambers parted with ferrous complaint, and a representative of the City Council emerged from behind them to meet the sudden hush of the crowd. The Council had agreed to address the Problem of the Monuments. The crowd resumed its boisterous discourse. There was to be a Memorial Advisory Board, continued the representative – a small, lonely figure in front of the gates, accompanied only by the stone personages of the city founders, flanking her to the left and right. Tear them down, demanded the crowd. The Memorial Advisory Board would be an independent body of experts, and the content of their meeting would be made public; and this information was now being pressed through the waves of the crowd's triadic chant into the waiting cameras and microphones that had sprung, unexpectantly, to life at the foot of the steps leading up to the chambers. The representative retreated behind the gates, leaving the silent city founders to confront the crowd without her.

The Memorial Advisory Board was convened quickly, in one of the several boardrooms of the City Chambers that were set aside for advisory matters. The independence of the meeting was to be ensured by the daily closing of the boardroom door – as though the weight of wood and decades of layered varnish could hermetically seal the room, hiding its contents from the surrounding chambers like a pill that could be ingested and forgotten. There was to be a reporting of proceedings, rendered from the screeds of a temporary stenographer and issued as a bulletin in the evening papers.

Its five members were selected for their experience and expertise in areas relevant to the matter at hand: first, the Head Curator of the City Museum, an art historian and classicist who had held responsibility for housing and maintaining the city's artefacts for several years. Next, the Chairman of the Municipal Heritage Trust, who oversaw the management of the grand buildings, estates and gardens that had been placed, at one time or another, by their erstwhile wealthy owners into the hands of trustees, thereby trading the cost of maintenance for the conditional grant of access to grounds in which the monuments of their old masters remained. The third appointee was the Chief Public Prosecutor, whose jurisdiction over criminal cases to be charged and tried was coupled with the duty of overseeing public order. It was felt by the Council that he ought to be appointed as a precaution: he would advise the Board on the likelihood of further unrest, should there be any oversight in that regard. As it happened, the Prosecutor enjoyed a long-standing friendship stretching back to his school days with the fourth Board member: a gregarious figure known colloquially as "Brutus", the President of the City Guilds Association. His presence on the Board had been necessary due to the large quantity of monuments commissioned over the years by Guild members, and in which the Guilds might have some sort of proprietary interest. The final appointment to the Board was the more reticent figure of the Senior City Planner, whose advisory role on questions of location and access was expected to be unproblematic and limited to the facts.

All five Board members were opposed to the destruction of the monuments, and from the outset: the question having been raised as the first point of discussion. The monuments were too valuable to be destroyed: many were priceless artefacts, exemplary of their craft and type, which bore the signature of master sculptors. Preservation, said the Curator, was the necessary antidote to the Problem of the Monuments: the City Museum would host those which were offensive; and the public would be free to observe them in the safe detachment of its galleries. This, she explained, would allow for the likenesses of those celebrated figures to appear in context: inscriptions would accompany them, recounting their deeds, demarcating who had been slave traders, exploiters of the weak and the vulnerable, the purveyors of conditional philanthropy. The city must confront its history, and discussion would be the city's talking cure. This is what our museums were for.

But if a cure was necessary, said the City Planner, the museum was not nearly adequate to encourage this, for it stood on the banks of the river near the outskirts of the financial district: travelling there, and entering, was a voluntary activity in which only those with a vested interest in seeing the monuments would ever participate. Any discourse would be partial, or one sided, and nowhere near ubiquitous enough to be effective. Only a self-selecting minority would be cured. The Chairman of Municipal Heritage, who had been waiting for the Curator's idea to fail on practical grounds, now seized the chance to return to the ideological: a talking cure was preposterous in any case. Obliteration, not of the monuments, but of their memorial function, was what was needed. For there was no such thing as a city psychoanalyst who could guide citizens through the recovery process: public discourse could not be influenced or contained by inscriptions and galleries alone, and more harm than good might very well come of it. Besides, the emplacing of the monuments in the museum belied the overarching rationale for preserving them: these were items of historic, as well as monetary, value. No, the monuments ought to be hidden from view for the sake of the peace; and the Chairman was willing to lease one of the more remote stately gardens to the city for the purpose of retiring them …

The Prosecutor's apparent indignation could no longer be contained. We were truly speaking of *retirement* now, he laughed, sardonically: "and a garden is such a pleasant place for the purpose, but we do not send criminals to live out their days in pretty gardens, Mr Chairman …"

"Indeed," interrupted the Curator, "we rehabilitate them."

The President of the Guilds, perhaps spurred to action by the familiarity of his friend as interlocutor, interjected with blustering impatience: he did not see why the monuments had to be retired at all. In fact, while he must admit that he was glad that they had all agreed not to destroy them, this was becoming ridiculous. The selection of monuments for retirement was too uncertain: what about those of which we should be rightly proud? Are we to relinquish all testament to our hard-won glory at the whim of the masses? The hands and minds immortalised in those statues are the same ones that built our industry, our finest halls, our roads, our democracy, *this very room*: they fathered this city. What patricidal misery are we to endure, witnessing the subjugation of our forebears to the ignominy of observation or oblivion like so many vanquished giants …

"Now, Brutus, we have to maintain order, and the public would never have it. You know very well that it is my responsibility not simply to prosecute but to ensure the peace …"

"They *are* gargantuan," said the City Planner, suddenly: "and public space is at a premium."

The City Planner had calculated that the only appropriate space left in the city with the capacity to contain all of the potentially objectionable monuments was the city square, right in front of the Chambers.

"Ugh, the square! That place makes me *weary*, just thinking of the sheer amount of public funding needed to call it to order over and over …" the jovial Brutus glanced at the Prosecutor to determine whether he would take up the challenge. Nothing. "We could fill it to the brim with our monuments, hey? Then where would the rabble go?"

"These issues must be discussed in the open," insisted the Curator, now unimpressed with the President of Guilds, and resuming her argument with the Chairman.

"But it is *irresponsible* …" the Chairman retorted, his hands splayed emphatically aloft while the Prosecutor gazed into the middle distance.

"Fill it right up! Give them nowhere to go! That'll put a stop to the nuisance!" Brutus of the Guilds gleefully continued to address the Prosecutor, and was now jocularly nudging the Planner, who failed to grasp the conspiracy. "You'd certainly be out of a job then, old boy …"

"A trial, then," replied the Prosecutor. A trial of the monuments, in the city square.

That evening's bulletin would therefore read: "Memorial Board agrees monument solution by four votes to one"; and, some days later, the City Council would approve the Board's recommendation unanimously. Monuments to problematic historic figures were to be held to account in a court of law. As with any other criminal trial, it was envisaged that each statue would be indicted and tried in a public forum; prosecutors would make representations on behalf of the city in accordance with procedure; there would be a right of defence, the production of evidence and the citation of witnesses. From now on, the offences of the monuments would be held up to the light of day, in accordance with the rule of law. Justice would be done, one way or another.

The first trial of its kind would require the construction of a new court, vast enough to contain the physical range of its subjects: for the more colossal the subject, it was feared, the more serious the charges might be. The Court Architect, appointed by the Board, drew plans for a large-scale replica of the nearby High Court; but with certain adjustments that were necessary to accommodate its novel purpose. This was not an easy task. Despite the logistical need to allow for the transportation of the accused by cranes and rails and pulleys, it was nonetheless essential that the new edifice should be self-contained and replete. The Architect had been instructed to ensure that the Court was clearly demarcated from the rest of the surrounding city, to avoid what the Board referred to as "contamination". Initial blueprints for an open-air court that would ease the burden of conveying the accused to the docks had been rejected immediately: "we might as well just take them all down to the square just now!" – and once the Court stood on the ground, this would *no longer be a public square.* For the point was to remove the statues entirely from municipal life, not least because any failure to contain the visual spectacle of the monuments would inevitably replicate the offences. Indeed, the accused could not belong to societyat all while they were at the mercy of the law: in the spirit of detention, if not consecration, they would be wholly immured between the walls of the Court. Yet the trial was to be a public event, and so the Architect incorporated a viewing area into the plans: a large window would separate the appurtenances of the Court at one end of the building from a cavernous public gallery at the other. There would be doors at each side of that public gallery to allow for the voluntary coming and going of citizens, who could view the proceedings through the large window at will. People would eventually pass through the gallery daily as they crossed the erstwhile public square (as was still necessary if one wished to cross from one point of the city to the next) – often without stopping, let alone watching the proceedings once the initial public curiosity over the trial had waned. No matter, said the Architect: any sight of the monuments, whether brief and peripheral or long and contemplative, would now be experienced through the lens of the Court, and endowed with the context of judgment.

The ground clearing works began in the first week of August, hindered only by the prone figure of the odd saboteur sprawled from time to time on what remained of the decreasing expanse of tarmac. Such occasional spurts of protestation would temporarily halt the din of the drills until the city police arrived to grapple with limp or flailing but always stubborn limbs. The building works commenced during the autumn months and trudged on through the winter and into the spring: sheets and beams of steel and iron were assembled into a dark, imposing skeleton which overshadowed the thawing city like a spectre until it was eventually clothed in dense columns of white, vernal concrete. The finished edifice stood much taller than the buildings in surrounding streets, separated from its neighbours only by a narrow circumferential passageway and pressing darkly up against the City Chambers. Even those who had lived their entire lives in the city experienced a temporary disorientation at its centre, for familiar navigational landmarks were now blocked from view as the towering walls of the court closed in on every periphery. Crossing through the gallery tended to make matters worse: for regardless of how certain one felt about one's navigation of that skyless place, the confusing multitude of small doors at each end of the hall combined with the vertiginous spectacle of the proceedings through the gallery window, to such discombobulating effect that it was quite common to emerge in the opposite direction as was intended.

In the meantime, the council appointed a panel of judges from among the city's extant judiciary: three justices, of crime, property and public law, respectively, would preside over the proceedings. In future months, they would be seen clambering daily up a series of ladders, coming to rest upon three absurdly towering chairs at the head of the vast courtroom. For the Architect had feared that the scale of the monuments would visually diminish the stature of the judiciary and sought to counteract this by elevating the justices above the heavy, unseeing heads of the accused. Through the gallery window, however, one could only dimly perceive three small, distant figures perching together like birds in the rafters.

The council had used exceptional powers to pass the foundational legislation of the Court, granting it special jurisdiction to hear the somewhat ill-defined charge of "Offences *Contra Memoria Civilis*". Before the trial began, counsel for the defence would submit preliminary pleadings as to the jurisdiction of the Court: the charges, she argued, conflated the crimes of the monuments with the deeds of their subjects; and those who had traded slaves or adopted despotic ideologies did so legally at the time. In any case, one could not raise and try the dead; and unless this was to be a ghostly forum, any jurisdiction of the Court had already been seized – albeit most certainly by Hell itself. But the Prosecutor had anticipated this preliminary argument, and he would reply in his turn, his voice raised to the lofty judges, that indeed, the relevant injury could not be historic when the law was not; but memory was a thing lived in the present, and it was the experience of the injury to civic memory, not history itself, that was at stake.

At first, there was a steady movement of public monuments from all corners of the city, dangling from ropes and chains attached to cranes and helicopters. For some weeks, a series of slow, awkward arrests transformed the city's atmosphere into a circus of suspended objects gliding through the air above offices and houses in the direction of the Court. The accused were to be manoeuvred by a series of pulleys and wheeled dollies that could convey them into the building through a large, rolling door reminiscent of an aircraft hangar. The team of construction workers who had built the Court would be retained in the seemingly constant task of lowering and hoisting the accused into a wide, concrete dock which took up the better portion of the courtroom: a tiered structure that allowed the monuments to be positioned in increasing order of size, the largest taking up the back, many of these defendants inseparable from their horses and chariots and, in some cases, their historic victims, who were cast irredeemably of the same rock and forced to attend patiently with the accused, despite their innocence.

The population of the dock would increase steadily in the first months of the trial. While the City Planner had indicated a list of possible defendants littered throughout the streets and municipal buildings, the special decree stated that it was for members of the public to nominate the monuments to be tried. Mornings were dedicated to new indictments, and the trial would then resume as fresh subjects were rolled into the forum to join their co-defendants. Witnesses for the defence would enumerate the greater deeds of the accused; reams of ancient papers would be produced as evidence that the prosperity of the city could be attributed to these great figures; and, now wise to the conflation of the subject with the medium, counsel for the defence would build instead the case that any wound in the civic memory had long been sutured by gratitude. For even if it was not something experienced consciously, such indebtedness was inextricable from the benefits experienced *here and now,* in the present, by all who lived in the city.

Concerned that this might be persuasive, the Prosecutor had issued an open citation to the public, certain that the balance would lie irrefutably on the side of those who could speak to their injury. Indeed, it seemed that all the prosecution had to do was to prove that there was injury *at all*, and that it could be attributed to the accused. Scores of witnesses answered the invitation, filing slowly through the Court and into the gallery, emerging one by one in the witness box, dwarfed by the scale of their surroundings. Some read carefully composed statements punctuated with dates and figures, while others favoured unscripted appeals to human decency. A continuous narrative of violence and contempt resounded in the Court – and yet its auditory force seemed to weaken as the words migrated from the epicentre of the witness stand, reverberating in layered snippets around the judges in the ceiling, floating past whatever cochlear ornamentation, if any, had once been fashioned for the accused, and neutralised, finally, by the vast pane of glass traversing the indifferent muteness of the gallery. Cross-examination was infrequent, but pressing all the same: counsel for the defence was quite sympathetic, of course; but could the lady or the gentleman establish a substantive connection between their suffering and any one of these monuments itself? One had to show this beyond reasonable doubt; and no living acolyte of the old racist ideas was standing in the dock: indeed, such people were nameless individuals, undefined groups, hidden in the city's multitude beyond the reach of the Court. Should the lady or the gentleman ever happen to identify these individuals, the Prosecutor will surely take up the incident as a criminal matter in the usual way, if he has not already done so …

Nevertheless, the witnesses continued to answer the citation, and the unspoken ugliness of the city now squeaked persistently through small tannoys distributed across the public gallery, whispering inexorably at the passing crowd, persevering to defy its indifference.

Perhaps feeling the shame of association; or perhaps because of some inherent notion of proprietorship, many of the families descended from the accused would eventually begin to remove the likenesses of their forebears from public view. Some descendants would gather their tools and meet in the night, sometimes with hired help and often with sympathetic associates of no relation, removing what they could of their ancestors' presence. Others were more forthcoming in their operation, openly repatriating the monuments to their own estates.

Each rescue was an exercise in safekeeping: some families locked their sculpted forefathers in basements or cellars; others attempted to bury or submerge them, with varying degrees of success, as copper-stained hats and hooves and pointing fingers began to protrude sporadically from the fields and lakes that surrounded the city. As this practice progressed, the council, acting on the Board's advice, would decree that a lack of public visibility was a complete defence: hidden statues ceased to be monuments, since perceptibility was a prerequisite for the specific *actus* of offending civic memory. Even the Prosecutor agreed that in the absence of any reminder capable of *inciting memory*, no injury was committed in the present; and wherever the living memory of the city had passed into its history there would be no case to answer. A spate of rescues then swept the town, the salvagers racing against the city police. By the end of the fifth month, the city was bereft of monuments, its plinths and alcoves barren. There were no more offenders at large.

And yet the trial wore on, and the colossal assembly of the hitherto accused remained in the dock, crowding the vast flight of concrete platforms: an absurd and anachronous horde. Smooth classical sculptures of white alabaster stood shackled to imposing bronze behemoths: prudish merchants eternally clutching their stiff lapels; pith-helmeted explorers brandishing blank copper scrolls; and a host of monstrous statesmen, steel eyes fixed no longer in condescension at the civilian masses, but in mortification at the hollow ground.

Outside, the novelty of the first weeks of the proceedings would gradually give way to the mundane omnipresence of the law. For even when the Court was out of view, its residue seeped into everyday life through television screens and newspapers and recorded announcements on radios and public transport; snippets of legal vernacular flitted incessantly through the air at school gates and in restaurant kitchens, at work and at home, in waking and in sleep. Under these conditions, the city soon found itself rent by a fresh division that nonetheless charted the scars of the old. Now steeped in municipal litigation, those who had once been unmoved by the Problem, or even defensive of the monuments, would now declare their satisfaction at the even-handedness of the Court. Meanwhile, those who had once called for the removal of the monuments became suspicious, for surely the new defence of invisibility was nothing less than an evasion of justice.

There had been no new indictments for weeks, and yet the ignominy of civic memory persisted. The sudden exile of the monuments from the city was immaterial if they had seized the public imagination first. And in the minds of citizens, they were still to be found, installed indelibly – untouchable, ineffaceable monoliths looming large in the civic conscience.

Aggrieved by an injury untempered by the law, small, covert gatherings of people began to form, concerned by the evasion problem. The accused in the dock did not represent nearly the entirety of its potential population, and the glory of those who had escaped remained unchallenged for as long as they were able to outrun the spectacle of the Court. Indeed, their happy existence would only ever have been staged against the backdrop of civic life, before they were returned to the earth from which they came, without reckoning. They must be reclaimed for the law. But initial attempts at excavation had been to limited effect: the practical difficulty of tracking down the fugitives aside, those who harboured them seemed to prefer their merciful destruction to the threat of extradition. What the evening bulletin would refer to as a "petri-cidal frenzy" soon gripped the noble classes: the residue of crumbled limbs peppered the fields and forests outside the city; weighty heads ground almost entirely to dust piled up in the cellars of the estates; and disfigured chunks of iron were used to anchor the drowned in perpetuity.

One morning in the seventh month, however, the city police received anonymous nominations for the arrest of three *monuments-at-large*. Reinstated overnight on her plinth in the university, the first of the three was found: a eugenicist, among other things, in her time, she had been rescued by some unknown disciples during the weeks of exile; but now she had returned, cold and intransigent in the morning light. The twelfth Baron of the historic district was also discovered, restored just as the nomination form had said, by the central fountain in the city park. And the founder of the City Museum, who had been among the first to be rescued, had suddenly reappeared that morning at the museum entrance, along with a two-word note: "for theft". Perplexed, the Prosecutor nonetheless ordered the arrests and, for the first time in months, the vehicles of the Court trundled once again through the city, their quarry sailing overhead.

In the following weeks, a recrudescence of monuments plagued the city. Abandoned plinths and niches were mysteriously reoccupied, as if their absent tenants had voluntarily returned to face arrest. Analysis by the Curator would reveal that these statues were new, which was to say, they were copies of the originals – and very good ones, save for the fact that they were made of fresh materials. Careful hands had fashioned these, and, assuming that this had been a coordinated effort, there was more than one skilled sculptor involved. Appraised of this evidence, counsel for the defence would lodge a fresh motion to the Court: the interlopers in the dock could not possibly be offenders; rather, they were symbols of contempt for the Court itself. To produce such imitations, counsel argued, was a mockery of the solemnity of the proceedings, and all charges, at least in respect of these new arrivals, must be dropped.

After some deliberation, the judges handed down their pronouncement – a rare occurrence in itself, and a brief one. The new monuments were genuine, they said, not in the sense of authorship or origin, but in their memorial quality. These were not effigies of the deceased: they had not been commissioned to disparage the memory of their subjects; they were not hasty articles destined for any vengeful, cathartic destruction. On the contrary: these copies had been crafted with care and attention; they were tributes, expressions of reverence, and thus they performed the same function as the originals. They were also, for that fact, capable of conflating shame with glory, and thus of offending the civic memory anew, and that was all that mattered to the Court. The charges against the proxy monuments would be allowed, and the copies would remain among the ranks of the accused. In the days and weeks and months that followed, more would join them still; for whatever cryptic network had produced the first of the counterfeits had become emboldened, and the city's alcoves were repopulated one by one. Anonymous tip-offs directed the city police to the locations of the new monuments; outstanding arrest warrants were reinstated; and new leviathans were manoeuvred into the now overcrowded docks, blocking the gallery from view.

A sudden cessation of the proceedings would afflict the ninth month of the trial, when a hairline crack, which had been creeping for weeks across the expanse of the dock, suddenly gave way under the now excessive weight of the defendants, splitting the Court in two. The ground shuddered and the monuments trembled. An unearthly tumult resounded from below the Court and into the streets; cars listed across pavements and the walls of the buildings shook. The tempered glass of the gallery window shattered in place, transforming the watchful lens of the law into a vast white cataract, blind to the proceedings beyond. The Court was evacuated, save for the accused; and the Architect was summoned once again. Of course, the sheer volume of the defendants was now far beyond the capacity of the Court: the only solution was to decommission the public gallery, and to transfer half of the defendants into the space instead. But this was not enough in the long term: the very building was in need of relief. Its foundations could not tolerate such a large and persistent load. Was there an end in sight for the trial?

The Architect could not have apprehended, at the time, the significance of this last question. But those who lived and dwelled in the city would eventually begin to suspect that the fate of the accused would never be known: not this year, nor the next, nor in anyone's lifetime. By the end of the fifth year, the headlines of the evening paper would read: "Memorial Trial to Outlast the City"; and "Who Will Remain to Remember?" All the while, an industrious labyrinth of sculptors would continue to forge false monuments. A quiet proliferation of the craft swept through schools and workshops and warehouses: for the fear had not abated that the monuments might abscond into oblivion. It became necessary, in the name of justice, to train a force of skilled workers to fashion multiple iterations of each figure in the hope that some would survive. Indeed, despite a renewed and steady trail of nocturnal destruction, several copies at a time would often come to rest in the halls of the Court, the new with the old, the first with the last.

The more numerous the copies that sprung up in the streets, the more intense the threat of obliteration became. Explosives entered into the arsenal of the saboteurs and coordinated attacks could reduce dozens of the copies to rubble in a single night. But warehouses grew into factories, filling the east side of the city; and soon half of the working population had taken up voluntary apprenticeships, taking turns to fill the workshop floors from morning until evening. Monuments continued to fill the Court, regardless, now, of whether they were duplicates of those already standing somewhere in the monstrous crowd. People had long since ceased to anticipate the moment of judgement, as witnesses of a new generation began to take the stand. And, seeing no end of the proceedings in sight, the Architect and the City Planner agreed that the Court would be expanded into the city. Rows of buildings to the north of the old square were marked out for demolition; the roof of the Court was extended, and a new wall erected from the ruins. Displaced residents attempted in vain to appeal to the judges for the immediate resolution of the trial. Some from neighbouring areas joined the saboteurs in a frantic effort to defer any further swallowing up of the city. Others appealed to the factories to stop creating copies altogether. But this was not possible: for there was a dawning understanding among the voluntary sculptors that it was the law itself that compelled the reproduction of the monuments.

Forgetfulness was unthinkable. True, while the ongoing, clandestine sabotage of monuments was not explicitly sanctioned by the law, neither was it contempt of the Court. Such obliteration was not condoned, but neither was it illegal, as long as it occurred out of the sight of the city. To this end, the law could still distinguish permissible oblivion from impermissible, public annihilation. But the former was unacceptable while the latter was forbidden. Perhaps, one day, the moment of judgement would arrive, and the monuments – perhaps some of them, perhaps all – would be destroyed judicially, and the city finally reclaimed for the living. But for now, there could be no forgetfulness *outside of the law*. What alternative was there, then, but to recall, over and over, these crimes in the open?

And this accompanied a second unavoidable truth: the witnesses and evidence before the Court would never be adequate to the charges. Indeed, this would later be cited by the official Court Historian as the primary reason for the interminability of the trial. For the prosecution had to demonstrate injury to *civic* – not partial, nor partisan, but public and wholesale *memory*. In the courtroom, witnesses could speak either of injury, or of gratitude, but always from one side of that division. No testimony of was ever heard of a singularly lived experience of dissonance – and it had not occurred to either defence or prosecution to look for one, to seek out those whose fractured recollection of both shame and glory might speak to the wider civic condition. Unbeknownst to the nascent Court in its early days, the injury outlined in the charges was not a simple one: it could not pass into history for one half of the city while it remained painfully alive for the other. Instead, the offences referred to a complex injury: one that inhered in the very substance of apology and excuse. Such an injury was irredeemably collective and continuous: suffered only by a totality and only in the present. One could not demonstrate that this was the case by juridical means alone. It had to be demonstrated outside of the Court, in the ever-present city. It was necessary to replicate the monuments, unceasingly and in public.

And so the repetitive works of memorialisation continued even as the city was captured by the law, the roof of the Court moving darkly over time towards the west, then the south. Within a generation, there would be those who lived and died within the walls of the Court. The gargantuan dock was interspersed with new passageways; buildings were retained for dwelling and working; finally, streets were left unaltered, and the intrusion into civic life was as minimal as waking up one day to a sunless morning, the exterior roof of the Court passing over trees and pylons and chimney stacks outside.

The factories to the east would continue to transport new prisoners of bronze and granite into the city. The original dock had long since filled, and the new accused now lined the skyless streets instead, standing sentinel along roads that ran north to south and across the city, cloistered beneath the shelter of the law. No monument was at large outside the Court; and the shrinking enclave of the remnant city was finally subsumed within its walls. All memorials were now before the law, awaiting judgment as they loomed obstinately over civilian life, gazing jealously through upper storey windows into daily scenes of domesticity. The intrusion of this ominous presence would become unbearable, the residential districts too cramped, the availability of inhabitable space increasingly usurped by a population of stone until the final exodus of their fleshly neighbours, family by family and building by building. A new world was to be found beyond the city walls: a suburban reformation in which one could exchange a life lived collectively in the pain of disappointed hope for a muted, gentle existence of dispersal and amnesia – for no monuments had ever been erected there. The abandoned dwellings in the city-Court would be filled, in time, with awkward stone impostors: a grotesque dioramic parody of the departed.

Years would pass. New judges would replace the old in the towering thrones at the heart of the city; until one day there was no judiciary left, with no public to exonerate or condemn. The factories would then submit a delegation of their own: three eternal justices, cemented firmly in their citadel above the sprawling accused. Those who could still remember the city would take the tram or the bus from the suburbs to the witness stand, narrating the continuation of their experience; but age and frailty would finally bring these outings to an end. The last Court Historian ordered that the narratives of the witnesses should be recorded and played in perpetuity throughout the unattended city-Court. Their testimony would resound forever in the avenues of unhearing giants. The ground would tremble from time to time.

16

LEXICON ACT 2020

Gary Watt

This is not a statute and it has not passed in stages through parliament. Statute and stage are stopping words, and this is a new movement. This is a law made by the people for the people. A parliament of people who just happen to pass by, just happen to be just. They are as fit as any to be passing laws. This is a law for the courts of popular opinion. Except this is not a law, but a primal act. The people have been unfrozen from the solid state in which since ancient times they have been locked. The old certainties have thawed. The trickle of popular opinion has risen to a tide. Now, the first thing we do is drown all the lawyers. We drown the lawyers' books. We drown the lawyers' language. We drown the law. The new world will be ex-lex, lex-less, un-lexed, unisex, sex-less. The city of men will sink to silence, submerged at last, and the standing stones will lie un-fathered, unfathomable. Lawyers will lie with their language, upon a briny bed among the wrecks. The law with the lie, the law with the language of lies. Lex con lexicon.

Section 1

There are henceforth no sections. We will not begin with a cutting. There will be no circumcision.

There will be no full stops

Only commas, so as not to break the flow, of the moon-drawn tide, the sun has been too harsh, dialling out our days in constant measures of extremes, the moon knows no degrees but a monthly cycle of reflections in imperceptible shades and beneath its gentle light infinite variable snowflakes gel to quilts of lace and are mocked not with melting glares

We drown the letters seriatim A to B to C as sea creeps in upon a beach to lap the lapidate stones of law, to wear them down as they have worn us down, to blunt with waters where they have whet sharp lawyers' points

Arbitro is will, is the beginning, as is the end, will, the arbiter passes the first judgment, the arbitress the last, let the arbitrary sea pass judgment on it all with the to and fro of varying tide

Barristers are barred and robed unless debarred and bared, but no barrier can bar the incoming wave, counsel may rail upon the bench like serried Cnuts enthroned upon the shore, but their barrier will break upon the beach with buffeting, their bulwark will slip into a dreamless wake, the advocate may shout against the sea as Demosthenes declaimed against the foam, but none will stop the incoming wave, their call will be drowned out, their counsel cancelled, plunging them in salty stew of their own stock, as crowing chanticleers plucked off, deplumed, un-penned, unclamouring, dis-claimed, vacated of vocation, uncalled-for, unnamed, no-men-clature, patrons uncliented

Compensation is con-spun-satisfaction, cash where a limb used to be, withering contracts with complicated and con-dictated conditions shrink everything but lawyers' purses, the black-caped outlaw-in-law stands like a statute, accosts the conveyance and its stage-weary passenger withstand and deliver, steers and stables their steeds like an arresting constable, and leaves them stalled to count the costs, standing is the lawyers' state, estate, establishment and constitution, not just in the instant case but constantly from case to case by stare decisis

Dispute will end only with the pugilists struck down and out, for even the defender puts up a fence and fights with fending, impaling his points in soft nature's febrile flesh

Evidence is always before your eyes, but can you see the vision in the advice of the wise, or in the guise of history, or in the visa where the visage doesn't fit, and in the supervisor's interview, in the oculus panoptical, or in wit and wisdom, wot, the world is still deceived with ornament, law writes a welt tattoo on skin in iron gall ink, it is a spectacular punched in braille, so trust your eyes, justice is blind, and must be seen to be done

Fee, fie, foe, fumblings in lawyers' drawers, files of life defiled, decided, handed down as deciduous leaf, a fiefdom of fields laid out in foolscap, I smell the blood of fees yearning, indenture jaws yawning, the giant picks up cattle like peas from green beds, counting chattels per capita of head pecuniary, the judge says there is something wrong with a state of the law which makes it necessary to create fairy tales, and yet giants stride the earth

Grant us a gleaning of the field, let us walk within a garden without walls, a homely letting in some hortus uncourted, let us wander creant creatures in a miscreant world

Hearing judicially, we strain to sift the garden songs, discerning the sweet voice of justice from within the chanting and the incantation of lawyers' cant, noting, amidst the clamour of claims, the ring of truth, and the silence of sound judgment

Interest is a lawyers' word for the thing that matters, but it is a materialist matter, imposing itself within the essence of us, a questionable inter-esse, between the to be and the not to be, like making money breed

Jury's in and jury's out, the judge said something and th'accused said nowt, conjure is a word to conjure with, it might as well mean con-jury, for the lawyer who manipulates a judge or jury with persuasive speech and dazzling gestures is demonstrating the legerdemain of law, and though it might be trickery, there's magic in it

Kings cannot withstand a tide that wrecks all ships, nor can a hollow crown hold in the sea

Law firms and barristers' chambers must drown, let the law be un-firm, let barristers not live in boxes, where claims clamour and counsel of three thousand years call echo with the be-all end-all climax of bed chambers and double-barrel gun chambers, let sink to silence the hunter and his clarion horn, pursue not, shuffle off the suit, let sleep the dogs of law, exclude their lie ability

Magistrate, and everyone else is prostrate, what is the matter is a very good question, ask the mother, the mater, the origin, and heart

Nisi, a decree to sigh and cry, unless …

Obligations are cut and law's ligatures and leather bonds are let and loosed

Personality is a metaphor, an actor's mask, a superfice impenetrable and unprobable as any proof, the persona represents the human, and passes on death to the personal representative, who becomes thereby a representation of a representation, the lawyer who represents the personal representative is a representation upon a representation upon a representation, if we kill the lawyers we might only make things worse

Q has come in proper order, it is the most orderly of all the letters, requiring u to line up with it

R in fact is even more regular, so let Q be the exception that proves the rule, we stand up to be dressed down, erected to be interrogated, corrected, for reckoning and rectifying is the prerogative right of those who rule, those of rank, of the regent and all who reign in the realm, Daumier's Gargantua was a king who passed laws from his rectum, which is certainly not the right and proper way to do things, which begs the question of right and power, wherein lies the power to make the right, for recall once that when the vicar "come to put the questions, he put 'em by the rule o' contrairy, like, and he says, 'Wilt thou have this man to thy wedded wife?' says he, and then he says, 'Wilt thou have this woman to thy wedded husband?' says he … I was all of a tremble: it was as if I'd been a coat pulled by the two tails, like; for I couldn't stop the parson, I couldn't take upon me to do that; and yet I said to myself, I says, 'Suppose they shouldn't be fast married, 'cause the words are contrairy?' and … I says to myself, 'Is't the meanin' or the words as makes folks fast i' wedlock?' … And he made light on it, and he says, 'Pooh, pooh … make yourself easy,' he says; 'it's neither the meaning nor the words – it's the re*ges*ter does it …'"

Suit follows naturally, as suitors do, and executors too, who are just following orders, and, having been assigned their task, prosecute and pursue the statute to the letter, sequestering and suing, like *La Justice et La Vengeance divine poursuivant Le Crime*

Tenuous it may be, and quite a stretch, but we are intent upon speaking of tenures and tricks

U as you know is unfair, that which is not pleasing to the sight, but who can say for a fact if it is fair today to speak of a fair maid if she is only fair by being made up and if she herself is made up to be so feted

Violence is the system of inheritance, hear the heart of her, Antigone, heaving handful earth, interring her brother, honouring his disinherited blood

> Had I had children or their father dead,
> I'd let them moulder, I should not have chosen
> In such a case to cross the State's decree,
> What is the law that lies behind these words?
> One husband gone, I might have found another,
> or a child from a new man in first child's place,
> but with my parents hid away in death,
> no brother, ever, could spring up for me,
> Such was the law by which I honoured you

Will all third parties passing by witness, that testaments weigh the dead by scales, striking the balance with bronze, engraving them in books crafted by dead bees, thus quoth the dying – as is written in these tablets of wax, so I give, so I bequeath, so I declare my will, and so do you, citizens, bear witness, and thus quoth the living – let your family and money pass into my charge and custody, and, in order that you may make your will properly in accordance with the public law, let them be purchased by me with this bronze

X is the state of law, the sign of the cross, the sign of the canceller, the sign of the chancellor, the signature of the illiterate, the name of the anonymous, and the ending of the Trial of the Pyx in which the Chancellor of the Exchequer checks in and checks out

Y is the question of what should come next in an unsequential world, a world that does not follow

Z is for the business of the bees and for the lazy drone, a honey-tongued fellow once said that honey bees are

> Creatures that by a rule in nature teach
> The act of order to a peopled kingdom
> They have a king and officers of sorts;
> Where some, like magistrates, correct at home,
> Others, like merchants, venture trade abroad,
> Others, like soldiers, armed in their stings,
> Make boot upon the summer's velvet buds,
> Which pillage they with merry march bring home
> To the tent-royal of their emperor;
> Who, busied in his majesty, surveys

The singing masons building roofs of gold,
The civil citizens kneading up the honey,
The poor mechanic porters crowding in
Their heavy burdens at his narrow gate,
The sad-eyed justice, with his surly hum,
Delivering o'er to executors pale
The lazy yawning drone

Workers of the air untie, go fly your several ways, pick pollen from the pendant, petalled purse, make bowers on silken blooms, for all things are better that could not be worse, put sun at your backs and follow the moon, wander where you will and fill your ears with your own merry, buzzing tune

17

CARRIER BAG LAW

Bernard Keenan

Law is a medium for the production of a certain type of subject who inhabits a certain type of world. This makes law appear to work as a technology. As the world of the singular heroic subject burns around him, is it possible to imagine a different kind of worlding? A different concept of the relationship between technology and culture may offer a way.

The departure point is perhaps to consider law as we know it as a technical project. The law understood as technology operates in two registers: social functionalism and normative representation. As a social function, law is a machine for producing specific outputs from given inputs. To re-imagine law while remaining within this register is to imagine a different set of machine programmes, whether at the level of a minor adjustment or at the level of radically reinventing the social order. As in Borges's story of the lottery in Babylon, the reader is invited to apply the law by thinking through the outputs resulting from whatever symbolic inputs are stated in the rules.[1] One imagines law like one imagines an algorithm, a process for making conditional jumps: if this, then that.

Law as a technology of normative representation means that law imposes or signifies some underlying political decisions, social customs, or moral values. Modern law also signifies its own legitimacy. The laws produced by a legislature are made via constitutionally mandated procedures and are enforced by courts that unfold disputes according to flexible procedural rules. Thus, law works technically to convert aspirations into actions and to inform an imaginary community about itself. An imaginary law in the representative register could serve

1 Jorge Luis Borges, 'The Lottery in Babylon', *Fictions*, tr. Andrew Hurley (London: Penguin 2000) 51–8.

to celebrate or satirise a political ideal or its perversion, or to indicate the values of some other metaphysical order.

By drawing attention to law as technology, we can see that both the functionalist and representational modes presuppose certain techniques by which a legal text may be made and actualised. In cybernetic terms, the functional view presupposes the first-order techniques of the jurist, who reads the law and applies it to the environment. The representational approach is then a second-order perspective, reading the law not simply for what it actively does but for the meaning that it holds in relation to a moral, cultural or political environment.[2] In both modes, the legal text serves as a metaphorical infrastructure for the enactment of something beyond the text. This is why for Lévi-Strauss, the lawyer's account of the world is "like an animal trying to explain to a zoologist the workings of a magic lantern".[3] Law is a rhetorical performance for those who are already captured by the misapprehension that law, "sandwiched between theology ... and journalism",[4] describes or enacts social reality. For Levi-Strauss, it ought to be noted, if one really wants to know the world or change it, law is the last place to look.[5]

The relationship between technique and cultural reproduction lies at the heart of the theory of cultural techniques. An elaboration on so-called "German" media theory,[6] this approach draws attention to the law's medial substrata and the techniques through which it is made to function as if it describes the world. Recent years have seen scholars turning to the study of the technicalities and materialities engaged by legal practices as a way of seeing how rhetoric and textual exegesis are in themselves modes of world-making, in which the law is assumed to act as a technology.[7] According to the outline provided by Cornelia Vismann, the law in its modern form operates through the enactment of textual media via particular and contingent sets of inherited and teachable cultural techniques.[8] Laws are not determined by the conditions media of transmission, storage, and reproduction, but law in its particularities and genealogies can be productively interrogated through media-technical analysis.

2 This alludes to Niklas Luhmann, (1992) 'Operational Closure and Structural Coupling: The Differentiation of the Legal System', *Cardozo Law Review* 13: 1419–41.

3 Claude Lévi-Strauss, *Tristes Tropiques*, tr. John Russell (New York: Criterion Books, 1961) 57.

4 ibid.

5 I owe this observation to Alain Pottage, (2014) 'Law after Anthropology: Object and Technique in Roman Law', *Theory, Culture & Society* 31, 2–3, 147–66.

6 Bernard Dionysius Geoghegan, (2013) 'After Kittler: On the Cultural Techniques of Recent German Media Theory', *Theory, Culture & Society* 30, 6.

7 For a summary, see Hyo Yoon Kang, 'Law's Materiality: Between Concrete Matters and Abstract Forms, or How Matter Becomes Material', in *Routledge Handbook for Law and Theory*, ed. Andreas Philippopoulos-Mihalopoulos (Abingdon: Routledge, 2018).

8 Cornelia Vismann, (2013) 'Cultural Techniques and Sovereignty', *Theory, Culture & Society* 30, 6: 83–93; see also Cornelia Vismann, (1999) 'Jurisprudence: A Transfer Science', *Law and Critique* 10, 3, 279–86.

In setting out her methodology, Vismann draws attention to the peculiar role of the "medium voice" in Greek grammar. In the medium voice, a verb's performance is not ascribed to the subject of the sentence but to the medium through which they act. Thus, for instance, a bather:

> "is carried by the water. As opposed to a spear, which is released from the hand of its thrower, the trajectory of bathing remains bound to the medium of water. The grammatical form of the medium indicates that very relational quality. Spear-throwing, on the other hand, represents a classic case of active verb formation."[9]

This is the media-technical precondition of scripting for a law that can be transmitted and simultaneously enacted over time and space. When legal scripts and protocols are technically performed, the peculiarly legal quality of law is reproduced: this is the re-inscription of the difference between the legal and the non-legal. In other words, the operation and continuation of modern law depend first upon protocols, which precede any symbolic effect.

One function of modern legal protocols is to mediate the idea of the active and singular legal subject. This is the same subject that projects its will onto the world, either as an individual or as an abstract sovereign legislator. The imaginary subject can serve to represent a community or an empire, or it can be the repository for a list of rights:

> "The ballistic perspective (the active voice, the spear) corresponds to the logic of the law, which continuously associates means with their ends. Moreover, it also partakes of a legal narrative according to which an operation may be attributed to an agent as the source of a conflict or a legal matter."[10]

This figure in turn underpins the law as a connector between means and ends, and the stability of this figure is what allows specific rules and procedures to be flexible, reflexive, archived and re-writable.

One could connect this to other critiques of law's foundational violence. It is consistent with law as the imposition of reason on the world and of the metaphysical idea over desire. The law reproduces the paternal master who monopolises not only violence but normativity and reason. The spear-throwing subject underlies the history of global law. Planetary modernity made it possible to conceive of one world legal system with regional variations. This in turn raised the problem known at least since Kant of speaking for the other via the same, which remains a problem even where others' indigenous legal practices are either

9 Vismann (n8) 85.
10 ibid., 85.

maintained or recuperated after decolonisation.[11] The reinvention or the maintenance of non-modern, non-individualistic modes of normative judgment can in themselves only be apprehended by the world system in contradistinction or comparison with itself so that the other becomes describable only in system terms, and recuperation is always reinvention.

But it is the comparison between law's subjectivity and the spear that I would like to draw out here.[12] If law is the technology that underpins the subject that *uses* technology to master the world, then the relationship between technology and political subjectivity might be reimagined via a different imaginary of law. And if planetary world systems are now in crisis and collapse, then such reinvention is urgently necessary. Is it possible to depart from a media-technical analysis to imagine a different world trajectory?[13]

One such departure might be found in Ursula Le Guin's carrier bag theory of fiction, which shifts attention away from the techniques of the spear thrown by a subject towards the techniques of holding, carrying, filling and reusing.[14] In an essay describing the ethics behind her authorship, Le Guin positions the container (as in a bag, a holder, a recipient) as the original cultural technology. She explicitly refutes traditional Euro-American origin myths in which primitive man ascended to mastery of the world through the tools he wields: the axe, the knife, the club, the spear; that is, the tool as the extension and projectile of the will of the subject. Hegemonic western culture rests upon the singular hero having radical struggles with alterity, discovering the unknown, surviving the outside, taming the different. Such narratives surround and infuse the legal order and sovereign power, and here lies the resonance with Vismann:

> "the Hero has decreed through his mouthpieces the Lawgivers, first, that the proper shape of the narrative is that of the arrow or spear … second, that the central concern of narrative, including the novel, is conflict; and third, that the story isn't any good if he isn't in it."[15]

The hero story of course persists, not least for its drama and its exceptionalism. But its continued triumph means the reproduction of the same and comes at the

11 For a recent example of comparative scholarship see, Hermann Amborn, *Law as Refuge of Anarchy: Societies without Hegemony or State*, trans. Adrian Nathan West (Cambridge, MA: MIT Press, 2019).

12 The isomorphism that Vismann and Krajewski elsewhere identify between law and technology should be understood in these terms, see Cornelia Vismann and Markus Krajewski, (2008) 'Computer Juridisms', *Grey Room* 29, 90–109.

13 Put differently, is a different "cosmotechnics" possible? See Yuk Hui, *The Question Concerning Technology in China: An Essay in Cosmotechnics* (Falmouth: Urbanomic, 2016).

14 Ursula K. Le Guin and Donna Haraway, *The Carrier Bag Theory of Fiction* (London: Ignota Books, 2020).

15 ibid., 34.

expense of stories and storytellers who do not conform and those whose worlds are occluded from its trajectory.

In contrast the carrier bag theory draws on a different type of story to establish different kinds of subjects. The theory is based on a simple observation: that culture did not begin with tools and weapons used to direct force outwards, but with devices for bringing energy home. The precondition of the hero-weapon is the humble carrier bag, the sling, or the basket. These tools assemble and contain whatever is needed. They allow seeds to be gathered and water to be collected and the baby to be carried all the while. And home, after all, is nothing if not a container for life.

Le Guin's suggestion is that fictions that dwell on the bag can germinate different imaginaries. This way, a more complex and nuanced account of human relations might unfold within it. In any case, the hero can no longer dominate. The hero "does not look well in this bag. He needs a stage or a pedestal or a pinnacle. You put him in a bag and he looks like a rabbit, like a potato".[16] The sovereign subject must learn to accept he is not sovereign but always needs to make and share space and time with other existing things. This way, an explicitly feminist technique of fiction-writing engenders a different cultural imaginary.

The use of fiction in worlding or re-worlding is gaining traction.[17] It matters, as Donna Haraway insists, what stories tell stories.[18] What would it mean for a legal order that consciously does not re-inscribe the singular hero, the active agent, the ballistic subject of law? What would it mean to start from the techniques required to stay with, in Le Guin's words, "what is in fact going on, what people actually do and feel, how people relate to everything else in this vast sack, this belly of the universe, this womb of things to be and tomb of things that were"?[19] It would not necessitate a revolution, but a shift in the technical parameters through which law reproduces itself. Perhaps it is merely a restatement of the "ethical" turn familiar to critical legal studies.[20] Techniques of complementarity, reciprocity, synchronous and sequential on-going-ness of the world, paying attention to the indeterminate interaction of persons and things. No more human exceptionalism. Irreducible to traditional ideas of anarchism, although perhaps sharing with them a certain ethical predisposition. A law of action, but

16 ibid., 35.

17 See Simon O'Sullivan, Henriette Gunkell and Ayesha Hameed, eds, *Futures and Fictions: Essays and Conversations That Explore Alternative Narratives and Image Worlds That Might Be Pitched Against the Impasses of Our Neo-Liberal Present* (London: Repeater, 2017).

18 A concept most fully developed in Donna J. Haraway, *Staying with the Trouble: Making Kin in the Chthulucene* (Durham: Duke University Press Books, 2016).

19 Le Guin (n 14) 37.

20 Luce Irigaray's hopes for an explicitly feminist law spring to mind, see Alain Pottage, (1995) 'A Unique and Different Subject of Law', *Cardozo Law Review* 16, 1161-1204; similar pitfalls may then apply, see, Nicola Lacey, (1996) 'Normative Reconstruction in Socio-Legal Theory', *Social & Legal Studies* 5, 2: 131–57.

the source and the effect of the action would be different; an action that does not ballistically project itself in time and space but aims to bring things home, so to speak. It seems worth a try. If teleological human progress is in a death spiral, perhaps it is time for critical legal thinkers to imagine a law – if law could still be the word – without the technical imperative of the hero's progress.

18

LAW IN THE ROUND

Linda G. Mills

For over two decades, I have imagined a space, a circle, where those who commit intimate crimes of a violent nature can go to understand their abuse, untangle its origins and seek to repair the harm this all-too-often intergenerational influence reaps. An imaginary development, option or law has begun to take shape in the round. A restorative approach to intimate partner violence brings those who have been harmed into a circle of recovery to take stock of the events and for all to witness the potential for change.

My own history is relevant here. Many years back, I was involved in a violent relationship with someone whose professional identity was to imagine programmes for the prevention of violence. As we learn very early on in psychological studies, the idea that someone who perpetrates violence might also spend much of their lives attempting to prevent it, is a paradox that should not surprise anyone. We often outwardly object to that which we do. This kind of over-reaction can paper over one's own guilt. In my case, my ex-lover's work in violence prevention both helped him cover up his own abusive proclivities, but also, in his mind, to mitigate them. His violence was no small matter. Tyres were slashed. I was pinned down. Very bad things happened. I repeat this story not so that the world can vindicate my victimisation, although this is certainly a common reaction these days. With no alternative pathway for expression or healing, there is only a singular and often unsatisfying outcome. My desire is to imagine a shelf of new possibilities for the cabinet of imaginary laws.

In this heterotopic world, the violent family member or lover is brought into a circle to redress the harm committed, surrounded by caring but nevertheless firm loved ones and community members to hold him, her or them responsible for the violence that has been committed. But accountability, as it is often referred to by prosecutors and victims' lawyers, is far from the solitary goal. It is in the process of revelation to others that recovery can begin, that one is helped and guided to a different standard or path and when a long history of injustices can finally be addressed.

In my own case, this circle would involve recognition of the harm done as well as accountability and would likely involve a full exploration of my ex-lover's own experience of violence, both the ever so seemingly meaningless slights by a judgemental mother, to the rejection and pain that this and other more brutal effects may have generated. And while none of this justifies the violence against me, it certainly provides a pathway for understanding it.

I am prepared to accept this outcome, as are others I know who do this circle work. Why? Because if we do not seriously grapple with the consequences – and causes – of violence, it will always be the perpetrator's legitimate form of expression. Violence is, for the most part, learned; it is our responsibility as members of civil society to help people find new methods of reacting and responding to whatever the violence generated, assuming our goal is to reduce violence, rather than just lock it away. The only way to look beyond the devastating singular incidents of the abuse we abhor, is to develop a method for interrupting its intergenerational transmission.

So what exactly does this imaginary shelf include? People who love violent people – or their stand-ins – and who are willing to hear their origin stories, and who will listen to the pain of all the unspeakable violence that leads to reproducing it. People capable of recognising that we can be both good and also bad, loving and full of hate, hurtful and protective. All these qualities are imprinted upon us during an age when we are too naïve or young, or just too fragile, to understand and make sense of it. This sense-making must come later and yet we do not create those opportunities for making sense. The damage has been done and that is it. Game over. Jail or prison for you.

The value of such a circle is opportunity. It is to give space to the many who see the good, loving and protective that is so painfully masked in the violent cage that can envelop a person and which they have now recreated. This is fighting back, finally, but surrounded not by courtrooms filled with people they do not know and who have no interest in understanding them, but by those who care enough to support a person through the change. On my shelf is the need to create a space to hear all aspects of the pain violence causes and to make sense of it. For everyone. As we build this muscle to listen, we also find new ways of helping people heal.

Because we fear violence, its effects and how we might become tangled inside of it, we are all too often blinded by its attractive or manipulative influences. And so we impose our views for theirs, replace their sense with ours. And in that imposition, we often beget more violence and the trauma that trails it. We force those harmed to inhabit the pain, rather than help them find their way out of it. Women all too often return to their violent lovers without the insight and strength they need (and can tap into) because we do not help them create a space for understanding the violence they have endured and making informed choices about how to address it. We leave those who have been harmed with only two choices: forcing them either to hold their painful history in secret or to fight tirelessly to send someone to jail. We need strategies that go beyond these options. We need to promote both healing and justice.

So in my law, there is, in addition to the prosecutor, the defender of what happened, why it happened, what caused it to happen, how did we get to this point and what histories are relevant to understanding the dynamics of escalation. These questions not only give those who were victims of this violent episode a new kind of voice, we also give those who perpetrated violence an opportunity to explain, to excavate a history that one can be given the opportunity to extricate from. In doing so, we all gain insight into how violence begins in the wee hours of a life, between parent and child, sibling and sibling, in the playground, between friends or so-called enemies, towards creatures, by burning ants or injuring pets. How it then mushrooms, balloons – for some, not all – into a world that can cultivate a life behind bars.

Some might ask: "What's the point? Why understand violence?" I believe that for those who experience violence in intimate relationships, an airing would provide them both with the support they need and the reality check they seek. In my own case, finally finding a couples' counsellor who would "talk it through" with me and my violent partner, gave me the pathway to leave the relationship. He also got the help he desperately needed, and I was liberated from my participation in it.

But the real point is that to understand violence in its particulars, means we can understand the collective roots and communal responses that are so desperately needed. This is the part of the shelf that is least developed and the most urgent. Each case makes up a piece of the whole and if we are unwilling to let any case go down this imaginary path of understanding, we will never reduce the violence we seek to eradicate. But to let go, case-by-case, in an imaginary world of justice, is to understand the whole and begin to chip away at its effect, to seriously consider reducing violence, not by prosecution or persecution, but by accepting the fact that abuse is perpetuated by one generation and then another.

Under this law, we are safer – all of us – because we can anticipate violence and its effects, we can step in earlier in the lifecycle, and we can actually prevent it. We are less afraid of it because we understand where it starts, what it looks like and how it feels when it begins. Imaginary or not, violence is real, its effects are reproduced, and our fear of it only makes the problem much worse. Paradoxically, standing up to violence involves sitting down with it, getting to know it and yes – making friends with the demon we currently seek to lock away. I have witnessed this unimaginable effect in the real circles I have helped to create.

Law in the Round Act

1.1 In the interpretation of this Act, diversity of input and participation is to be privileged, recognising the traumatic effects of violence and its history.

1.2 All personal pronouns in this enactment are mutable and changeable and all formations of partnership are invited to participate.
1.3 A circle is constituted of a trained facilitator and the community of those close to the couple: family, kin group, neighbours, friends, colleagues, co-workers who participate to bear witness to the violence and its impact and influence. Those who both reproduce violence and experience it, are to be included, particularly if the goal is to interrupt its transmission across generations.
1.4 Intimate violence is defined, herein, as any vocal, emotional or physical abuse of another, wheresoever occasioned.
1.5 Intimate violence is presumed herein to be a communication that either results in insults or in the failure of words, as well as in the physical manifestation of pain.
1.6 Punishment is to be replaced or at least supplemented by considered treatment in the form of circles that untangle the meaning of the harm caused and why accountability and consequences for the behaviour become necessary.
1.7 To prevent future violence calls for an understanding of the physical manifestations of the triggers of violence and a concrete plan for mitigating or preventing those triggers or a means for safely walking away from them.
1.8 Circle members commit to an open and difficult dialogue. The circle endeavours to help participants appreciate how their learned behaviours can influence an entire constellation of people and generations. Family members, biological or otherwise, act as helpful monitors to help prevent escalation when it begins to occur.
1.9 A circle is an elastic community and will remain in place for an indefinite time, or until the facilitator and participants are persuaded that the history is adequately addressed and understood and that the future holds not only the promise but a reality, that new forms of communication have become the norm, as the pathway to a meaningful cessation of violence.

19

Καὶ μηδὲν μόριον ἀποκεκρύφθαι

The bare life of the Stoic sage

Phillip Mitsis

… vain Covering if to hide
Thir guilt and dreaded shame; O how unlike
To that first naked Glorie.

John Milton, *Paradise Lost* 9.1113–15

The Stoics have often loomed significantly, if somewhat remotely, over the origins of Western ethical and legal thinking. The great Victorian ethicist, Henry Sidgwick, for instance, credited them with furnishing "the transition from the old Greek view of ethics, in which the notions of Good and Virtue were taken as fundamental, to the modern view in which ethics is conceived as primarily a study of the 'moral code'".[1] By the same token, their jural conception of morality in combination with their theory of divine natural law has commonly been taken to have laid the intellectual foundations of Roman jurisprudence.[2] This is heady, if somewhat abstract stuff, so I think it may be worthwhile to have look at one of their particular laws in order to gain a more nuanced sense of their contribution. Evidence for particular laws, real or imaginary, is rather hard to come by, but I want to focus on what seems to be one of our very few surviving positive prescriptions from the founder of Stoicism, Zeno of Citium. From what we can tell, it formed part of the legal structure of his *Republic*, which in many

1 Henry Sidgwick, *Outlines of the History of Ethics for English Readers* (London: Macmillan and Co. 5th edition, 1906), p. 97.

2 See Paul A. Vander Waerdt, "Philosophical Influence on Roman Jurisprudence? The Case of Stoicism and Natural Law" in Wolfgang Haase (ed.), *Philosophie, Wissenschaften, Technik. Philosophie*, (Berlin: De Gruyter 1987) pp. 4851–901.

ways was a critical response to Plato's and presumably attempted to cast doubt on central Platonic claims.

Before turning to Zeno, though, it may be helpful to briefly mention a bit about Stoicism's contemporary reception, since by any stretch of the imagination, the gap between what many nowadays are finding important in Stoicism and what our evidence suggests about them is striking – perhaps even more striking, I think, once we have a look at this particular law. So, for instance, over the past few decades the Stoics have become the darlings of the American military. A strange turn of events for antiquity's original peaceniks, but one to be attributed almost entirely to the exemplary life of U.S. Navy Vice-Admiral James Bond Stockdale, who after being shot down in Vietnam, stood up to years of torture in the infamous "Hanoi Hilton" by taking to heart the precepts of Epictetus that he had studied as a philosophy grad student at Stanford.[3] So too, Wall Street's warriors, always big on manly courage, except perhaps when facing cuts in their annual bonuses, climbed on the Stockdale bandwagon, and Epictetus reading groups were soon formed in some of the plushest hedge fund lounges in New York. This, remember, is the Epictetus, a Stoic slave, who observed:

> You ought to treat your whole body like a poor loaded-down donkey; if it be commandeered and a soldier lay hold of it, let it go, do not resist nor grumble. If you do, you will get a beating and lose your little donkey just the same. But when this is the way in which you should act as regards the body, consider what is left for you to do about all the other things that are provided for the sake of the body. Since the body is a little donkey, the other things become bridles for a little donkey, little pack-saddles, little shoes, and barley. Let them go too, get rid of them more quickly and cheerfully than the little donkey itself.
>
> *Diss.* 4.1.79 (trans. Oldfather)

However little Epictetus seems to be giving prescriptions about how to be Lazard's employee of the month, nonetheless he is regularly held up as an exemplum on the Street. Go figure.

Conversely, prominent liberal academic philosophy professors, such as Martha Nussbaum and Anthony Appiah, have found in the Stoics founding charters for their own particular brands of cosmopolitanism, communitarianism, cosmopolitanism with a communitarian twist, communitarianism with a cosmopolitan twist, etc. I must confess that the thought of academic liberals on safari waking up in the same tent with admirals and ultra-high net worth equity managers offers some tantalisingly wry opportunities for ideological deconstruction, but

3 James B. Stockdale's powerful accounts of his experiences are to be found in *Courage under Fire. Testing Epictetus's Doctrines in a Laboratory of Human Behavior* Hoover Essays no.6 (Stanford: Hoover Institution Press, 1994).

being an old-time philologist I will limit myself to turning to a text. I say "a text" because we basically have only one that seems to be even modestly reliable as a report of an actual Stoic work, in this case a snippet from Zeno's *Republic* and its seemingly spare cabinet of nomothetic prescriptions for an ideal society of concord, virtue and happiness.

The text is a report by Diogenes Laertius of one of Zeno's critics, Cassius the Sceptic, who complains:

> Again, in the *Republic*, making an invidious contrast, he (Zeno) declares the good alone to be true citizens or friends or kindred or free men; and accordingly in the view of the Stoics parents and children are enemies, not being wise. Again, it is objected, in the *Republic* he lays down community of wives, and at line 200 prohibits the building of temples, lawcourts and gymnasia in cities; while as regards a currency he writes that we should not think it need be introduced either for purposes of exchange or for travelling abroad. Further, he bids men and women wear the same dress and keep no part of the body entirely covered.
>
> R. D. Hicks, 1925[4]

One can quickly see that however useful Stoicism might be in helping one stand up to torture or in facing a downturn in the market, Zeno's own conception of an ideal world includes neither the military, nor Wall Street. By ridding his city of gymnasia, he is consciously abolishing the most important institution for young men not only to come to wrestle naked together and to strengthen their bodies along with their social bonds, but also to prepare themselves for military service to their city. And by abolishing currency in the next breath, there is at least an underlying hint of the standard ancient philosophical connection between war and money. But at any rate, at least for Zeno, there will be no truck with money; hence no bankers allowed.

As for cosmopolitanism, even Carl Schmitt might find rather pessimistically severe the Stoic claim that all parents and children are enemies if they have not attained wisdom. Moreover, given the Stoic view that a wise man is "as rare as the Ethiopian phoenix", a world in which it is extremely likely that every single living individual is wallowing in unending enmity with every other seems rather infertile ground for the kind of tolerant, open-minded-conversation-based cosmopolitanism cum communitarianism touted in the liberal academy.

4 [33] *Πάλιν ἐν τῇ Πολιτείᾳ παριστάντα πολίτας καὶ φίλους καὶ οἰκείους καὶ ἐλευθέρους τοὺς σπουδαίους μόνον, ὥστε τοῖς στωικοῖς οἱ γονεῖς καὶ τὰ τέκνα ἐχθροί: οὐ γάρ εἰσι σοφοί. κοινάς τε τὰς γυναῖκας δογματίζειν ὁμοίως ἐν τῇ Πολιτείᾳ καὶ κατὰ τοὺς διακοσίους <στίχους> μήθ' ἱερὰ μήτε δικαστήρια μήτε γυμνάσια ἐν ταῖς πόλεσιν οἰκοδομεῖσθαι. περί τε νομίσματος οὕτως γράφειν, 'νόμισμα δ' οὔτ' ἀλλαγῆς ἕνεκεν οἴεσθαι δεῖν κατασκευάζειν οὔτ' ἀποδημίας ἕνεκεν.' καὶ ἐσθῆτι δὲ τῇ αὐτῇ κελεύει χρῆσθαι καὶ ἄνδρας καὶ γυναῖκας καὶ μηδὲν μόριον ἀποκεκρύφθαι.* (Diogenes Laertius 7.33)

Notice, however, that our passage concludes with a Stoic regulation that, at least as far as I know, rarely gets recommended as much as it might to budding generals, titans of finance, or professors of Kant. R. D. Hicks's rather notional translation from the world of 1920s Trinity College, Cambridge misleads and would cause such cross-linked sartorial complexity in practice that it is not clear that even a sage could manage the fashion design. Our titular sentence actually recommends something much more simple and reads, "and he commands that men and women wear the very same clothes and that their genitals not be covered."[5] However much we might think that the benefits of same-sex egalitarian garb might be profitably espoused by the army, Goldman Sachs, and All Souls, the added Rick Owens fashion touch of exposed genitals probably packs too much of an ontological wallop – or in some cases, perhaps too little – to be likely adopted and run with.[6]

What we might find especially puzzling, however, is why would a Stoic, who finds things like property, clothing and everything else a matter of indifference except for moral virtue, require his ideal citizens to wear these kinds of outfits? One easy answer – well perhaps not so easy, since it flies in the face of the views of Heidegger, Levinas, Agamben, etc. about the founding of ethical and legal systems on a sense of bodily shame – is that Zeno is merely reversing in rather antinomian cynic fashion the standard institutions and customs of the Greek polis. By abolishing temples, gymnasia and money, he essentially denudes his city of the customary foundational Greek legal and political structures. So, perhaps we should infer that by having the genitals of his ideal sages uncovered, Zeno is merely reversing the normative grounding of non-ideal societies in *aidos*.[7] But the argument of mere antinomian reversal seems to have some holes. Can we imagine these ideal citizens sitting around in caparison clubs watching dancers teasingly playing with covering their unnaughty bits while a drunken sage in the back yells "Come on, luv, cover it all up"? A mirror theory backfires, I think, since the mirroring of signifier and image, as Lacan discovered, begins to dissolve in the tension between signifier and psychological drive.

Classical scholars have been titillated by Zeno's fashion sense and, rather than, say, being worried about its practicality once the cold winter winds set in, have typically viewed it as a prescription for easier sexual congress. But such an inference, perhaps, mostly reflects the kind of Christian post-lapsarian preoccupations and repressed titillation encapsulated in our epigraph from *Paradise Lost*.

5 Aristotle, *Parts of Animals* 689a21; Diod. 1.85.3; Sextus *P.* 3.205; *membrum virile* Plutarch *Fort. Rom* 323b.

6 Some fashion reporters at the time observed that the male models wearing Rick Owens bare crotch pants failed to create a powerful effect and some included such deflationary descriptions of the stars of the show as "peeping timidly", "unimpressive", etc. See https://www.scmp.com/lifestyle/fashion-watches/article/1695788/rick-owens-bared-crotches-spark-full-frontal-mens-fashion (Accessed 20 July 2020).

7 "Modesty, shame, respect, sense of honor, dignity, majesty; genital organs".

In this same passage, we have the common Greek utopian claim that women (wives?) will be held in common, though unlike in Plato, it is unlikely that for Zeno this was a necessary consequence for a eugenics project. In Plato's *Republic*, sex with the best is a crucial reward for better performance on the battlefield and it helps insure the genetic purity and betterment of the best. For the Stoics, sex is just a matter of flesh rubbing against flesh and it does not matter whether that flesh is one's mum, sister, daughter, brother-in-law, etc. Moreover, the Stoics tend to hold to the egalitarian thought that anyone from any gene pool can hope to make sage, even if they have twagged geometry class. Further indifference to the standard Greek bodily boundaries is evidenced in the Stoic view of the dead. Rather than burying the dead and wasting the meat, they recommend the kind of funeral feast that includes the deceased on the menu. Again, a dead body is just so much flesh, and what is important about human beings – their moral autonomy – is in no way connected to it. Thus, given their indifference to the body, there remains the question of why there is this concern for a regulation with dubious practical benefit, either from the point of sexual convenience or protection from the elements, and that seems to stick out like a sore thumb on two counts. First, it is one of perhaps only two surviving positive requirements[8] among a list of prohibitions. And second, it seems to carry on like a two-bob watch about something that should be a matter of indifference and, in keeping with Epictetus's metaphor, is like fretting over the reach of a donkey's pack saddle.

Here, of course, we can only offer a few speculations. The first cuts across the discussion of Agamben and others about the nature of bare life and nudity. Zeno seems to want to collapse public and private life by mandating a homogeneous dress code of cookie-cutter conformity. We might initially think Zeno is Mao with a wicked sense of humour. But more serious strains of analysis beckon. Agamben, for instance, might perhaps claim that Zeno's prescription brings into being a zone of indistinction of the sort that the state of exception creates in order to turn the exception into an absolute norm.[9] Yet, ungendered dress that reveals

8 We do not know how extensive Zeno's legal code might have been; however, it is plausible to presume that, like Plato in the *Republic*, his emphasis was not on a detailed list of laws, since laws are held to be only as good as those enforcing them, and the bulk of the worry is about producing the right sort of character in citizens. More important in the case of the Stoics, since all citizens in the ideal state are already good, there would seem to be little need for laws, except for a few, perhaps, to coordinate interests. The report says that Zeno (δογματίζειν) the community of wives, which can have a stronger sense of "decreed" or something weaker in the sense of "to express a view in favor". However, he commands (κελεύει) that men and women wear the same clothing. This strongly suggests that wearing this kind of clothing will be in accordance with a legal requirement and not just a descriptive claim about the sort of garb that sages will naturally come to wear once they join together into a community. At the same time, of course, one of Zeno's goals in setting out his ideal city was criticising contemporary practices. Unfortunately, we have no evidence explaining why sages covering their genitals would present a problem for their living a good life.

9 I owe this observation to Ioannis Ziogas.

gendered private parts remains slightly off-kilter, I think, as a state of xxxeption. Zeno, of course, is creating his city of sages against the backdrop of an Athens in which one can meet naked representations of the phallus in temples, gymnasia, commercial centres, and through religious Hermai on your average street corner. The pudenda (to thumb forward to a medieval term) do not carry in this context the same kind of signification *per se* that grounds the discussions of Heidegger, Agamben, etc. At the same time, Zeno does not turn his city of sages into a nudist colony, so we have to assume there is a philosophically motivated point in putting the fashion spotlight where he does.

One possible suggestion is that the effect of his clothing is to desexualise the genitals and in the case of the phallus, to deflate its symbolic power. So too, it moves female sexuality into the public realm, and by exposing it to everyday view, undercuts the kinds of patriarchal preoccupations and protections that kept women cloistered in private seclusion. By shining a light on the problem, Zeno, in keeping with his demystification of sexuality and his indifference to the body, creates not a zone of indistinction, but one of indifference – which is after all the Stoic goal in the first place. Exactly how such garb would prepare one for the military or Wall Street or dinner at All Souls remains an interesting question, but this forgotten *motu proprio* from Zeno's imaginary cabinet perhaps deserves more of an airing among our contemporary Stoic enthusiasts if they might want to try real Stoicism on for size.

20

MOVE OVER, FELIX

Addressing the impact of the domestic cat

James Attlee

Some time ago I found myself at a table with a group of people I had not met before. They mainly worked in one of two fields, financial services or the oil industry, neither of which I have personal experience in. It was a happy occasion; many of those present had flown from locations around the world to be there: friendship and family clearly meant a lot to them. But as the evening progressed and they spoke among themselves of their work, something became clear to me. Their sense of duty, connection and responsibility was strong, but it was limited to their partners and immediate circle – beyond that, the world would have to take its chances. This, I realised, is how they are able to do what they do – extract and sell fossil fuels, help multinational corporations avoid tax – without examining the effects of their work on the wider community. They flip a switch in their heads. And what I thought was, *I bet they all have cats.*

I myself am not immune to feline charm: the eyes, the sinuous, expressive body, the hypnotic, helicopter-drone of the purr; the sense a cat somehow projects that it is a *privilege* to be allowed to pet them, that they are present as long as it is convenient but that they may leave at any moment on business elsewhere. It is clear they make wonderful companions, especially for old people living otherwise lonely lives. Stroking them is apparently therapeutic; at least the number of visitors to the cat cafés of Japan would seem to suggest so. Nevertheless I have never desired to own one myself, both for the reasons explored in this essay and also, and I share this in the spirit of full disclosure, because I am allergic: or rather, I am allergic to the allergens produced in cats' sebaceous glands and in their saliva, deposited on the dander they detach in the grooming process that drifts, adhering to carpets and furniture or hanging suspended in the air, alerting a sensitised person to the presence of a cat as soon as they pass through a dwelling's front door.

"Are you a dog person or a cat person?", people ask, rather in the manner they enquire about your star sign: in other words, as if the answer was written in the heavens. The question suggests a divide in our affection for animals that many would find over-polarised: we may own both a dog and a cat,[1] or have no interest in owning either. However, the difference in our treatment of these animals, mainly expressed in the level of responsibility expected of those who possess them, constitutes a strange anomaly in Western culture. Dog owners are required to keep their pets under control in public and clean up after them, while the owners of cats are allowed to let them wander free, 24 hours a day, without supervision. It is rather as though those who favour cats do not believe they truly "own" them at all.

A cultural attitude is one thing: to have it enshrined in the legal system is another. In the United Kingdom for instance all dogs must be microchipped by law, their owner's details registered on a database, and they must wear a collar inscribed with their owner's name and address on it whenever they are in a public space. Those who do not clear up their dog's mess can receive on-the-spot fines of between £50 and £80 (around US$69 to 111); if they refuse to pay, they will be taken to court and fined £1,000 (US$1,392). Dogs are further restricted by Dog Control Orders that can be issued by local government bodies, banning them from certain areas or types of land, requiring them to be kept on leads, specifying the number of dogs one person is allowed to walk in specified locations and so on.

Cats on the other hand, like ramblers in Nordic countries, have a legally recognised right to roam. Although *The Code of Practice for the Welfare of Cats* published by the UK's Department for Environment, Food and Rural Affairs (DEFRA) advises that "microchipping a cat gives them the best chance of being identified and (makes them) more likely to be reunited with their owner if injured or lost",[2] the practice is entirely left to personal discretion. Cat owners, while arguably having a duty under common law to avoid their pet causing a nuisance, cannot be held legally responsible for where their cat goes, or for what it does when it is there; wandering freely, killing birds and other wildlife, entering neighbours' houses through their cat flaps and urinating and defecating on their property are all regarded as "normal" behaviour for cats under British law. When pressed to justify these contrasting scenarios, cat owners argue that, unlike uncontrolled dogs, cats never pose a threat to the personal safety of human beings. In this, I hope to demonstrate, they are very much mistaken.

Imagine the scenario: *Felis catus* (a domestic cat), fed and housed by your neighbour, makes a habit of coming over the garden wall and defecating in your

1 According to the American Pet Products Association's 2017–2018 National Pet Owners Survey, there are 94.2 million domestic cats and 89.7 million domestic dogs in the USA. *Insurance Information Institute*, https://www.iii.org/fact-statistic/facts-statistics-pet-statistics, retrieved 15 October 2018.

2 See: https://www.gov.uk/government/publications/code-of-practice-for-the-welfare-of-cats.

toddler's sandbox and in the freshly turned earth of your vegetable bed. Your own research has made you aware that contact with cat faeces puts you and your child in danger of contracting toxoplasmosis and potentially therefore of developing eye cysts that result in glaucoma and blindness; it also places your family at higher risk of various mental illnesses including depression, bipolar disorder, OCD, suicidal tendencies and schizophrenia – the *Toxoplasma* tachyzoites localise in muscle and nerve tissue, especially in the brain.[3] Finally, a widely circulated article in the *Journal of Clinical Psychology*[4] has informed you of a possible link between toxoplasmosis and intermittent explosive disorder (IED), the behaviour most typically displayed in contemporary society as "road rage". As a resident of a leafy suburb in New Jersey you are understandably disturbed to learn that 1.2 million tons of cat faeces are deposited in the environment in the United States every year. *Toxoplasma* can survive in soil and even water for periods ranging from months to years and only one, minute, two-celled organism needs to be ingested for infection to occur. Infections to pregnant women can cross the placenta, invading foetal tissue causing acute or chronic disease.[5] Humans and rodents are not the only mammals affected by the disease; deer are also susceptible, along with sheep, goats and pigs, leading to a further risk to humans consuming under-cooked meat;[6] while cat faeces flushed away into the ocean have been implicated in the steep decline in the sea otter population in California, as well as fatally infecting whales, dolphins and porpoises.[7] But toxoplasmosis is not the only unsolicited gift you may receive from your pet: cats are also the number one carrier of rabies among domestic animals in North America, presenting a "disproportionate risk of human exposure" as urban dwellers are more likely to

3 See Chapter 5, 'The Zombie Maker: Cats as an Agent of Disease' in Peter M. Marra and Chris Santella (2016) *Cat Wars: The Devastating Consequences of a Cuddly Killer,* Princeton and Oxford: Princeton University Press, pp. 75–94. See also 'Toxoplasmosis-Schizophrenia Research' at the Stanley Medical Research Institute: http://www.stanleyresearch.org/patient-and-provider-resources/toxoplasmosis-schizophrenia-research/, accessed 10 April 2018.

4 Emil F. Coccaro, MDa,*; Royce Lee, MD; Maureen W. Groer, PhD; Adem Can, PhD; Mary Coussons-Read, PhD; and Teodor T. Postolache, MD, '*Toxoplasma gondii* Infection: Relationship With Aggression in Psychiatric Subjects', *Journal of Clinical Psychology,* https://www.psychiatrist.com/jcp/article/Pages/2016/v77n03/v77n0313.aspx, accessed 26 October 2018.

5 Aguirre, A.A., Longcore, T., Barbieri, M. et al. (2019) 'The One Health Approach to Toxoplasmosis: Epidemiology, Control, and Prevention Strategies' EcoHealth 16, 378–390 https://doi.org/10.1007/s10393-019-01405-7, accessed 20 May 2019.

6 Gregory A. Ballash et al., (2014). 'Seroprevalence of Toxoplasma gondii in White-Tailed Deer (Odocoileus virginianus) and Free-Roaming Cats (Felis catus) Across a Suburban to Urban Gradient in Northeastern Ohio', *EcoHealth* 10: 1007, October 1, https://www.ncbi.nlm.nih.gov/pubmed/25269422, accessed 20 May 2020.

7 Conrad, P. A. et al., (2005) 'Transmission of Toxoplasma: Clues from the study of sea otters as sentinels of Toxoplasma gondii flow into the marine environment', *International Journal of Parasitology,* volume 35, pages 1155–1168 http://www.marinemammalcenter.org/about-us/News-Room/2017-news- archives/toxoplasmosis.html, accessed 15 May 2020.

interact with their pets than wildlife.[8] Allowed to wander freely, cats, then, pose a very real threat to the safety of your loved ones, yet you have no legal recourse through which to protect them.

The relationship between the toxoplasmosis parasite and those it infects is a fascinating one. Its aim is to colonise animals that might become the prey of cats and other feline species, making them easier to catch, thereby facilitating its return to the cat's intestine to complete the cycle of its development. One effect the parasite has on the brains of rats, for instance, is to change their response to the scent of cat urine from one of fear to one of attraction, supressing their flight response and making them more likely to stay in areas in which they can easily be caught. The same changes have been observed among man's closest relative the chimpanzee: those infected with *T. gondii* lose their aversion to the urine of their only natural predator, the leopard.[9] Scientists call this effect of parasitic presence "host behavioural manipulation". Cats meanwhile are engaged in their own manipulative behaviour, seducing their hosts into providing all their material needs while in many cases retaining a freedom of movement that is unique among domesticated animals.

A year or two ago, my wife and I were invited for dinner at the house of a writer and academic in Oxford. We sat at a long table looking out into the garden through floor-to-ceiling French windows, along with the other guests. It was summer and shadows extended slowly across the suburban lawn as evening progressed. Our hosts knew I was allergic to cats and, with the best intentions, had pushed theirs out into the garden on our arrival. At a certain point in the evening it appeared the other side of the glass, staring in at us with a brilliantly-coloured goldfinch still fluttering in its jaws, the vividness of the bird's plumage giving the scene the quality of a vision, as if the goldfinch had broken the chain that held it captive in Carel Fabritius's famous seventeenth-century painting and fluttered to earth in this garden only to be pounced on by its captor. Our hostess got up swiftly and pulled a curtain across the window. "He's naughty, he's always doing that" she said, and the conversation continued as if nothing had happened. Goldfinches, of course, are not unique in being at risk from cat predation. In over half of the sites monitored in one study in the UK, the number of dunnocks, robins and wrens killed by cats exceeded the number of juveniles fledged. Similar

8 A.D. Roebling., D. Johnson, J. D. Blanton, et al. (2013). 'Rabies prevention and management of cats in the context of Trap-Neuter-Vaccinate-Release programmes', *Zoonoses and Public Health:* HYPERLINK https://onlinelibrary.wiley.com/doi/abs/10.1111/zph.12070, accessed 15 May 2020.

9 Clémence Poirotte, Peter M. Kappeler, Barthelemy Ngoubangoye, Stéphanie Bourgeois, Maick Moussodji and Marie J. E. Charpentier, (2016) 'Morbid attraction to leopard urine in Toxoplasma-infected chimpanzees', *Current Biology 26*, R83–R101, February 8, https://www.cell.com/current-biology/fulltext/S0960-9822(15)01517-1, accessed 9 April 2019.

impacts were observed among house sparrows, blue tits, common blackbirds, great tits and starlings in other locations.[10]

The threat to the wild bird population due to industrial farming methods is well documented: a decrease in diverse habitats, the loss of hedgerows and the use of chemical sprays that impact insect and plant food sources have all contributed to their decline. To the hazards they face in flight from tall buildings, wind turbines, power lines and low-flying planes have recently been added the presence of drones, while climate change is having increasing and unpredictable effects on habitat and migration patterns. In search of a safe haven in which to feed and breed, a number of bird species have come increasingly to rely on the suburban and urban gardens which form a fragmentary but nonetheless vital nature reserve, rich in food and very often free of the noxious chemicals used on agricultural land. Concerned as we profess to be about nature, it is into these reserves we choose to release the predators we have fed, bred and nurtured in our homes.

Rather than eating the prey they have caught, cats sometimes bring it home, perhaps in an attempt to teach their human owners to hunt; scientific estimates of the deaths they cause are often based on these offerings. However, retrieved carcasses represent only a proportion of prey taken: researchers at the University of Georgia using miniature video cameras attached to the collars of free-roaming cats observed that they only brought around 25% of prey home, either eating or discarding the remainder uneaten;[11] while some hunting cats are known not to bring prey back to their owners' homes at all, the deaths resulting from their activities going unrecorded. The latest estimate in the UK is that cats kill 220 million prey items a year, 55 million of which are birds, the remaining 165 million small mammals, reptiles and amphibians; BBC journalist and naturalist Chris Packham has called these figures "conservative"[12] Figures in the US are, if anything, more

10 Philip J. Baker, Susie E. Moloney, Emma Stone, Innes C. Cuthill, Stephen Harris, *Cats about town: is predation by free-ranging pet cats Felis catus likely to affect urban bird populations?*, https://onlinelibrary.wiley.com/doi/10.1111/j.1474-919X.2008.00836.x, accessed 26 October 2018

11 "Forty-nine percent of prey items was left at the capture site, 28% was eaten and 23% was brought home to the residence. The proportions of prey brought home versus abandoned were significantly different ($\chi 2 = 4.51$, df = 1, $P = 0.03$). Individual cats manipulated different prey in more than one way, such that a cat might eat one item, and bring the next one home. The multinomial regression model is estimated to be of adequate fit ($P = 0.53$). The model suggests that prey size has a significant influence on prey fate (i.e., what the cat did with the item); as prey size increased it was more likely to be left onsite than consumed ($\beta = -1.261$, SE $\beta = 0.063$, odds ratio = 3.533, $P = 0.037$". Kerrie Anne T. Lloyd, Sonia M. Hernandez, John Carroll, Greg J. Marshall, *Quantifying free-roaming domestic cat predation using animal-borne video cameras*, http://digitalcommons.unl.edu/natrespapers/649, accessed 15 May 2020.

12 Chris Packham et al., *A People's Manifesto for Wildlife Draft 1*, http://www.chrispackham.co.uk/wp-content/uploads/A-Peoples-Manifesto-for-Wildlife.pdf, accessed 15 May 2020; and Chris Packham *Changes for Cat People?* BBC Springwatch, blogpost 19:34 UK time, Thursday, 7 June 2012, https://www.bbc.co.uk/blogs/natureuk/2012/06/changes-for-cat-people.shtml, accessed 5 November 2018.

startling. Scott Loss of Oklahoma State University, together with Pete Marra of the Smithsonian Migratory Bird Centre in Washington and Tom Will of the US Fish and Wildlife Service undertook a systematic review of data from studies of cat predation in the US, Europe and other temperate regions, including Australia and New Zealand. Their conclusion was that cats allowed to roam outdoors kill between 1.3 to 4 billion birds and 6.3 to 22.3 billion mammals in the US every year, far exceeding other causes of avian mortality.[13] This is a substantial increase on estimates scientists had made in previous studies.[14]

But does this really matter, the dispassionate may ask? Nature, Tennyson has told us, is red in tooth and claw; the behaviour of cats merely one manifestation of its bloody agenda. What we have to remember is that cats are not part of "nature" at all: they are an invasive, non-native species, only introduced to sensitive natural environments with the arrival of man. Birds, on the other hand, are more than colourful additions to the landscape: they play a vital role in the wider ecosystem, pollinating plants, spreading seeds, controlling insects, and fertilising the soil. Furthermore, the effects of cat predation are not limited to the avian kingdom. It is probable cats began their symbiotic relationship with humans when hunter-gatherers settled down and began storing grain, attracting the attentions of rodents in the vicinity. Cats may well have played a useful role in keeping down the rat population in the past, particularly perhaps on long sea voyages – a key method by which both cats and rats have spread around the globe – during which there would not be a choice of other prey. However, recent research reveals their reputation as rat-killers has been exaggerated; behavioural studies show they prefer to take smaller rodents, many of which are endangered, and shy away from confronting the large and omnipresent urban rat,[15] the numbers of which are increasing: rats in New York are now said to outnumber humans in Philadelphia.[16] In the southern hemisphere, Australian zoologist Chris Johnson has identified the predation of cats and foxes with "a succession of waves of extinction" in Australia over the past 200 years. "They continue to threaten mammals", he believes, "and might well cause more extinctions in the future".[17]

13 Rachel E. Gross, *The Moral Cost of Cats,* Smithsonian.com, 20 September 2016, https://www.smithsonianmag.com/science-nature/moral-cost-of-cats-180960505/ accessed 5 November 2019.

14 See Scott R. Loss, Tom Will and Peter P. Marra, (2014) 'The impact of free-ranging domestic cats on wildlife of the United States', *Nature Communications*, 29 January, https://www.nature.com/articles/ncomms2380, accessed 26 October 2018.

15 See *Cats are surprisingly bad at killing rats,* Smithsonian.com, https://www.smithsonianmag.com/smart-news/cats-are-surprisingly-ineffective-keeping-urban-rat-populations-check-180970428/ retrieved 08 April 2019.

16 Ben Guarino, 'As cities report more rats than ever, scientists find eastside and westside rodents', *Washington Post,* 5 June 2018.

17 Chris Johnson (2007) *Australia's Mammal Extinctions: A History,* Cambridge: Cambridge University Press, at p. 228.

Domestic cats are most active as hunters outside between dusk and dawn. Logic would suggest that their owners – their cats microchipped, and their details registered in the same way those of dogs are – could be legally required to keep their cats inside during these hours, at the risk of severe fines and the confiscation of their cats if they do not comply. Keeping cats in at night is thought to cut predation by 50%. Curfews for cats are already in place in cities around the world, particularly in Australia. Cats' success in taking prey can be further restricted by fitting them with collars with bells or incorporating a sonic device.[18] However, recent research has highlighted that the presence of cats in gardens, even during daylight hours and whether or not they are fitted with a collar, has a negative effect on birds, reducing the amount of food brought to chicks.[19] Male birds spend their time making alarm calls or feint attacks on the cat rather than gathering food, losing weight themselves; the number of chicks in a clutch is reduced over time and the alarm-calling behaviour increases the risk from hawks and other predatory birds as it pinpoints the location of hidden nests. It is therefore clear that the imposition of feline curfews will not be enough.

Two fundamental duties of government are to protect their citizens "in the enjoyment of life, liberty and property", in the words of the Pennsylvania Constitution of 1776; and to protect the territory they inhabit from invasion or degradation. In view of the danger cats pose both to human health and wildlife, a law requiring cat-owners to keep their pets inside or in secure enclosures at all times, to walk them on a leash and always clear up their mess – in other words to treat their cat more like a pet dog – appears unarguable. When observed in a feral state, cats will spend as much as 18 hours out of 24 resting or asleep when food is plentiful. Many domesticated cats already live inside around the clock with no ill effect,[20] requiring only sufficient space and adequate stimulation.

To minimise their impact, more must be done than controlling the movement of cats; feline population growth must also be addressed. Cats have evolved to be highly prolific. A female becomes sexually mature at between four and six months old and can produce as many as three litters a year, each containing two to four kittens. In the UK there are thought to be 10 million cats, one to every 6.6 human beings, while in the US there are about 86 million cats, one to every three households. Legislation should be backed up with the requirement that all

18 RSPB, *Collar that Cat to save Wildlife!* https://www.rspb.org.uk/birds-and-wildlife/advice/gardening-for-wildlife/animal-deterrents/cats-and-garden-birds/stop-cats-catching-and-killing-birds/, accessed 15 May 2020.

19 Colin Bonnington, Kevin J. Gaston and Karl L. Evans, 'Fearing the feline: domestic cats reduce avian fecundity through trait-mediated indirect effects that increase nest predation by other species', *Journal of Applied Ecology*, 30 January 2013, https://besjournals.onlinelibrary.wiley.com/doi/full/10.1111/1365-2664.12025 accessed 20 November 2018.

20 Ellen C. Jongman, 'Adaption of domestic cats to confinement', *Journal of Veterinary Behavior*, Vol. 2 Issue 6, pp. 193–196, 2007 https://www.journalvetbehavior.com/article/S1558-7878(07)00227-4/abstract, accessed 20 November 2018.

cats be microchipped and neutered;[21] by the impounding of cats found roaming outside; and by the removal of colonies of feral cats from urban and rural environments where they do much harm to wildlife, with accompanying fines for those who feed and encourage them.

Carrying through legislation will require steadfastness and political will. Any move to confine *Felis catus* to the home is bound to be met with vociferous resistance from the pro-cat lobby, despite the fact that roaming cats are at risk of being struck by cars, attacked by other predators and contracting diseases and parasites, not least *T. gondii* itself. What is required is a shift in public perception on a scale similar to the changes of attitude that have occurred around smoking in public. When smoke-free legislation was in draft in both the US and the UK it was met with huge protests from smokers and tobacco industry lobbyists, while a decade-and-a-half later the new world these laws have created is almost universally welcomed. Opponents at the time described restrictions on smoking as an infringement of liberty – despite the fact smokers were imposing their smoke, with its attendant health risks, on others without their consent. In a similar way, pet owners talk about the rights of their cats while ignoring the rights of the animals they slaughter and the humans they infect with disease. Key to the success of any legislation would be the legal requirement for all cats to be microchipped, allowing the behaviour of individual cats to be instantly and irrefutably made the responsibility of their owner.

Addiction, we know, undermines clear thinking. So, it seems, does affection for our undeniably charming feline companions. However, we should not forget that many cat owners are nature lovers, deeply concerned about the natural world.[22] Presented with the facts relating to the impact their pets have on the environment as well as the risks their pets run when allowed to wander freely, made newly aware of the dangers of ignoring zoonoses (animal-borne diseases) by the arrival of Covid-19, they will come to accept the necessity of change, just as smokers have done. Some among them, given the greater responsibilities cat ownership will entail after legislation, may decide against keeping a cat at all.

This is not the place to discuss what penalties should be brought to bear on those who continue to allow their feline charges to roam; I leave the detail of detection, legal administration and burden of proof to others. One piece of

21 As well as controlling the feline population, there is another reason to neuter cats: neutered felines roam far less far than un-neutered ones, liberated from the compulsion to seek out mates or patrol territory to defend it from rivals.

22 Indeed, this is seen by some as the reason that UK charity The Royal Society for the Protection of Birds, the largest wildlife charity in Europe with an annual income of £130m, has been so reluctant to support calls for restrictions on the free movement of cats, arguing in an online document that only weak or ill birds are taken through cat predation (an argument that is effectively contradicted elsewhere in their online content: see above). Many of their approximately one million members are cat owners. See https://www.rspb.org.uk/birds-and-wildlife/advice/gardening-for-wildlife/animal-deterrents/cats-and-garden-birds/are-cats-causing-bird-declines/ accessed 15 May 2020.

poetic justice with attendant environmental benefits does suggest itself: arriving at an airport to go on holiday or make a business trip, those whose cats have been detected roaming unsupervised outside would find themselves barred from entry. Deprived of flight themselves, they might pause to reflect on the other flights cancelled through their pets' activity.

The author acknowledges the scientific advice of Claire Nemes, research student at the University of Maryland Center of Environmental Science. You can read about her research into cat predation here: https://www.umces.edu/al/nemes

21

THE PROOF OF JUDICIAL OMNISCIENCE ACT (UK)

*David Campbell**

Explanatory note

Constitutional reform under the governments of Mr Tony Blair placed Parliamentary responsibility for the administration of the legal system under a newly created Ministry of Justice. Primary legislation regarding the courts now has to be introduced into Parliament by this ministry. In response to a perceived gap in the constitutional framework left even after reform as extensive as Mr Blair's, the Ministry engaged the charity *No Wrong Answer Ltd* to carry out a preliminary investigation into the feasibility of a Proof of Judicial Omniscience Act. *No Wrong Answer* is an independent, non-governmental organisation concerned with the promotion of human rights which has its main offices in Bloomsbury, London and lower Fifth Avenue, Manhattan. It is in constant contact with the Ministry of Justice – most senior staff have worked for both organisations – and in receipt of large government funding. A draft of the executive summary of *No Wrong Answer's* report to the Ministry unfortunately was left in The Ivy restaurant after a lunch given by the Ministry at which the draft was discussed with senior figures in the charity, the legal profession, legal academia and in the media. His sense of discretion having perhaps been weakened by the Ministry's hospitality and so unable to resist professional temptation, one of the media figures has leaked the draft to his newspaper's webpage.

* This chapter was drafted whilst I held a Visiting Professorship in the Auckland University of Technology (AUT) Law School, New Zealand and I should like to thank AUT for its hospitality. I should also like to thank the editors for their suggestions, in particular Peter Goodrich's naming of the ducking apparatus.

Executive summary: Proposal for a Proof of Judicial Omniscience Act

No one familiar with the modern history of the appellate courts of the UK will be in any doubt that, though suffering from a reputation for employing what Llewellyn called the "formal style" of adjudication, those courts have throughout that history showed themselves wholly capable of departing from that style. Two of the clearest precepts of the formal style were that "policy is for the legislature, not for the courts, and so is change, even in pure common law".[1] And yet even the relatively mundane sphere of private law has seen remarkable departures from these precepts. The most remarkable came, of course, in 1932 in *Donoghue v Stevenson*,[2] when an all but unreported judgment in the Scottish court of first instance[3] seems to have prefigured the statement, by a majority of the House of Lords, of what we now have as the general principle of negligence. And in 1963 in *Hedley Byrne & Co., Ltd v Heller & Partners Ltd*,[4] the House of Lords did what it had been encouraged to do in the unreported first instance judgment and found that negligence liability could extend to misstatement.[5] The facts in *Donoghue v Stevenson* were never proved; the facts in *Hedley Byrne v Heller* disclosed neither negligence nor misstatement; the Appellate Committees of the House of Lords hearing both these cases were fully conscious that they were stating a new principle, and this principle has profoundly affected the lives of millions in a way that only very little primary legislation could ever possibly do.

After the UK Government, about to embark on the most extensive social security programme the world had ever seen, mercifully failed to summon the necessary resolution to abolish the private action for personal injury,[6] it has proven entirely possible for *Donoghue v Stevenson* to undermine the universal welfare state. The unfortunate socialist aspiration to provide mutual aid against want,[7] which would have acknowledged that accidents are a question of common hardship, has been countered by preservation of a proper regard for self-interest regardless of social cost expressed in the individual right to the private action,

1 K. N. Llewellyn (1960) *The Common Law Tradition*, Boston MA, Little Brown, at p. 38.

2 [1932] AC 562 (HL).

3 The perfunctory and very limitedly available "report" of the judgment of Lord Moncrieff is at 1932 SN 117 (OH).

4 [1964] AC 465 (HL).

5 It has always been possible to discern the thrust of the judgment of McNair J in the Commercial Court from reference to it in the reported appellate judgments, but that judgment has recently been made publicly available: see Barker, K. et al. (eds) (2015) *The Law of Misstatements*, Oxford, Hart, at p. 345.

6 *Final Report of the Departmental Committee on Alternative Remedies* (Chairman: Sir Walter Monckton) Cmd 6860 (1946) para. 25. It is deplorable to have to report that the decision to retain the damages system divided the Committee and was taken despite the Committee as a whole finding that: "substantial advantages would be gained were it found possible to abolish the remedy by action and to substitute for it rights to benefits under national insurance".

7 Lord Beveridge (1948) *Voluntary Action*, London, George Allen and Unwin, at pp. 8–9.

and even to expand self-interested litigation into a widespread compensation culture. Courts believing they have the competence to bring about change which had the potential to yield consequences of this magnitude have, undeniably then, long found the power of the widest-ranging judicial legislation within themselves, and have had little difficulty with the implicit claim that, when legislating, they knew the right policy to adopt.

Since the passage of the Human Rights Act 1998, the demand for judicial omniscience has, however, grown astronomically. The UK was one of the original signatories to the European Convention on Human Rights, and in that sense the European Court of Human Rights has been legally sovereign in the UK over matters within its competence since 1953 when the Convention entered into force. Though appeal to the Court of Human Rights when recourse to the UK's domestic courts has been exhausted remains extremely important, the 1998 Act sought to incorporate the Convention rights into UK domestic law and thereby make legal action in reliance on them a far more practical possibility. Nevertheless, the 1998 Act regrettably could be passed only on the basis that Parliament would remain the legal sovereign of the UK, and this is principally reflected in the way that, under s. 4 of the 1998 Act, the UK Supreme Court[8] has no formal power to strike down primary legislation. The UK Supreme Court may only declare primary legislation incompatible with the 1998 Act, and in itself this has no effect on the legal status of the legislation.

But (leaving aside the same point as it had long been made since the convention itself was debated) it was obvious even during the passage of the 1998 Act that the compromise between sovereignty of Parliament and the supremacy of the courts over matters which could be regarded as falling under the convention rights was completely unstable. We may be grateful that it has been resolved very thoroughly indeed in favour of the courts. Not only has government never sought to enforce legislation declared to be incompatible, but a strike-down power is now in the process of being developed,[9] and though it is still vestigial by comparison to the power under the US Constitution, the direction of travel is clear.[10] This, however, is almost by the by,[11] because s. 3 of the 1998 Act requires that, "So far as it is possible to do so [...] legislation must be read and given effect in a way which is compatible with the Convention rights", and it has so far proven "possible to do so" to the extent that all the UK's courts, even those

8 The various senior courts of the UK may make declarations of incompatibility: Human Rights Act 1998 s. 4(5). But it is not misleading to generally speak of the UK Supreme Court exercising this power as appeal by the Government to this court against a finding of incompatibility is all but inevitable.

9 *R (Miller) v Secretary of State for Exiting the European Union* [2017] UKSC 5; [2017] 2 WLR 583.

10 Campbell, David and Young, James (2002) "The Metric Martyrs and the Entrenchment Jurisprudence of Lord Justice Laws" *Public Law* 399 and Campbell, D. (2018) "*Marbury v Madison* in the UK: Brexit and the Creation of Judicial Supremacy" 39 *Cardozo Law Review* 921.

11 Heydon, John Dyson (2014) "Are Bills of Rights Necessary in Common Law Systems?" 130 *Law Quarterly Review* 392.

which are at the foot of the hierarchy of courts and tribunals,[12] have enthusiastically used this power to "remould" legislation in a way which has conveyed greater power to counter the intention of the legislature than is possible under the US Constitution.[13]

These great achievements make it clear that in the era of the Human Rights Act the claim to omniscience made only intermittently and implicitly by the senior judiciary that handed down the likes of *Donoghue v Stevenson* and *Hedley Byrne v Heller* has to be regularised and made explicit. When policy decisions of great complexity and importance become the normal business of the senior courts, it is essential that those courts be staffed by a judiciary capable of executing that business, and the quality that is necessary is a routine omniscience. UK citizens used to seeing such decisions as political matters falling under the sovereignty of parliament have long been prepared to accept that limited competence will always be part of political decision-making. This deplorable acceptance of imperfection probably should be traced to that lamentably pragmatic strain in British moral philosophy which led Adam Smith, for example, a representative of the Scottish so-called Enlightenment, to allow that there may be ends which are indisputably right, but that "it has not been intrusted to the slow and uncertain determinations of [human] reason to find out the proper means of bringing them about".[14] Nothing could show the necessity of transferring truly important decisions to courts which of course enjoy the force of law in the sense that the judgments must be and will be right. And so we cannot now shirk from declaring what is necessary in clear terms. The logic and legitimacy of replacing political decision-making by legal decision-making in areas of fundamental policy requires proof of judicial omniscience. This proposed Act will provide a mechanism – the dipshit – for those elevated to senior judicial office to give this proof, both to those appointing them and, thereby, to the citizens of the UK, who we can only hope will rise above their normally deplorable views and grasp what is being done for them.

The obvious, indeed logically entailed, means of establishing omniscience is, of course, simply to ask those who are to exercise their omniscience when sitting to self-identify as omniscient when making their application for senior judicial office. But any hope that what reason shows to be obvious and logically entailed would therefore readily be adopted was, of course, forlorn in a legal system which has never fully recognised the implications of *iura novit curia*. It was only to be anticipated that the difficulties raised by citizens still romantically attached to obsolete nostrums such as *nemo judex in sua causa* unfortunately

12 Campbell, David (2015) "'Catgate' and the Challenge to Parliamentary Sovereignty in Immigration Law" *Public Law* 426 and Campbell, David. (2018) "Decency, Disobedience and Democracy in Immigration Law" [2018] *Public Law* 413.

13 Campbell, David and Allan, James (2019) "Procedural Innovation and the Surreptitious Creation of Judicial Supremacy in the United Kingdom" 46 *Journal of Law and Society* 347.

14 Smith, Adam (1759) *The Theory of Moral Sentiments*, Oxford, Clarendon Press, at p. 77.

would, as a practical matter, have to be given some weight. One remembers that as recently as 1998 the House of Lords encountered great difficulty just because it allowed the chairman of the charitable arm of a socially valuable organisation which was an intervener in an extremely politically contentious case to sit as a Lord of Appeal in that case. The Lord's judgment had to be overturned![15]

This sort of thing thankfully now seems to come from a very distant age. More recently the then Deputy President of the UK Supreme Court, Lady Hale, saw fit to convey a very clear indication of how she was minded to decide *Miller*, the most important constitutional case since the Second World War, in a public lecture given shortly before the appeal reached her court. What could be clearer indication of the improved atmosphere in which the courts now hand down their decisions than that she saw no reason to recuse herself from later hearing that case. No question of her recusal obliging her to give up any ambition she may have held to become the court's president could then arise, and she did, of course, go on to assume that office,[16] from which she has only recently retired, and during her tenure of which she thankfully was able to impress such masterpieces as the judgement concerning Northern Irish abortion law shortly to be discussed. Despite this, it is to be feared that romantic public attachment to the natural law of correct procedure, even when it would inconvenience having the right persons in the right place to do the right thing, is still not an entirely irrelevant consideration.

But the problem that has actually caused most difficulty during trialling of self-identification of judicial omniscience was not anticipated. There proved to be a most unfortunate excess supply of candidates. It turned out that all, save some antediluvians whose main interest had been in commercial law, were highly likely to self-identify as omniscient. In fact, every candidate who had had a practice focused on domestic or international human rights law, and (an overlapping but far larger category) every candidate who had taken an optional course in domestic or international human rights law during university studies, self-identified as omniscient. As we remain far from the ideal state in which all the most important policy questions are immediately referred to rights determination, there simply is not enough judicial work for all those self-identifying as omniscient. A filter unfortunately is required.

Although, as has been discussed, the UK has actually surpassed the US in granting to its courts power over the electorate as represented by its legislature, it can hardly be denied that a principal driver of the developments in the UK since the passage of The Human Rights Act has been an attempt to emulate what has been accomplished in the US. Reflection on this led one to think of drawing on US wisdom for possible guidance over proof of judicial omniscience. And, coincidentally, this impulse has recently been given great force by the UK having

15 *R v Bow Street Metropolitan Stipendiary Magistrate and Others* [2000] 1 AC 119 (HL).
16 Campbell, n. 10 above, at pp. 934–45.

had its own *Roe v Wade*.[17] At the volition of the people of Northern Ireland under a devolved system of government, the legislation under which an abortion may legally be obtained in the province has been much more restrictive than the comparable legislation in the rest of the UK. On grounds which need not be discussed here, the UK Supreme Court had to find, obviously most reluctantly, that it could not properly hear a challenge to the Northern Irish legislation under The Human Rights Act.[18] Nevertheless, a majority of the Court, including Lady Hale, who had then become its President, very correctly said in their judgments, though the Court had just concluded that they had no power to say this, that the Northern Irish legislation was indeed incompatible with the Human Rights Act. Their brave defiance of the stuffy rules defining their competence in the case[19] undoubtedly was of major assistance to the UK political campaign to change the Northern Irish law, and to the joy of all who have viewed the matter in the correct way, the necessary legislation has been passed.

What, then, is the guidance about a satisfactory method for proving judicial omniscience that US history may disclose? That history is, in fact, very rich, and, though it reaches back to early European settlement in North America, important developments are of a very recent vintage. When suspicious of a maleficent, indeed diabolical, presence in their community, North American settlers of the late seventeenth and early eighteenth centuries would test whether Satan had indeed taken possession of the suspected person, usually an elderly woman, by a number of means, the one of interest to us being ducking. Ducking itself was subject to many variations, but in the "pure" method the suspected person was tethered to a "stool", the nature of which is better conveyed by describing it as a chair, which was fixed to one end of a beam centred on a pivot, the other end of the beam being held by a number of strong men. The stool was suspended over a pond of water into which the men could lower it, to the point where the suspect was completely submerged. If the suspect survived a submersion which would have drowned a person not given supernatural endurance, then, of course, this was proof of diabolical possession, and the suspect would be taken from the ducking stool and disposed of in other ways.

There are very few recorded cases, and they themselves are disputed, of such ancillary disposal being required, and a measure of dissatisfaction with complete maintenance of the belief that only the guilty were ever placed on the stool led to a certain relaxation of the pure method. Under the "moderate" method, the period of submersion was shortened to the point where a person of robust constitution (not, say, the constitution of an elderly woman) would survive even if not supernaturally protected. But this moderate submersion was repeated, and a

17 410 US 113 (1973).

18 *Re Northern Ireland Human Rights Commission's Application for Judicial Review* [2018] UKSC 27; [2018] HRLR 14.

19 Campbell and Allan, n. 13 above, pp. 359–64.

person could bring the repetition to an end only by confessing whilst out of the water. Though the 100% rate of success in identifying the possessed by use of the pure method could not, of course, be achieved by the moderate method, the number of confessions was sufficiently high that this method was all but universally found to be satisfactory.

Recent developments in US judicial appointments procedure (and there are parallels to the treatment of candidates to and holders of other high office) happily show how ducking may now be put to the purpose of proving judicial omniscience. Those seeking senior judicial appointment in the UK will be subject to ducking, but the process will feature a number of modern improvements: and so will be called the "improved" method. Ducking apparatuses – dipshits – will be built in a factory, of better materials, and will be operated by an electric motor. Recalling the basic problem of the number of applicants which made necessary a method of proving omniscience, it is greatly to be welcomed that the relative cheapness of the factory production of the apparatuses will allow the great benefit of large volume ducking. And so it will be possible, on any practical assumption of the numbers involved, that all candidates for a particular appointment can and will be ducked simultaneously. The successful candidate will be the one who has lasted through the largest number of submersions, those submersions being, of course, of moderate duration, for proof of omniscience using the pure method would yield very few or no successful candidates actually capable of discharging their office. It will not even matter if there are so many candidates that all the necessary duckings cannot be carried out in one location. Modern forms of communication will readily allow all the duckings to be, in various ways, the subject of simultaneous, "real-time", national spectacle.

The most important improvement, however, has been in the choice of ducking medium. The higher general level of health since the early days of ducking (and the different demographic profile of the candidates) might be feared to lead to undue prolongation of each appointment process. Ducking now, however, will not now be into mere water but into pools of human excrement. An aversion to ducking in this medium even greater than the aversion to being ducked in water might well be expected to shorten the duration of the appointment process. Furthermore, such aversion might also be expected to shorten the process indirectly by placing some limit on the number of candidates prepared to go through that process. Early trials have, in fact, exceeded expectations. Successful candidates have invariably been found to have been possessed of a Herculean self-confidence – those mired in obsolete understandings predictably have called it megalomania – that distinguishes them from the merely grossly self-satisfied candidates who failed. It was just this Herculean quality that allowed the successful candidates to prevail, and it is this quality that is, of course, highly desirable in those called on, not merely actually to be omniscient, but to have the confidence to exercise their omniscience so as to bring desirable changes to the lives of the great numbers subject to the jurisdiction of their courts.

It is perhaps particularly to be welcomed that potential candidates who, though believing in their omniscience, have such nice sensibilities that they are unprepared to have their family, friends and acquaintance watch them undergo the process, weed themselves out at an early stage. It is true that there have been unfortunate incidents when, whilst attending the process, family members in particular have themselves been, not of course ducked, but incidentally spattered with the excrement. No process, unfortunately, can be expected to work entirely without mishap. It is welcome that candidates insufficiently self-confident to be prepared to accept this on their family's behalf should withdraw their candidacy.

Of the two principal concerns raised whilst the proof procedure was being initially devised, one has proven to have no weight whatsoever and the other has not yet appeared to be a great difficulty, but it must in fairness be said that some time will have to elapse before a final judgment may be reached. Though, as has been mentioned, ducking apparatuses can easily be provided, it was initially a concern, given the basic problem of the number of candidates, whether a sufficient supply of excrement could be obtained to test them all. This has proven to be no difficulty. It has not even normally been necessary to draw on the public finances to provide the supply. Once a person's candidacy has been announced, a large number of private parties have, sometimes by funding organised political groups, been very anxious to furnish excrement, and modern media of communication have again proven very advantageous in that they have allowed the dissemination of a vast superabundance of material. One can have every confidence that some party or group will always be able to find and provide more than sufficient excrement to submerge any candidate who comes forward.

The second concern has not been so happily allayed. It is alleged that, even after the successful candidate has been raised from the pool and exhaustive efforts made to clean her or his person, a certain taint of the excrement continues to cling to her or him for some time, perhaps throughout the entire period of their occupation of judicial office, perhaps for life. The only relevant consideration here must be whether this affects the performance of their judicial duties. And one is happily able to report that, by a most fortunate circularity of cause and effect, routinely giving the force of law to the decision of issues which formerly were regarded as political is giving the entire legal system an atmosphere of excrement, into which the personal taint of the successful appointees to judicial office will, it is predicted, become entirely subsumed.

The introduction of a Proof of Judicial Omniscience Bill giving effect to the improved ducking method is recommended to the Ministry of Justice.

Thomas Kavanaugh, for No Wrong Answer Ltd (a charity)
pursuant to UK Ministry of Justice grant number 666

22

THE RULE BOOK OF A DREAMER

Niall Brooks

There is one predicament we all know so well; it isn't worth thinking about. Breathing is in a league of its own. I'll deal with breathing first, then I'll mention the dark politics of my age. I'll finish with a proposal for constitutional reform called *The Rule Book of a Dreamer.*

Breathing is disruption that begins at birth. It is the foremost experience of suffocation. This seminal gasp for life never really goes away. Until it does. The longer I continue to breathe the more likely it is that I will suddenly be reminded of my abject reliance on the function.

I first stopped breathing unexpectedly on a beach. I recall being barefoot on a stretch of hot sand, aged no more than six. A few mild breakers lurched up the shelf that mounted the beach I was on. Each one collapsed with a pleasing thud. There was a boiling sun, and the spray cooled my body. Aware that my mother was sitting nearby, I must have thought it was safe enough to venture just a few more steps into that soft froth the waves were giving up.

My wonder was almost crushed. As I stepped closer to the ocean it yawned skywards. I was sucked under and rolled out to sea. I swallowed the contents of a saltshaker, and my sense of up and down was replaced by my first memory of terror. Almost as abruptly as this watery abduction began, I was hauled from the shallows, yanked upwards by my spindly arms. I recall gobbling for breath and trying to wail bitterly. I remember the laughter of the stranger who had rescued me. He stood me upright on the sand, a juddering wreck for my mother to sweep away and console.

I consider the consolation I received to be the best reaction to life's disappointments. Today, it isn't the prospect of death, but the darkly political pursuits of my age that combine to crush my spirit. I feel horrified. When I look down from this height, I don't see what's below. I only see the fall.

The way consolation works is simple. It rewards and nurtures wonder. In the face of such a fragile moment in history, there are some consolations that can still have a calming effect. *The Rule Book of a Dreamer* is no more challenging than the soothing words of a mother to her child. I propose it as the preamble to any good constitution:

1. Everything imaginable is possible,
   but it can never be known unless it's imagined
2. What is possible is anything capable of coming into existence,
   though not necessarily by reference to a single lifetime
3. To imagine is to merge what is known with the unknown
4. The unknown has forever been ready to be thought of
5. Even what is not imaginable is possible

23

THE DISMANTLER

Karsten Schubert

The carpet in the office has a surprisingly symmetrical pattern, made entirely from old coffee stains. The desks are antiquated, too, but not dirty. Our secretary tried his best to make the offices look nice with plants and some random posters of old book launches and events, mostly from local anti-racism and queer organisations. This is our interim office, and I am not sure if, after the recent political scandals, we will ever move into more permanent facilities. I work for the Office of the Federal Commissioner for the Dismantling of Normalising Power and Structures of Privilege that was created through the *General Act for the Dismantling of Normalising Power and Structures of Privilege* five years ago. My boss, the Commissioner Robert Richardson, was just forced to resign. Now we have someone new, from the conservative party, and she has never hidden her hate for the Office and her plans to dismantle it, instead of dismantling privilege. And to be honest, I am not sure anymore, maybe that would not be too bad after all. I mean, of course I support our cause to fight for equality and against "normalising power" and "structures of privilege", but maybe it is just not possible to institutionalise it – or at least not in the way it was done.

When the Parliament decided on the *General Act for the Dismantling of Normalising Power and Structures of Privilege*, it was a huge surprise that they voted in favour of this law, which was mainly an idea of the left and Green Party opposition. But after a huge wave of new social criticism of social media that spilled over to the established media, and hardly any opposition from the right wing and conservative parties, the government felt pressured to endorse it. They said that it would help to foster a new dialogue on social justice and – eventually – also help to realise it. And when they created the new office in a breathtakingly fast process of only one year, I thought it might be a nice opportunity to get out of my old job as chief of accounting in the Federal Railway Administration that had bored me to hell. I thought it would be great to actually contribute to social progress, and not only to manage "irrational technical rationality". That is also why I encounter a weird bureaucratic irrationality now, I always want to research where the concept actually came from, but then I never do it. Anyway, I am quite happy that I am only responsible for the accounting, and not involved in the policy-making processes here, like Frieda. These were way less stressful in the rail sector, even though the environmental activists used to give us a hard time. But that was nothing compared to the political trench warfare that came along with the "Dismantler", as everybody quickly started to call the *General Act for the Dismantling of Normalising Power and Structures of Privilege.*

The "Dismantler" is a pretty complicated law, so let me try to explain its rationale. It is directed against what leftists call the "liberal consensus", that is, the belief that our democratic institutions and the rule of law overall work fine and are the rational outcome of the deliberation process of free people. It reminds me of this social contract thinking we discussed in high school: if there were no state, people would still build one, one pretty much exactly like ours, out of free choice, because it is the rational thing to do out of their own self-interest. And now the leftists say that this is an ideology – which, they say, is obvious already in the fact that such an idea is taught in our schools, in order to make the current regime *seem* legitimate. What is actually structuring our institutions and law, according to them, is exploitation, repression and systems of privilege, upheld by an array of social norms, that even pervade sciences and the structures of knowledge. And this is where the "Dismantler" comes in: it is aimed at making these norms and privileges visible, at getting them out of the ideological blur of liberalism, at shedding light on them and thereby helping to rebuild the system in a more just and equal way. I wanted to join the Office, because I was fascinated by this approach to institutionalising such processes of critique *within* the law. Because, if you look at it, it is squaring the circle: how can you use the very legal and administrative structures that are the root of the problem to solve the problem? Before I started working here, I talked about this puzzle at a dinner with friends, who are mostly academics, one just commented laconically "Well, it's dialectical". Everyone nodded. I did not dare to ask what he meant and it was only later that I realised that most people refer to something as "dialectical" to hide that they don't have a clue about it. Be that as it may, I can tell you that the "Dismantler" is doing two things mainly.

On the one hand, it establishes a principle within the law to control any law or jurisdiction for normalising power and privilege. This forces judges to consider these issues in their jurisdiction. And on the other hand, it installed the new Commissioner and our Office to supervise legal processes and to campaign for such issues. Our Office is necessary because effectively the "Dismantler" cannot really "force" the judges to follow the principle to control for normalising power and privilege since the whole construction allows for a huge margin of appreciation in counterbalancing proportionality and privilege control. Our job is to advocate for the "Dismantler" and to encourage judges to take privilege into account; and also to sanction a judge if they disregard the "Dismantler", although it has to be noted that most cases are too complex to hold judges accountable in that way.

Robert Richardson was the first Commissioner for Dismantling Normalising Power and Structural Privilege. Regarding his experience, he was a perfect choice. He was not a member of any political party but had worked in social justice organisations for 20 years. After he received a PhD. in critical social theory, he had consulted the government in mainstreaming intersectionality for a couple of years before he was appointed as Commissioner. His positionality was a bit more contested and did not fit well with the position, as he is a white middle-aged cishet man. You can imagine the criticism. Nevertheless, I originally thought that he was a smart choice because in appointing him the government was able to appease the conservatives who criticise "positional fundamentalism", showing them that when in conflict, content and competence matters more than social position. It turned out I was wrong, because in the end, he was not competent at all, or somehow "lost" his competence.

After the initial wave of media attention and heated debate over the Office and Richardson's appointment, things calmed down, and the first cases of problematic jurisdiction we – that is, my colleagues from the legal department – objected to went largely unnoticed in public discourse. Then, one judge, a certain Marcelo Escoto, who is also an outspoken conservative, managed to initiate a scandal and to mobilise a huge wave of right-wing protests against us, after we forced a revision of his sentence. The case was about Patricia Marble, a 28-year-old tech person working in a start-up, a typically privileged expat – and a black *Black Lives Matter* activist. She was under surveillance by the police as they (wrongly) suspected her of dealing. While they found some drugs, it was just a bit of cocaine and not the weed they suspected her to deal with. In the process she was charged with the possession of illegal substances and was sentenced to pay an unusually high penalty. The penalty was that high because Marble defended herself by accusing the police of having racially profiled her, which Judge Escoto interpreted as lack of remorse and general disrespect of the legal institutions, thus justifying the higher penalty. Of course, this jurisdiction was not only ignoring the principle to control for normalising power and privilege, but also actively reinforcing racial privilege by punishing the critique of racism.

When we ordered the revision, Judge Escoto went public, and virally so. He accused our Office of ideological and violent political correctness, which is inhibiting open debate in general and effective police work in particular. The police unions joined in, affirming that police suspicion is never based on race, but on reasonable hermeneutics that are the result of policing experience. Soon after, a shattered alliance from the right and conservative spectrum mobilised seemingly out of nowhere, claiming that nowadays every white person was automatically charged with racism.

For some time, the leading narrative in this scene, especially on *YouTube* and *Twitter*, was that the mainstream media were infiltrated by a network of anti-racist liberals and "gender ideology" feminists, all orchestrated by Mossad, to split up the Western (or White – it was never clear for which of these *#WEC* stands) Enlightenment Consensus. Once, in a coffee shop, I got into a discussion, or argument, with a guy who believes this. It was just impossible to communicate, because he just produced one unfalsifiable statement after another, and to my demands for proof, or coherence, he just replied with more of such statements. The centre of this ideology was a grumbling suspicion that the mainstream media, the politicians, and the academic experts lie and that they only prouce "narratives". They switch deliberately between this total scepticism without claiming that they know what is really going on and advancing a clear and specific "alternative truth" regarding particular questions. Regarding the attacks on the Commissioner, the latter was the case, with the conspiracy spectrum allied in the conviction that the "Dismantler" is Mossad's project to dismantle "Western/White Enlightenment".

Of course, nobody in the established institutions actively pushed such conspiracy theories, but it nevertheless put us in the spotlight. We – that is, the colleagues from PR – still managed pretty efficiently to position the Office well in the debate, especially with the help of our new social media manager, Joan, whom I brought into the Office and who is a master in their field. Joan is a former classmate of mine and was fed up with their PR work for a huge car manufacturer and wanted "to do something good" in their life and "give back a little"; and Joan emphasised their sincerity about that by stressing how enormous the pay gap between their old and new job was. I felt an unspecific antipathy towards Joan because of this. When I think about it now, it must have been because our reasons for changing jobs were so similar, and their juvenile and shallow discourse about it made me confront the actual shallowness of my own justifications. It was good that I never showed this antipathy: Joan is not only good in their PR work, they are also a perfect communicator and socialiser. Joan made more friends throughout the Office in one month, than I managed in the whole year I worked here before their arrival. I would have hated them for this, normally, alas they introduced me to everyone, and most importantly Frieda. Before Joan, I had lunch alone, or with my colleagues from accounting. The others did not see us as part of the political project of the "Dismantler", but just as accountants – random people essentially. And to be honest, that was fair. My other colleagues from accounting did not even switch to the Office out of political interest, as I did, and quite often they gossiped about the politics that the Office was pushing, and which they did not understand, but in any case rejected. With Joan's help, I was suddenly well connected to colleagues from nearly all departments, and especially the fancy ones; and, crucially, I had lunch with them – no more isolated accountancy lunches for me. Apart from Frieda, it is these people, and the talks they have over lunch, that are the source of my moderate insight into the political dramas taking place in our organisation.

Such dramas, particularly the trouble Richardson created soon after, even Helge with his magical skills could not help. The case against Marble was revised as we ordered, but then, to our extreme surprise, the revision exactly confirmed Judge Escoto's sentence. This was very surprising, because the "Dismantler" demands that revisions on its grounds are not decided by a judge, but by a standing jury that consists of judges selected by the most important minority organisations, and *Black Lives Matter* was very influential in this appointment process. One of the initial tasks of the Office was to set up this jury and to organise the selection processes. I can tell you: it was hard. You cannot imagine the fights among the minority group organisations over the influence that my colleagues from the jury department told me about. Many minority groups claimed that due to the systematicity of their oppression and its structural involvement with liberal capitalism, they deserve the largest say in the process. Others argued that you cannot counterbalance suffering and that you need equal representation. Often it was not clear at all who could legitimately speak for whom. For example, there were four Muslim organisations, with different agendas, and the three feminist ones were not able to agree on anything at all after the fights over trans politics back in the 2010s and 2020s. For me, this looked all weird, and I was just annoyed over how unproductive the debates were, how mean and violent the discourse was, and how little real solidarity there was. Why can't they just cooperate? I mean, there are blatantly evident common enemies, yet nobody could act in unity. Sometimes I thought about changing positions again, and returning to accounting for the Federal Railway Administration, but my old job was now taken and there was no other leading accounting positions open in the whole federal administration. I could have only changed position by accepting a huge loss in pay and retirement privileges, and if I learned one thing here, it is that privileges are important, and I really did not want to lose them.

So why did the standing jury, appointed by the minority organisations, confirm Judge Escoto's sentence? The reason lies in the fact that the jury members, despite their appointment by the minority organisations, still need to be professional judges. And that means they are mostly white and bourgeois, and most importantly, socialised in the liberal legal culture that is the root of the problem. At least this is the official rationale of the Office. I was always a bit sceptical of this explanation, it sounded too simple and schematic. It sounded like the "positional foundationalism", that identity politics were always charged with, and the conservatives always accused the "Dismantler" and the Office of the Commissioner of such positional foundationalism. What they mean by "positional foundationalism" is the idea that social position and political views are necessarily connected, and that even some positions necessarily lead to certain views. It is a crude version of the classic feminist standpoint theory, and the complex analysis of the entanglement of knowledge and power that was developed by critical theorists and French theorists in the second half of the 20th century. However, nobody professional holds such a simple position – it is more of a straw man made up by the conservatives. But still, there seems to be something like a real tendency in such critical theories to fall back into a crude, or "vulgar" thinking, as the few remaining Marxists in these debates like to say.

The complicated thing is how to operationalise these overall very reasonable and realist social theories, without falling into this kind of foundationalism. And

I think the Parliament did a good job with the construction of the jury: to let the minority organisations select the jury members is to acknowledge that social position matters, yet to require everyone to be an actual judge takes into account that you cannot reduce qualification to social position, but instead that expertise matters.

Well, the Commissioner did not see it that way. In the weekly heads of department meetings, he got angrier and angrier over the questionable decision of the jury. He said that the "Dismantler" in the current state does not dismantle anything, and effectively works as a cover-up for the ongoing wrongs done by the system by adding to its legitimacy. If criticising the system "from within" works at all, he said, it would be only through installing really subversive institutions, that is, something completely different from the jury that is already "corrupted in the totality of its thinking by bourgeois legal rationality". One curious thing is that in his rage, he referred more and more to radical political and legal theorists, especially from the old U.S. critical legal studies movement, that pushed the critique of liberal law as a totality being corrupted by capitalism, and sometimes he even, shouting, cited Marx. It was a bit caricaturesque and reminded me of this Netflix show about the 1968 student protests that was very popular at the time. First, the other department heads, especially Frieda and the head of and General Legal Questions, challenged Richardson, but he shut them down, saying we would have to keep our lines closed in these times of crisis, and that the Office needs to be aligned in the position to reform the "Dismantler" to the effect that the professionalism requirement of the jury is lifted. I did not participate in these debates, of course. After all, I am only an accountant.

Richardson now concentrated on political lobbying for this reform and realigned our resources to this end. We started a political campaign exposing and attacking the legal system as a whole with slogans like "Racism – The Core of Legality", "Dismantle Professional Judges", or "No Community Justice, No Peace". From there it went downhill really quickly. There was no chance any of the parties, not even the left party, could still support Richardson after that, and the government made him resign only a week after we started the campaign. The new Commissioner is Frederica Kemp, really conservative. As I said, she was always fundamentally opposed to the "Dismantler", and we fear that she is trying to dissolve the Office from within, but so far, the regular work is continuing, though without any executive decisions. Everything feels very much up in the air and no one of my colleagues knows what will happen. What is clear is that nobody wants to work for a ghost institution and against the leadership. We cannot quite imagine how to run the Office without the full political commitment of the Commissioner.

Of course, among us colleagues, we talk a lot about what happened. Two weeks ago, I met with some of them, whom I would by now even call friends, in a bar and we discussed why Richardson failed. Obviously, it was because of his overreaction and quite simply his bad political judgement. He just seemed to have abandoned all realist political struggle, understood as the messy process of working on compromises and improvised solutions that makes it necessary to cooperate even with people who are political enemies. He was not able anymore to give in and accept anything other than his ideal vision of dropping the professional requirement for the jury judges – it was all or nothing. But especially Frieda thought there was more to it, something more structural.

Frieda claimed that it was the corpus of social theory on which the "Dismantler" was based that had opened up the "conditions of possibility" (she was a philosopher by training) for Richardson's failure. The problem is that this theory operates, in one form or another, with a "hermeneutics of suspicion". This means that it is sceptical of the surface and the hegemonic narratives with which we explain the world, and looks deeper, for hidden mechanisms and forces. The two main concepts the "Dismantler" uses, "normalising power" and "structures of privilege", are exactly such forms of a hermeneutics of suspicion. The problem is, now, that once the decision is made as to the fact that the surface level cannot be trusted and that there is some kind of deeper stratum, it is not clear where exactly this scepticism ends. I was reminded of my discussion with the right-wing conspiracy theorist: even though fundamentally different, he also had something like a "hermeneutics of suspicion" with an "alternative truth", as they call it. The difference was mainly that the conspiracy theory was way more random in its scepticism and more fixed in the particular truth it came up with, the Mossad explanation, bending everything according to this story, leaving no room for falsification. Frieda explained that the social theories the "Dismantler" uses are not that random, of course, but the result of an intersubjective, academic and political discourse that is producing plausible insights about the social situation and not just conspiracies. But still, we all also know that these theories are complex, often contradictory and far from being consensually agreed upon. And being interpretations of the social and political world, they cannot be falsified or verified in the "correspondence" way, but are only more or less plausible. And what is plausible for someone is heavily dependent on their overall theoretical and political worldview. According to Frieda, the problem was that Richardson somehow shifted an intersubjective and pluralist hermeneutics of suspicion to a version that was more like the conspiracy theory, with a unified and somewhat absolute idea about what is the cause for the problems: for Richardson the "ideological liberal law" and its judges.

I liked that explanation, especially because it allowed me to stick to the core ideas of the "Dismantler". The overall idea is good, but Richardson just took a bad path. Yet, the more I thought about it, the more I became sceptical (I guess my job here had an impact on me, after all). You see, Richardson's explanation was not that far-fetched, and also because it seems a cheap way out to just solve this problem of the "conspiracy fallacy", as Frieda put it, by just referring to intersubjectivity. After all, that is also what the conservatives say all the time: intersubjectivity, reason, universality. I recently read in a quite plausible analysis of this conservative universality talk that they use it to cloak the fact that they just want to defend their privileges: they invoke intersubjectivity to suppress minority perspectives. So it seems that intersubjectivity does not solve the problem either.

By now, I am frustrated and annoyed, because I do not know anymore if this work makes sense, in the end. Not only because of the political mess, but because of the conceptual confusion: the hermeneutics of suspicion seem to open up the possibilities for bad conspiracy theories, but intersubjectivity stabilises the status quo. When I came here I just wanted to contribute to social progress. I did not imagine that this would entail such political and even conceptual struggles - it is really exhausting. I might call my former boss from the Railway Administration tomorrow – I heard that my old post might become vacant again soon.

24

BREATHING LAW – REAL IMAGININGS OF WHAT IT MIGHT MEAN TO MATTER DIFFERENTLY

*Daniela Gandorfer**

How *real* can – and should – imaginary laws be? What are the ethical and onto-epistemological implications of imagining, of picturing, of representing law, and what modes of existence are excluded by the very form of imagination, imitation, and expression of fancies of the mind? If imagined differently, can (and should) law make a difference? In addressing these questions, aiming to collapse image and imagination onto a spectral realm of ontological relationality that necessarily calls mattering into question, I propose to attend to breathing and breath *differently*. In doing so I wonder: what would it mean to imagine law *matterphorically* by thinking it with and through every breath, perhaps viewed from (with) not a mind, but a lung as one of many virtual beginnings of a different kind? What other modes of thought does breath(ing) as a matterphorical concept offer, and how does it change the way we can think and imagine law? What kind of existence(s), necessarily exceeding mind and lung, would an aerially imagined and atmospherically entangled law make possible, even under – or perhaps precisely because of – the most stifling and suffocating conditions of the present moment? For in the density of this present, it can hardly be denied that respiratory arrest – whether a consequence of institutionalised violence (*#icantbreathe*), air pollution, or highly selective access to mechanical ventilation during the Covid-19 pandemic – is a physical condition whose possibility is built into the politico-legal system in which it occurs. This system, I argue, compares,

* I wish to thank the remarkable editors of this volume, Peter Goodrich and Thanos Zartaloudis, for their invitation and careful reading, as well as Zulaikha Ayub and Karen Barad for their feedback.

analogizes and differs entities according to representational modes of thought as it relies on a particular image of thought, based on a notion of ontology that - even before considering particular laws and concepts – regulates conditions and possibilities of existence.

Every breath you take, every move you make
Every bond you break, every step you take (I'll be watching you)
Every single day, every word you say
Every game you play, every night you stay (I'll be watching you)
Every move you make, every vow you break
Every smile you fake, every claim you stake (I'll be watching you).[1]
[The Police]

"I breathe, therefore, I am,"[2] Irigaray states her rejection of the Cartesian mind which is forgetful of air, of the state of matter, of nitrogen, oxygen, argon, carbon dioxide, neon, helium, methane, krypton, hydrogen – and dismissive of the entangled matter(s) of breathing, thinking, and being. Irigaray's axiom not only cautions to think (of, with and in) air and thereby undermines the mind/body dichotomy, but also unsettles the notion of a clearly bounded subject existing in and yet separate from the enveloping atmosphere. Continuing to think thought, concept, and potentially an imaginary law with air and breath, we might ask where the human body is, "if it is viewed from within the lung". This question, raised by Elizabeth Povinelli, provocatively points to the onto-epistemological[3] dimension of breathing, rendering it a material practice of knowing that as such can neither be forgetful of air, nor easily reproduce the outlines of the body that has historically been considered the thinking subject's material shell. A lung, Povinelli notes, *knows* the larger, massive biotic assemblage, "including green plants, photosynthetic bacteria, nonsulfur purple bacteria, hydrogen, sulfur and iron bacteria, animals, and microbes", intimately.[4] How does a lung *know* law and what does law look like if viewed, sensed and conceptualised from with a lung?[5]

Breathe in through your nose for a count of four;
hold your breath for a count of four

1 The Police, "Every Breath You Take", in *Synchronicity* (A&M, 1983).
2 Luce Irigaray (1999) *The Forgetting of Air in Martin Heidegger*, trans. Mary Beth Mader (London, UK: Athlone), p. 163.
3 The neologism *onto-epistemology* denotes that "knowing is a material practice of engagement" and as such not detached from but a part of the world in its differential becoming. Karen Barad (2007) *Meeting the Universe Halfway: Quantum Physics and the Entanglement of Matter and Meaning* (Durham, NC; London: Duke University Press), p. 89.
4 Elizabeth A. Povinelli (2016) *Geontologies: A Requiem to Late Liberalism* (Durham, NC: Duke University Press), p. 42.
5 For an example of how matterphorical concepts matter-forth see Elizabeth A. Povinelli, Daniela Gandorfer, and Zulaikha Ayub, "Mattering-Forth: Thinking-with Karrabing," *Theory & Event* 24, no. 1 (2021).

(one bomb, two bomb, three bomb, four);
exhale through your mouth for a count of four;
hold your breath for a count of four
(one bullet, two bullet, three bullet, four),
and then restart the cycle.
Breathe deeply and methodically –
completely filling and emptying your lungs during each cycle.[6]
[Omeima Sukkarieh]

Shifting perspective from the individual ("I") to the lung that knows interiority and exteriority as inseparable from each other certainly and importantly undermines the idea that bounded entities are exterior to an atmosphere which they simply use and internalise as needed. This conceptual break, however, does not touch the most intimate political matters at stake. For lungs, too, matter differently. Not every respiratory process counts. Which lung is deemed capable of holding the most of every breath?[7] Even gas exchange, we learn, has to be efficient; what is not usable for exchange is already cut out of the conceptual field termed life: Dead space.[8] Almost naturally. Respiratory arrest, positional asphyxiation. What cannot breathe, cannot *be*. At no time and in no space. Prepositions, too, matter. Can law be thought *of* time and space, *of* matter? Is outer space far enough to challenge the pitfalls of dominant earthly modes of thought and their (legal) concepts?

Breathe out, breathe in
American oxygen
Every breath I breathe
Chasin' this American Dream
We sweat for a nickel and a dime
Turn it into an empire
Breathe in, this feeling
American, American oxygen. [9]
[Rihanna]

If, as Irigaray states, the dominant mode of thought could for centuries operate in a vacuum and yet colonise, occupy, and appropriate bodies and matter(s), it shall not surprise that even upon the thought of being bereft of air – as is, for

6 Omeima Sukkarieh (2011) "Unsewing My Lips, Breathing My Voice: The Spoken and Unspoken Truth of Transnational Violence", *Somatechnics* 1, no. 1: p. 125.
7 Lundy Braun (2014) *Breathing Race into the Machine: The Surprising Career of the Spirometer from Plantation to Genetics* (Minneapolis, MN: University of Minnesota Press).
8 "Dead space represents the volume of ventilated air that does not participate in gas exchange."; https://www.ncbi.nlm.nih.gov/books/NBK482501/, accessed 20 March 2020.
9 Rihanna, "American Oxygen," in *ANTi* (Westbury Road, Roc Nation, 2016).

example, the case with considerations of laws in outer space – the Cartesian cut and the analytical gaze remain still the preferred tools at hand. Air is partitioned into pieces, oxygen is commodified, breathing becomes a matter of commercial exchange. When it comes to atmospheres other than the earth's, the concept of gas exchanges expresses its underlying semantics most obviously: "[W]hat will be the price of the air that the [space] colonists breathe?"[10] Although law is currently imagined as being carried through outer space as attached to bodies and the legal systems they are subject to, we still do not know how legal thought and concepts travel through different atmospheres, attracted by and through different fields of force and thought. Nevertheless, Elon Musk expresses his ideas. "Keep law short", he suggests when asked about the possible legal and political system he imagined for Mars after having successfully created a breathable atmosphere. As an "adjustment to the inertia of law", laws should, he adds, be difficult to create and easy to remove because, if not "taken away," laws have "infinite life". What needs to be rigorously controlled and decided upon in advance, Musk explains, is every law's *expiration* – lest it exists for too long.[11] Needless to say, his imagined laws are less imaginary than indicative of an attempt to enhance the capitalist grip on law, already, and by no means metaphorically, suffocating bodies and stifling breath. Titles he could imagine for himself, Musk reveals presumably jokingly and ironically in two interviews, are "King of Mars" and "Emperor or God-Emperor". Musk laughs. Both respiratory rate and oxygen consumption increase sharply as he seemingly enjoys the atmosphere in the room while imagining how "humanity" might exist and structure its existence on Mars.[12] The audience joins him. Inhalations, expirations. Breaths worthy to be breathed. Musk, by now self-declared "Technoking of Tesla" and exposed as "a man with feudal aspirations,"[13] continues to undermine international space law. In his most recent – more of less ironical, more or less humorous – attempt he is reminded by a law student that "Mars is not a legal vacuum." The article concludes matterphorically: "While Elon is welcome to the table, he can't keep sucking the air from the room." It leaves us space lawyers just shouting into the void."[14]

10 Adam H. Stevens (2015) "The Price of Air" in *Human Governance Beyond Earth: Implications for Freedom*, ed. Charles Cockell (Cham: Springer), p. 55.

11 Musk suggests that "*every law* should come with an in-built sunset provision," for if a law "is not good enough to be voted back in [by more than 40 percent of the people voting], then maybe it should not be there." [my emphasis] Recode, "Martian Democracy, Elon Musk, Spacex, Code Conference 2016", (YouTube, 2016).

12 The South by Southwest (SXSW), "Elon Musk Answers Your Questions! Sxsw 2018", (YouTube, 2018).

13 Akin Olla, "Elon Musk declared himself 'technoking'. He's just a hyper-capitalist clown," The Guardian, May 20, 2021, https://www.theguardian.com/commentisfree/2021/mar/20/elon-musk-declared-himself-technoking-hes-just-a-hyper-capitalist-clown?CMP=Share_iOSApp_Other. Emphasis is mine.

14 Cristian van Eijk Sorry, "Elon: Mars is not a legal vacuum – and it's not yours, either," Völkerrechtsblog, Nov, 5, 2020, https://voelkerrechtsblog.org/sorry-elon-mars-is-not-a-legal-vacuum-and-its-not-yours-either/.

On Mars, however, where oxygen will be scarce, breath, space researchers imagine, has to be kept short, too: "Suppose that a [space] colonist is down on their luck and cannot afford to purchase their required air … for the month. They could choose to purchase less than their needed oxygen and ration themselves to breathe lower than the standard 21% oxygen mix", that is, people could be "moving in and out of a low oxygen 'diet' as demand varies".[15] A mode of thought, appropriative of air and at the same time forgetful of how its and the thinker's existence is inextricably entangled with aerial matter(s), applies its concepts regardless of its spacetime, and is inattentive to the onto-epistemological questions that arise from the matters of space and time. It is in this sense that the importance of Irigaray's intervention in Western metaphysics can be understood when she asks: "What if he who gives you air gives you air so rarefied, or compressed, or pure, or polluted, or … or … that he, in effect, gives you death?"[16] Gas exchange will continue to have its price. Breathe in, this feeling, American, American oxygen. Whitey on the moon,[17] SpaceX on Mars. Thought deprived of oxygen, breathless ontology.

Can law *be of* (rather than in) time, and *of* (rather than in) space? How to think this breathable air, the sensitive flow of oxygen, the exchange of gases, the inseparability of atmosphere – thick with gases, subject to physical, legal and social pressures – and various, differently affected bodies as well as modes of existence? And can we perhaps push thought – including its modes, its histories, its habits – further, to think what cannot, and yet has to be thought?[18] Irigaray warns that in order for dominant, post-Enlightenment modes of thought to exist, they have to be forgetful of air. The metaphysician becomes "a trafficker in airs", while air remains "unthought, by him".[19] Logic fails: "Is air thinkable?" Does thought, she provocatively asks, "need an other air than the living do?" And "[i]f so, how does the living thinker make do with these two airs?"[20] How, I wish to add, does the legal thinker, the thinker of law and legal concepts do it? How, to rephrase that question, not to fall for an image of thought[21] that produces imaginary laws

15 Charles Cockell (2015) "Extraterrestrial Liberty: Can It Be Planned?", in *Human Governance Beyond Earth: Implications for Freedom*, ed. Charles Cockell (Cham: Springer), p. 31, p. 40.

16 Irigaray, *Forgetting of Air*, p. 7.

17 Gil Scott-Herold, "Whitey on the Moon", in *Small Talk at 125th and Lenox* (Flying Dutchman/RCA, 1970).

18 Gilles Deleuze and Félix Guattari (1994) *What Is Philosophy?*, trans. Janis Tomlinson and Graham Burchell III (New York, NY: Columbia University Press), p. 59.

19 Irigaray, *Forgetting of Air*, p. 6.

20 Ibid., p. 6, p. 12.

21 Throughout his work, Deleuze, later also in collaboration with Guattari, argues that the dogmatic and moralistic image of thought prevents actual thought from coming into being. Thinking has thus to break free from it. In *Difference and Repetition*, Deleuze sets out to identify the postulates of this image, which preconditions what thought is and how thinking operates. Most importantly, thought based on this image – be it in view of Plato's *Theaetetus*, Descartes's *Meditations* or Kant's *Critique of Pure Reason* – is deeply committed to the "model of recognition". The image is necessarily representative, because it accepts the subjective preposition of

as repetition of this forgetfulness, of deliberate erasure, and as reinstatements of the very possibility to take not only breath, but air, an atmosphere even, away – again and again, until legal concepts are devoid of oxygen, designed to reside in a created vacuum, nevertheless delineated, bounded? Can anything *matter* from the perspective of thought coming from a space devoid of matter, that is, from a space in which pressure is assumed to be so low that processes carried out are not affected by it?[22] The construction of the vacuum, the narration that determines that only one mode of thought, and nothing else, matters, and that takes away the very possibility of material existence, is an appropriative act: "The vacuum that they create by using up the air for telling without ever telling of air itself: chasm at the origin of their thought's appropriation?"[23]

While thinking in and from a vacuum as devoid of matter and unconcerned with various kinds of pressures is, according to Irigaray, philosophically questionable, Karen Barad shows in their essay on Quantum Field Theory (QFT) and vacuum fluctuations that it is also physically not tenable. For vacuum fluctuations – ontological indeterminacy in action – matter. Whereas classical physics inherits a Democretean ontology, considering particles, fields, and the void (assumed to contain neither matter nor energy) three separate elements, QFT states that they are in fact *intra*-related.[24] According to Barad's interpretation, intra-actions (measurements or observations as material-discursive practices of mattering that determine different forms of *being* rather than *reacting*)[25] resolve the ontological indeterminacy at the core of quantum physics only partially in the materialisation of specific phenomena and its constitutive exclusion (which must remain indeterminate).[26] Put differently, intra-actions undermine an ontology that assumes pre-existing individual entities and objects with determinate boundaries and properties, observable and measurable from a detached outside.[27]

---

a universal, cognitive faculty that speaks for – or: in the place of – others. Hence, thought that relies on recognition and re-presentation will, so Deleuze, necessarily reproduce the image of thought and its laws: the unquestioned common sense according to which everyone knows what it means to think, the belief that thought has a natural relation to truth, the assumption of the good will of the thinker, and ultimately the superiority of the thinking subject. Gilles Deleuze (1994) *Difference and Repetition*, trans. Paul Patton (New York, NY: Columbia University Press), p. 134.

22 See "Vacuum", in *Encyclopaedia Britannica*, https://www.britannica.com/science/vacuum-physics, accessed 20 March 2020.

23 Irigaray, *Forgetting of Air*, p. 7.

24 Barad, Karen (2012) "On Touching : The Inhuman That Therefore I Am", *differences: A Journal of Feminist Cultural Studies* 23, no. 3: p. 210.

25 Barad (2012) writes: "In other words, measurements are intra-actions (not interactions): the agencies of observation are inseparable from that which is observed. Measurements are world-making: matter and meaning do not preexist, but rather are co-constituted via measurement intra-actions." *What Is the Measure of Nothingness? Infinity, Virtuality, Justice/ Was Ist Das Maß Des Nichts? Unendlichkeit, Virtualität, Gerechtigkeit*, 100 Notes—100 Thoughts, Documenta (13) (Hatje Cantz), p. 6.

26 Ibid., p. 7.

27 Ibid., pp. 6–7.

In writing on the quantum vacuum, then, Barad uses QFT to rethink not only the ontology of matter, but also that of nothingness,[28] as it calls into question the very "conditions of im/possibilities for non/existence".[29] It is because the indeterminacy principle allows for quantum fluctuations (the vacuum's intra-action with itself, leading to virtual particles as "*quantised indeterminacies-in-action,*" or also with matter) that the vacuum cannot be determinately nothing.[30] Virtual particles, then, are not in but *of* the void.[31] As such, they "do not traffic in a metaphysics of presence", as they do not "exist in space and time".[32] In an attempt to express in and with language that which by its ontology cannot determinately be captured by it, Barad writes that virtual particles "are ghostly non/existences that teeter on the edge of the infinitely thin blade between being and nonbeing". Accordingly, the vacuum is far from empty, "a spectral realm with a ghostly existence".[33]

The use of "ghost" here is significant (yet not signifying). Ghost, etymologically tied to "gast", shares its first signification with the Latin noun "spiritus", both also denoting "breath". So much for etymological ties, but what does it, or perhaps even more importantly, what else *can* it mean – and how? Taking the ghostly existence(s) of the quantum vacuum (intra-acting with itself) seriously, Irigaray's axiom ("I breathe, therefore, I am") finds *expression* in a different onto-epistemological field, undermining the Cartesian concept of subjectivity and boundedness expressed by the "I", and of causality referenced by "therefore". If breath is inseparable from the im/possibility for existence, not only for an individual, or a group of individuals, but for existence as entangled with and immanent *in* the fluctuations of no/thingness, how far do we have to consider the implications of "I can't breathe"? And what potential implications for imagining laws differently could result? Raising this question is, however, not to say that a single utterance – even in the most literal yet matterphorical way – denoting and registering the act of being choked to death, is not already significant (and signifying) enough to expose the inexpressible injustice(s) it aims to ex-press with the last breaths breath-able. It *matters*. Rather, it asks whether (in)justices might only be thinkable if imagined, sensed, thought, expressed *from*, *in*, and *with* a different kind of vacuum, neither forgetful of a particular state of matter (or

28 Barad argues that ontology, as imagined and inscribed by Western philosophy, namely as "an already given there-ness" and as such "strictly a matter of being . . . separate from non-being," ought to be questioned and problematized further. According to them, ontology is better understood as "'the theorizing of what is' by materializing things in certain ways, a particular form of intra-acting, and as such part of the world." Karen Barad and Daniela Gandorfer, "Political Desirings: Yearnings for Mattering (,) Differently," *Theory & Event* 24, no. 1 (2021): 16–19.

29 Ibid., p. 12.

30 Ibid., p. 11.

31 Ibid., p. 13.

32 Ibid., p. 12.

33 Ibid.

spacetimemattering),[34] nor of the ontology of matter, which not only still *is* in question, but in fact *is* indeterminate.

The relation between expression and (in)justices is intimately tied to the modes of thought which think it, and to those of meaning production. The implications of quantum indeterminacy as a ghostly matter of non/existence for sense-making, and as such also for the question of expression, are not only directly addressed by Barad in their attempt to describe the (quantum) vacuum. The question of expression is introduced as an onto-epistemological matter. Expression is *matterphorical*, that is, not a specific form of signification, but rather a material-discursive practice of bringing matter and meaning into *being* – partially determined and never once and for all. The vacuum is "a lively tension, a desiring orientation toward being/becoming," a "jubilation of emptiness" teeming with im/possibilities that "yearn for expression".[35] It is here that we can also find resonance with Deleuze and Guattari's plane of immanence, where "an electron crashes into language", and "all that consists is Real".[36] It is also no coincidence that Deleuze and Guattari write that that which "dances upon the plane of consistency [immanence], carries with it the aura of its stratum, an undulation, a memory or tension."[37] Aura too denotes "breath" and "air in motion" and as such also inhabits the onto-semantic field of ghostly expressions closely entangled with the call for a relational ontology or, as I argue elsewhere, an onto-epistemology of difference.[38] What Barad and Deleuze, in his monog-

34 See also: Barad, Karen (2019) "After the End of the World: Entangled Nuclear Colonialisms, Matters of Force, and the Material Force of Justice", *Theory & Event* 22, no. 3: pp. 524–50.

35 The full quote reads: "The void is a lively tension, a desiring orientation toward being/becoming. The vacuum is flush with yearning, bursting with innumerable imaginings of what could be. The quiet cacophony of different frequencies, pitches, tempos, melodies, noises, pentatonic scales, cries, blasts, sirens, sighs, syncopations, quarter tones, allegros, ragas, bebops, hiphops, whimpers, whines, screams, are threaded through the silence, ready to erupt, but simultaneously crosscut by a disruption, dissipating, dispersing the would-be sound into non/being, an indeterminate symphony of voices. The blank page teeming with the desires of would be traces of every symbol, equation, word, book, library, punctuation mark, vowel, diagram, scribble, inscription, graphic, letter, inkblot, as they yearn toward expression. A jubilation of emptiness". *What Is the Measure of Nothingness? Infinity, Virtuality, Justice/ Was Ist Das Maß Des Nichts? Unendlichkeit, Virtualität, Gerechtigkeit*, 13.

36 Gilles Deleuze and Félix Guattari (2014) *A Thousand Plateaus: Capitalism and Schizophrenia*, trans. Brian Massumi (Minneapolis; London: University of Minnesota Press), p. 69. Consider also Deleuze and Guattari's description of the plane of immanence (or: consistency) which is "is in no way an undifferentiated aggregate of unformed matters, but neither is it a chaos of formed matters of every kind. It is true that on the plane of consistency there are no longer forms or substances, content or expression, respective and relative deterritorialisations. But beneath the forms and substances of the strata the plane of consistency [...] *constructs continuums of intensity* [...]. Beneath contents and expressions the plane of consistency [...] *emits and* combines particles-signs that set the most asignifying of signs to functioning in the most deterritorialized of particles." Ibid., p. 70.

37 Ibid.

38 Daniela Gandorfer, *Matterphorics: On the Laws of Theory* (Durham: Duke University Press, (forthcoming)).

raphies as well as in his work with Guattari, seek to break by attending to the inseparability of ontology and epistemology, is representationalism as the dominant, Western mode (or: image) of thought and sense-making. While Deleuze warned of the constant repetition of the moralistic image of thought that underlies Western philosophy and its legal, political, social concepts, Barad points to the ontological implications reproduced by this image (or mode) of thought.[39] And indeed, it remains questionable if theories and modes of thinking that rely on forms of representationalism – that is, for example, the idea that "the world is composed of individuals presumed to exist before the law, or the discovery of the law-awaiting or inviting representation"[40] – can possibly attend to the issue of breath(ing) in relation to the im/possibility for non/existence. Can law and (in) justices perform cuts and delineations from a place where neither air nor breathing actually *matters*?[41] Can concepts, including legal concepts, based on a vacuous metaphysics of individualism reach matters of entangled relationality, and if not, why are they still used to structure our understanding of who or what matters – and why? Who are what makes (the) difference?

> [I]f there was going to be justice, it would have been at the point
> when he said "I can't breathe."
> [Gwen Carr]

For Barad, questions of justice are entangled with questions of space, time, and matter. For "[b]eing in touch with the infinite in/determinacy at the heart of matter, the abundance of nothingness, the infinitude of the void that is threaded in, through, and around all spacetimemattering opens up the possibility of hearing the murmurings, the muted cries, the speaking silence of justice-to-come."[42] To see that these are not simply philosophical and physical considerations detached from the matter(s), and even law(s), at stake, it might suffice to listen to Gwen Carr, Eric Garner's mother who – upon learning that Daniel Pantaleo, the police officer that choked Garner to death, will not be charged with a federal rights violation – said that: "[t]here *is* no justice at all for Eric ... They murdered him and if there was going to be justice, it would have been at the point when he said 'I can't breathe'."[43] The inexpressibility of not only the pain of centuries of violence, suffering, lived injustices, of, as Frantz Fanon states, occupied

39 See Chapter Three ("The Image of Thought") of Deleuze, *Difference and Repetition*.

40 Barad, *Meeting the Universe Halfway*, p. 46.

41 This question becomes especially pertinent when reading Jacques Derrida's "Force of Law", which metaphorises spacetime and equates deconstruction with justice.

42 Barad, *Meeting the Universe Halfway*, p. 216, p. 36.

43 Gwen Carr as quoted by The Guardian. My emphasis. Laughland, Oliver. "'It all takes a toll': Eric Garner's family suffers indignities of trial process." The Guardian (US Edition), June 5, 2019, https://www.theguardian.com/us-news/2019/jun/05/eric-garner-trial-nypd-daniel-pantaleo.

breathing, combat breathing,[44] but also of the spatio-temporal conditions of (in) justice within current political and legal systems, finds its articulation in the very structure of the sentence. The specific temporalities, tying the present to both past and future, and the collapse of "the point" (indicating the particular location and the ghostly time between being and not-being alive) and "when" (referring not only to Garner's expression of the violently afflicted impossibility of breathing, but also to that of being upon his existence), ex-press the lived impossibility of justice in the current (il)legal atmosphere. The matter(s) of expression and expiration – the process of air moving out of lungs as the pressure in the lungs becomes greater than in the outer environment; the coming to an end of a law or contract; the action of breathing a last breath – are not only entangled, but differentially embodied. How far *can* #icantbreathe push the matter of meaning when expression can only ever follow pre-structured content(s) and a solidified chain too signifying to leave any air for what might come to matter? Perhaps it is time (and space) to, as Barad writes in regard to the quantum vacuum, "let the emptiness speak for itself", and to, as Deleuze and Guattari argue, understand expression as that which "precedes content and draws it along", as "materially intense" and nonsignifying. And perhaps it is time (and space) for difference to speak, rather than what is always already rendered different?[45] It is in this sense that #icantbreathe might also, with every entangled breath, call for "[a]nother justice, another movement, another space-time"[46] – one that cannot easily be appropriated by representationalist dynamics, expresses matter(ing) differently, radically challenges the onto-epistemological assumptions that underlie thinkability, and thus also attends differently to the im/possibility for non/existence(s) and mattering.

How, then, might another justice express law differently? Or, to rephrase Irigaray's aforementioned question, does legal thought need (not another but) an other justice than the living do? And if so, how to make do with these two justices? What is (the) difference?

Even more concretely, how might an other justice express difference, calling on law to become sensitive and response-able to the im/possibility for existence and its underlying dynamics, neither already recognizable nor represented, at (space)times not even representable? Given everything – or carried by the philia for wisdom that assumes everything as already given – is justice in the air – descending from the skies, hovering in the critical zone, or rising up from the ground? And if so, how do its movements matter for the uncountable injustices in their specificity and multiplicity; injustices that are entangled, incomparable,

44 Frantz Fanon (1994) *A Dying Colonialism* (New York, NY: Grove Press), p. 65.

45 Barad, *What Is the Measure of Nothingness? Infinity, Virtuality, Justice/ Was Ist Das Maß Des Nichts? Unendlichkeit, Virtualität, Gerechtigkeit*, 4. Gilles Deleuze and Félix Guattari (1986) *Kafka toward a Minor Literature*, trans. Dana Polan (Minneapolis, MN: University of Minnesota Press), p. 19, p. 41.

46 *A Thousand Plateaus*, p. 353.

often incommensurable, in (each and) any case non-universalizable? And if justice, as imagined and thought by thinkers forgetful of air and indifferent to the thinning of the Earth's atmosphere, cannot be in the air, perhaps cannot come to matter, might it be injustices in their specificity that law ought to attend to? Indeed, what if legal thought were to approach injustices neither as the other of justice, nor another justice, but as that which onto-epistemologically ex-presses entangled desires for an other justice – one not simply different, but in and as difference? For this other justice, then, difference cannot be a matter of representation or analogy, a question of applicability or non-applicability, inclusion or exclusion, representability and non-representability. And injustices cannot simply be considered divergences from universalized concepts (such as, but not only, justice and legal subject), but specific onto-epistemological expressions of the world in its (political, social, historical, physical, economic ...) entanglements. Difference, as Deleuze writes in *Difference and Repetition*, which aims to break the moralistic and representational image of thought, is aerial.[47] It is neither oppositional nor a matter of negation or comparison, let alone mediated and represented. In fact, difference has nothing to do with sameness and similarity. It is light and affirmative. Difference in breath is not expressed by a distinction between and categorization of different breaths. In other words, difference is not what describes the relation between pre-given entities and thereby re-inscribes hierarchies and value-judgments. Rather, Deleuze states in his attempt to formulate an ontology of difference as a different kind of relationality, "[e]ach difference passes through all the others;" it must "find itself through all the others." In fact, everything is difference and "behind difference there is nothing."[48] Nothingness, as we learn from Barad, is always already expressing (itself), "a field of differencing (differencing entangling)," flush with the yearning to be/come, that is, towards existence/existing.[49] It is thus difference, far from being the result of comparison, oppositional logic, or judgments from a declared beyond, that expresses non/existence as matter of onto-epistemological relationality.

Bibliography

(SXSW), (The South by Southwest), "Elon Musk Answers Your Questions! Sxsw 2018." YouTube, 2018.

Barad, Karen (2019) "After the End of the World: Entangled Nuclear Colonialisms, Matters of Force, and the Material Force of Justice." *Theory & Event* 22, no. 3, pp. 524–50.

——— (2007) *Meeting the Universe Halfway: Quantum Physics and the Entanglement of Matter and Meaning*. Durham, NC; London, UK: Duke University Press.

47 Deleuze, *Difference and Repetition*, 54.
48 Deleuze, *Difference and Repetition*, 57.
49 Barad and Gandorfer, "Political Desirings," 43.

——— (2012) "On Touching: The Inhuman That Therefore I Am. " differences: A Journal of Feminist Cultural Studies 23, no. 3, pp. 206–23.

——— (2012) *What Is the Measure of Nothingness? Infinity, Virtuality, Justice/ Was Ist Das Maß Des Nichts? Unendlichkeit, Virtualität, Gerechtigkeit.* 100 Notes – 100 Thoughts, Documenta (13). Hatje Cantz.

Barad, Karen, and Daniela Gandorfer. (2021) "Political Desirings: Yearnings for Mattering (,) Differently." *Theory & Event* 24, no. 1, 14–66.

Braun, Lundy (2014) *Breathing Race into the Machine: The Surprising Career of the Spirometer from Plantation to Genetics.* Minneapolis: University of Minnesota Press.

Cockell, Charles (2015) "Extraterrestrial Liberty: Can It Be Planned?". Chap. 1 in *Human Governance Beyond Earth: Implications for Freedom*, edited by Charles Cockell, 1–8. Cham: Springer, 2015.

Deleuze, Gilles (1994) *Difference and Repetition.* Translated by Paul Patton. New York, NY: Columbia University Press.

Deleuze, Gilles, and Félix Guattari (1986) *Kafka toward a Minor Literature.* Translated by Dana Polan. Minneapolis, MN: University of Minnesota Press.

——— (2014) *A Thousand Plateaus: Capitalism and Schizophrenia.* Translated by Brian Massumi. Minneapolis, MN; London, UK: University of Minnesota Press.

——— (1994) *What Is Philosophy?* Translated by Janis Tomlinson and Graham Burchell III. New York, NY: Columbia University Press.

Gandorfer, Daniela. *Matterphorics: On the Laws of Theory.* Durham, NC: Duke University Press, (forthcoming Duke University Press, 2022).

Gandorfer, Daniela, and Zulaikha Ayub. (2021) "Introduction: Matterphorical." *Theory & Event* 24, no. 1, 2–13.

Goodrich, Peter. (2021) "Transhumusians: On the Jurisography of the *Corpus Iuris.*" *Theory & Event* 24, no. 1, 117–30.

Fanon, Frantz (1994) *A Dying Colonialism.* New York, NY: Grove Press.

Irigaray, Luce (1999) *The Forgetting of Air in Martin Heidegger.* Translated by Mary Beth Mader. London, UK: Athlone.

Police, The. "Every Breath You Take." In *Synchronicity*: A&M, 1983.

Povinelli, Elizabeth A. (2016) *Geontologies: A Requiem to Late Liberalism.* Durham, NC: Duke University Press.

Povinelli, Elizabeth A., Daniela Gandorfer, and Zulaikha Ayub. (2021) "Mattering-Forth: Thinking-with Karrabing." *Theory & Event* 24, no. 1, 294–323.

Recode. "Martian Democracy, Elon Musk, Spacex, Code Conference 2016." YouTube, 2016.

Rihanna. "American Oxygen." In *ANTi*: Westbury Road, Roc Nation, 2016.

Sal, Intagliata, Rizzo Alessandra, and Gossman, William G. (2020) "Physiology, Lung Dead Space." In *StatPearls.* Treasure Island, FL: StatPearls Publishing.

Scott-Herold, Gil. (1970) "Whitey on the Moon." In *Small Talk at 125th and Lenox*: Flying Dutchman/RCA.

Stevens, Adam H. (2015) "The Price of Air". Chap. 5 In *Human Governance Beyond Earth: Implications for Freedom*, edited by Charles Cockell, pp. 51–61. Cham: Springer.

Sukkarieh, Omeima (2011) "Unsewing My Lips, Breathing My Voice: The Spoken and Unspoken Truth of Transnational Violence." *Somatechnics* 1, no. 1, pp. 124–33.

Weizman, Eyal. (2021) "Epilogue: Theory, Momentarily." *Theory & Event* 24, no. 1, 399–410.

Williams, Patricia J. (2021) "Skittles as Matterphor." *Theory & Event* 24, no. 1, 356–98.

25

UNTITLED. UNRELIABLE. UNCONFIRMED

Deepak Unnikrishnan

I've heard a rumour. It's good.

At the mall by IKEA, they're hiring again; not the usual personnel HR have got to hire to get any mall to run period – people like valets and toilet cleaners and sweepers and minders. They're looking for people willing to work with the high-roller-alpha-dog type, with the pay to match.

It starts with the card, whatever the shopper qualifies for after his/her/their first purchase. Apparently, once the shopper gets past the Premium, VIP Premium, and Platinum Premium tiers, someone pays them a visit to offer them a demonstration of a more useful shopping experience. And here's where I'm telling you I'm not responsible for the veracity of what you're about to read.

Like I said, I heard a rumour. And it's good.

After addressing the shopper by name, the visitor explains the mall sent him. And because this person's bespoke suit and footwear makes an impression, the person's invited in.

And as the shopper is asked to sit down because the news is big, the visitor in bespoke gear shares the shopper's status has been upgraded. I mean, *really* upgraded – shinier bells, louder whistles. And, to raise the stakes mind you, the visitor will add that if the shopper wishes to keep the privilege, they will need to abide by two rules. Basically, a) tell no one, and b) if they're cool with the first rule, submit to the terms of the second rule if they dig their present.

Present?

Bear with me; I'm getting to that part.

Then, before any beverages are offered or drunk, or phone numbers exchanged, the visitor explains it's best to talk business, because he doesn't want to keep his other clients waiting. By this point, the shopper has questions, none of which will be asked, because the visitor will zip the shopper's lip, then say:

Ask for something/anything. If you're not following, the shopper is being set up for their present.

Flustered, the shopper will acquiesce to be polite, often naming something quantifiable, like a gift card, or if they're really bold, pricy electronics. And the visitor will sigh before getting straight to the point: Ask for something you aren't allowed to buy. The shopper may/will laugh, and say something stupid, like love.

Be specific, the visitor will insist, Love, as in comfort, or Love, as in lust? And the shopper will pause and say something like, Love as in quiet. Okay, the visitor will say, then leave, knowing fully well that soon the shopper will have another visitor, someone who will fulfil those needs.

The following day, said shopper will be at the mall, revisiting the past 24 hours, and thinking about what's to come. Fact is, shopper's hooked, damn be the terms and conditions of the second rule, as long as the presents keep coming.

Anyways, at the mall, on cue, the shopper is going to be greeted by another mall rep. This person will greet the shopper with an immediacy and formality reserved only for the privileged and then place a shiny-looking card into the person's palm. Tap when ready, the shopper will be told. And if there's anything you're looking for, be sure to mention that out loud.

At this stage the shopper assumes dark/wild/forbidden wants could be had on tap. And so this individual will say something banal or silly, like Victory, or, sigh, Vice, because people are boring. And, well, nothing happens. But the mall rep, trained to wait this moment out because the shopper hasn't named a product, will wade through the embarrassment and the confusion on display and guide the shopper to, what else, a store. There, the mall rep will request the shopper to pick something worthy of acquisition. As the shopper makes the selection, an observant sales assistant of the Filipino/Indian/(or)Egyptian variety will dart into view.

Before any of the aforementioned nationalities are allowed to disturb the shopper, the mall rep will goad the shopper to fish out the new card and tap it three times.

At the shopper's third tap, the sales assistants, in mid-stride or mid-sentence, will disappear, as though airbrushed out of existence.

The upgrade, if you haven't figured it out by now, is privacy/seclusion, the elimination of small talk until the point of purchase, and the entry into another dimension where the only inhabitants are customers. And to keep your status, the mall rep will add, you continue to shop at the mall until you've hit your monthly/yearly targets. I mean, at this point, the shopper's intrigued but not too impressed. Frankly, it's not exactly beneficial to eliminate the help completely. I mean, what if you've got questions? Or if you'd like some flattery/honesty as you coax those trousers past your hips or wrap your feet in calf leather. At this point, the mall rep inspects your purchase-to-be. Let's presume it's something you've grabbed on the fly, like perfume. And the rep will say, Request for assistance. As the shopper does, someone far more sophisticated will appear and will dab the scent on his/her body, slowly/carefully. And will proceed to explain why the scent works, where its ingredients were sourced, how the fragrance will transform your day to day. And because these people are trained, you will feel as though nothing else matters in this individual's life, except you; and that's probably true. But what you're really thinking about is what you're going to ask for after you've met your targets because you've discovered you've got wants supermarkets/stores don't produce on demand. Plus, to sweeten the deal, the mall rep will add, regular sales assistants will be on call too. However, the client, and that would be the shopper, will also be able to decide the race, age, gender and build, of the mall rep.

But last week, there was a bit of a fuck-up. An elite shopper had met her targets and was waiting on a present, but she didn't know what to ask for. After weeks, she decided she wanted something different and settled on a request that would show her what her future could have looked like if she hadn't experienced loss. The shopper, if we're to believe the rumours, was confident the mall wouldn't be able to deliver; it had been a bet – a month's salary with a friend who had been upgraded too. Within hours, someone brought a ten-month-old baby boy that had just learned to crawl. Seven hours later, when the aforementioned someone returned to collect the present, which had (obviously) been a rental, the shopper and the baby couldn't be found. Since the incident, there have been speculations. The empathetic posit the shopper may have miscarried in the past or couldn't conceive. The less polite sink their fangs and tongues into the possibility of an aborted foetus, perhaps multiple ones if her legs parted on demand. Truth is, much remains obscure.

When they found the lady and the baby, all parties eschewed drama.

After the baby was returned, the shopper was taken to the mall, where she continues to be kept.

Apparently, they bring her out when the shortlisted candidates for elite mall reps are being interviewed. At least that's what they did for this round of interviews, seating her in front of them, as they're asked questions about their knowledge of Glashütte horology to the importance of diplomacy in the shopping experience. By then the candidates know her story since she would've been referenced repeatedly. And as they respond, she smiles at them. And they're not sure what to do or feel. They know it's a test, but a test of what? They won't wait long to find out.

Now remember I told you the pay's good. And the opportunity to work a gig like this doesn't come around every day. So when the last part of the interview is to give candidates the opportunity to ask this woman anything they'd like, what do you think she gets asked the most? The why, right? I mean, why take the baby! And where was she headed? But to expect her to tell them the truth, now that's putting too much faith in the world, and its people. And that's what the committee is looking for – to see how these aspiring candidates interact with this woman, especially when the candidates believe they're in charge.

On top of that, the committee also pays close attention to the candidate's reaction/response after the question's been posed, especially when/if the woman confesses she only took the baby to get rid of it, because she couldn't stand the noise or the smell.

Or what a candidate may do when the woman explains she gave the baby to a guy who had contacts in the recesses of the deep web, those who'd know what to do with and to a baby that she assumed was hers for keeps. And believe you me, she'll look at these aspiring men and women, and say something different every time. It's as though she's keeping herself entertained, or perhaps (if I may say so) acting on an order from mall leadership. Either way, the truth feels irrelevant. And since the candidates wish to impress their future bosses, they feel obligated or even required to hear her out, even if she says she wanted to know what it was like to have a baby cooing in the back seat as she drove around town, but then the little shit started screaming … as she tells another she had only left her boy – not the one they sent her, who looked nothing like her child by the way – in the tub for seconds and had done everything in her power to revive him but he just stopped breathing, as though she had left him in the ocean in the middle of a hurricane. Or she could claim, before she made her money, she'd been a refugee, raped at the border, forced to leave the baby she bore at an orphanage.

But at some point, as the woman says her piece, the candidates will realise, she's the one in charge.

And once the committee members have everything they need, they turn to the (often) exhausted candidate and will ask this person to carefully consider the woman's confession, and to contemplate her trustworthiness. Then they'll share the number of shortlisted candidates they were hoping to get, perpetually capped at ten, and explain every single one of their competitors were given a different version of events by the woman they were all asked to converse with. The woman isn't a pathological liar, they'll confirm, just crafty. However, they'll add, she may have lied during her Q&A.

And as much as *why* she committed the offence seems relevant they'll admit they're interested in something else, consequences.

She broke the rules, they'll tell every candidate, but we are interested in how rule breakers must be dealt with.

First, they'll continue, tell us whether you think she lied.

Second, tell us how you believe she should be handled, because there's opportunity here to set an example.

Third, the woman's not an actor. Irrespective of your decision, her punishment has been decided.

Before the candidate can think, or answer, the committee will share they've got one more thing to add. They'll say, we've also asked the woman to evaluate *you*, whether she believes you're ruthless enough to see through con artists, or to shake people down, whether you are gullible, an easy mark. Because she's been taking notes too, and if her input proves useful, her sentence gets reduced, so don't feel you've got to go easy on her, because you don't have to since she doesn't give a shit about any of you.

And then they'll mention a number, the salary the candidate is expected to make if the job's theirs. And they'll mention another number, the yearly bonus. Then as they share the perks of the gig, it becomes clear that the candidates won't have opportunities to apply again. No call-backs, wait-lists, nothing. On cue, someone from the committee will say – We could be barbarians, break her legs, strangle her cat, but all of that would feed off clichés; we're interested in something more.

And as though by reflex, every candidate will lean in, to drink in every line, because they know time's running out and they need to think how to proceed.

The committee would be least bothered, because someone on behalf of the collective will still be talking. The question here, this person will say, is to determine what sort of example ought to be set to act as a deterrent. The penalty shouldn't be soft, because we don't want her being a repeat offender, and we certainly don't wish others to try their luck. Therefore, the penalty needs to be something that makes sense, something that preserves our secrets, yet highlights our determination to track people down, if we must, then to set them straight. For example, you know that baby we gave her for a few hours? We took that from a member and we are keeping it until the infant's ten, maybe eleven. We're going to make this child do things for us. And inevitably, we are going to do things to it. Then we're going to send it back, eleven years on, to the member we took him from, a member who continues to be a valued customer, we should add. And when we send it back, we're going to make sure the kid knows he became what he did, in mind and spirit, because of the sins of his father. So now we cede the floor to your brain.

And it's possible as some of these candidates take their leave, they weigh the ethics of taking and raising someone else's baby. And for a few seconds they'll wonder about the perpetrator and his crime.

But what they'll really ponder for years, whether they get the job or not, would be the most direct of questions – Tell us, what must be done to this cheat, what are your laws?

And they'll need to look them all in the eye, especially the woman they're about to sentence, and tell them – This is what I believe.

26

LEGAL FICTIONS: A DIALOGUE IMAGINING LAW

*Elizabeth Cowie**

First Woman: Surely laws aren't imaginary, and they don't produce fictions.

Second Woman: But they are and they do. Bentham – the guy who thought up utilitarianism – argued that "fictions and fictitious entities" are necessary for speech and thought beyond that of "brute creation".[1] It was a matter of utility for him, arguing that "a fictitious entity is an object, the existence

* Acknowledgement: In writing this I was inspired by Anne Marie Miéville's brilliant three-part film titled *Nous some tout encore ici* (1997). Originally devised for theatre, the first part is an adaptation of Plato's *Gorgias*, performed by two women, iconic actresses of the modern French cinema, Aurore Clément and Bernadette Lafont, set in an ordinary middle-class kitchen, and which they perform with a theatrical naturalness, much as we might expect people speaking loftily and philosophically to each other – full of inflection and of passion. Lafont, as Callicles, is in her own home, doing domestic chores and putting on makeup while Clément, as Socrates, is the guest. Jonathan Rosenbaum writes: "The discussion starts with the merits of philosophy itself; it veers toward goodness and justice, and ends with a question that arises like a plea, for the definition of the good man. Miéville films their discussion with a deft drawing-room vivacity, as if Plato had stuck to his original calling as a playwright and became the Athenian answer to Philip Barry." (https://www.chicagoreader.com/chicago/were-all-still-here/Film?oid=1070305, accessed 7 June 2020). In the second part Jean-Luc Godard is on a theatre stage reciting a monologue condensed from Hanna Arendt's *The Origins of Totalitarianism,* and in the third part, Godard and Clement play a couple who see a film, go home, where she complains about everything he does, and he apologises.

1 Jeremy Bentham, "Essay on Language", in *The Works of Jeremy Bentham*, (Edinburgh: William Tate, 1843) vol. 8, 325: "To language, then – to language alone – it is that fictitious entities owe their existence; their impossible, yet indispensable existence" (198). Elsewhere he writes, "There are no real entities that are not species of fictitious entities: there are no fictitious entities that are not species of real entities", in "Draft letter to d'Alembert", unpublished manuscript (UC clxix, 59), as cited in Emmanuelle de Champs "The Place of Jeremy Bentham's Theory of Fictions in Eighteenth-century Linguistic Thought", author's translation, at http://eprints.ucl.ac.uk/647 (Accessed 11 June 2020).

of which is feigned by the imagination, feigned for the purpose of discourse, and which, when so formed, is spoken of as a real one." Of course utility itself is a fictional entity since it isn't an object in the world but an experience of a state, of being useful, hence electricity companies are "utilities". Without propositions that refer to fictitious entities, Bentham argued, there could be no medicine, no art, no poetry, no engineering, no chemistry or other sciences. In short, some legal fictions, and some legal fictitious entities, can be justified on the ground that their use tends to bring a net utilitarian benefit, though you have to be careful about that.[2]

First Woman: So fictions in the law are useful, and therefore they are kind of real, but how is law imaginary?

Second Woman: Well, an imaginary law might just be a law imagined but not yet enacted. Its imagining might be spoken of between friends or at political rallies. Or it may have material presence in a written document readied as an Act of Parliament but not yet law.

First Woman: Good, so these imagined laws become real.

Second Woman: Yes, and such imagined laws also figure desire, for the imagined outcome to be achieved by the imagined law. Figured here as well is a desire for the community and its social system in which a law can be imagined and thus enacted by those recognised as able to speak and to make laws. Because laws are not, usually, material objects that you can touch, hear or see. They are not "natural" phenomena either but exist as social acts and facts created by those recognised as entitled to do so, however that entitlement might be constituted.

First Woman: So only special people can imagine laws?

Second Woman: No, not only, for laws can be imagined that are not, or not yet enacted, because they are desired by those not recognised as entitled to speak, that is, to make laws.

First Woman: That doesn't seem fair, we should all be able to have our say. But going back to this fictional thing about law, surely once in the statute book they are real?

Second Woman: Well, not entirely, because even imagined laws enacted are nevertheless still fictions in that they imagine – constitute – a subject that is, or will be, the entity addressed by the law. Such a subject – you and me – will be prohibited from undertaking certain actions, such as murder, or theft, or child abuse, but also actions like racial discrimination. So lawmakers are also imagining law as not only affecting people's actions but also their ideas about their actions.

2 Colin Tyler, "Jeremy Bentham, Social Criticism & Levels of Meaning", *UCL Bentham Project*, http://www.ucl.ac.uk/Bentham-Project/journal/Tylerl.htm. See on this, as well, Slavoj Žižek in *Tarrying With the Negative: Kant, Hegel and the Critique of Ideology* (Durham: Duke University Press, 1993), pp. 83–89.

First Woman: So the law wants us to take actions.

Second Woman: Yes, as subjects we can be required in law to undertake specific actions, such as registering a child's birth. Laws also construct specific fictions in recognising certain legal subjects that are non-human entities – limited companies and corporations, or dogs and cats which can inherit property.

First Woman: That's pretty unreal, for sure, but a dog can't use a credit card or access its money at a bank, so who does?

Second Woman: Well, in that case the law recognises – or one could say, imaginatively constructs – certain categories of people as the subjects who can act for another as if them, which can specifically affect us women. For while as a woman I can have an abortion, I am not the subject in law who can authorise my abortion, unlike any other medical procedure where I have to sign a form of permission. Nor is the man who fathered the foetus. Instead it is doctors, two in fact, acting in "good faith", on one (or more) of the grounds legally specified, and with each needing to agree that at least one and the same ground is met. Only then can I have the abortion.[3]

First Woman: So women must continue to imagine a law that in fact – and in law – really does give women the right to choose?

Second Woman: Yes, we still desire the right to choose, to be ourselves the subjects who can action our abortion in law. At the moment such a law remains imaginary, it can only be enacted in the realm of writing that we know as "fiction", of possible worlds, people and actions.

First Woman: So what other laws do you imagine?

Second Woman: Well, I can think of something against which there should be a law.

First Woman: Against what?

Second Woman: Giving ground relative to one's desire.

First Woman: Don't you mean *not* giving way to one's desire, surely the law is meant to curtail desire not allow it to prevail? I mean I know you are into Freud but I thought that he was pretty down on desire, with his idea of a super-ego prohibiting and all, and sublimation as a way of getting your desire but displacing it onto something else, like religion, I guess, or art.[4]

3 In the UK the law on abortion, enacted in 1967, renders lawful activities that would otherwise constitute a crime under the Offences Against the Person Act (OAPA) 1861. The OAPA makes it a crime for a woman to "procure a miscarriage", or for another person to help her do so. The Abortion Act 1967 (as amended by the Human Fertilisation and Embryology Act 1990) states that an abortion is legal if it is performed by a registered medical practitioner (a doctor), and that it is authorised by two doctors. For more on this see: https://www.bpas.org/get-involved/campaigns/briefings/abortion-law/.

4 Freud distinguished between drives, the push for satisfaction (such as the sexual drive), and desire in relation to external objects of desire. Lacan develops Freud's concepts, using the term *jouissance* for Freud's drive, an enjoyment as such, outside of any sexual relation of desire, and thus outside the social. Desire always involves an object desired which, once obtained, does not itself deliver

Second Woman: Yes, but this other psychoanalyst, a French guy called Lacan, started re-thinking some of Freud's theories and came up with this peculiar idea of *not* giving ground relative to one's desire.

First Woman: But it would be impossible to enforce!

Second Woman: Maybe, but still, I would like to imagine a law against giving ground relative to our desire.

First Woman: But don't laws prohibit behaviours that involve desire, rather than require us to keep hold of our desire?

Second Woman: Laws prohibit actions, not desires. What prohibits desire is that voice in us which tells us not to want something and makes us feel bad when we go on wanting certain things. We think of it as our conscience telling us we shouldn't do or have something that we desire. Yet it is not just a feeling of being wrong, or in the wrong – doing a crime – but feeling another's gaze that is critical; and finding oneself and one's ideas of oneself wanting in the other's gaze. So, we are caught between an idealised idea of ourselves that Freud called an ideal ego, and an idea of ourselves that would be ideal to the other we care for, the other whose care for us we desire – an ego-ideal.

First Woman: Yes, I know what you mean, there's always a gap between how we see ourselves and how we think, or fear, that others see us.

Second Woman: For Lacan this ego-ideal is not a single person, but the other of our first carers – mother, father – whose desire for us we desire, so that we desire to be what they desire, which we take to be what they want us to be, and this sets us on the path, on the network, of norms and ideals, social and symbolic, that society sets forth for us to internalise through our upbringing and education. Lacan calls this our ego-ideal, which we put together from what we understand that the other wants of us and to whom we look for a gaze and speech of affirmation. It is that sense of a demand on us to be this or that, to turn the other cheek, to do unto others what you would do unto yourself, as the Christian Bible has it.

First Woman: I know what you mean!

Second Woman: But Lacan also saw that there is an obverse to this positive role of the ego-ideal, of the other, which is the sense of guilt that arises, of doing too little, or not doing it in the right way. Thus, our actions are at the same time not our own but are what we do to placate an overbearing sense of

---

the satisfaction of enjoyment, instead it will be replaced by another desire. Desire arises in the split in the subject of self, the ego, and the other to which it addresses its desire to be desired and from whom the image of what he or she should be arises. Desire, thus, involves a relation of desire, it arises in our social relations, in contrast to jouissance. And the law, in its essence, Lacan writes, seeks "to divide up, distribute, or reattribute everything that counts as jouissance [...]. Jouissance is what serves no purpose" in Jacques Lacan, *Encore: The Seminar of Jacques Lacan Book XX*, New York: Norton, 1975. p. 3.

obligation in relation to an other's felt demand or rebuke. This is Lacan's super-egoic Big Other.

First Woman: Wow, this sounds really heavy. Our desires are overseen by this overbearing Other?

Second Woman: Yes, so that your desire is no longer your own but the Big Other's desire, to be what it wants of you. It sounds really silly, but what this Big Other also demands is that we enjoy.

First Woman: Well that's a relief, we have got back our enjoyment then?

Second Woman: Not really, in fact, not at all! Because we are now enjoying *for* the Big Other, not for ourselves, so that our desiring and desires have been hijacked.

First Woman: In that case there really does need to be a law against this, we shouldn't give up on our desire!

Second Woman: Right, because what we are guilty of is giving ground relative to our desire. Our sense of guilt is a kind of masochistic self-beating for giving up on our desire in a blame-game, because the Big Other's demands are always right, so if I don't want what it wants, I must be wrong. Pretty shitty!

First Woman: Right, so how do we get rid of this dreadful Big Other and get back to the nice little other, the ego-ideal?

Second Woman: Ah! That's the problem with laws, they are all or nothing and what Lacan talks of is two sides of a coin, so they are indivisible. So maybe a law against giving way to one's desire would throw up too many other problems. I think that this may be what Lacan was on about when he talks of Antigone not giving up on her desire to bury her brother Polyneices, though at the cost of her life.

First Woman: Oh my goodness that doesn't sound good, a bit like your money or your life!

Second Woman: Yes, because in giving up on her duty to honour her brother in death by burying him, at the same time she loses what sustains her in life, namely being there for her brother, and indeed for her parents.

First Woman: So who was this Antigone woman and why was she trying to bury her brother even if it would cost her life?'

Second Woman: She is the heroine of the play by a guy called Sophocles in ancient Greece, in which Antigone's uncle Creon has become king of Thebes after the civil war ignited by the conflict between Antigone's two brothers, Eteocles and Polyneices, who died at each other's hands. Creon chooses one, Eteocles, to honour with burial and all the rites, while he condemns Polyneices to the shame of no burial and forbids anyone to go against his order or risk death.

First Woman: Ah, that's pretty heavy, but if Creon is the king and he makes the law, and Polyneices caused the conflict, Creon is in the right, isn't he?

Second Woman: Well that's what the play's chorus says, that while she is right in seeking to respect the dead, the power of the king is not to be thwarted.

First Woman: So why is Antigone so dead set on burying him if it will cost her life?

Second Woman: Well that is the question so many since have asked and found no answer that really satisfies.[5] Antigone herself declares that it is a matter of honouring the gods by honouring her brother in death, and that her family in death is more important to her than the possible husband and children she could have in the future. Perhaps she holds to her desire for the living who died and are lost to her, and this weighs on her more powerfully than the rule of law and the risk of death in defying it. She desires their desire.

First Woman: She does not give ground relative to her desire then?

Second Woman: Exactly, because in some important way holding to her desire is the same as her very being.[6]

First Woman: Then maybe we need to have imaginary laws as well as real ones, to work through what we really hope for in what we want to prohibit and how it may risk our desire, our being?

5 Notably Johann Wolfgang von Goethe and Georg Wilhelm Friedrich Hegel, and many other philosophers but also artists, authors and playwrights, such as Bertolt Brecht, in the twentieth century.

6 It is in the context of Lacan's discussion of Sophocles' *Antigone* that he declares "the only thing one can be guilty of is giving ground relative to one's desire" and that, "desire is understood here, as we have defined it elsewhere, as the metonymy of our being"; in *Ethics of Psychoanalysis 1959–1960: The Seminar of Jacques Lacan* (London: Routledge, 1992), at p. 321. For Lacan, Antigone as a hero is one who does not give up on her desire, and thereby dies, yet instead of a law - to not give up on one's desire - Lacan sees sublimation, a change of aim and not of object, but for which one must, still, pay a price, not of one's life but of one's jouissance. (ibid., p. 322)

27
COIL

Justin Clemens

If true, as some thinkers have thought,
That all of our thinkings are caught
In language's net,
Then laws that we get
Are downstream of words we were taught.

As such, the transcending of law
Is immanent to its rapport
With what it is not –
Its health and its rot
Depend on what seeps from its maw.

Whatever law says, it retracts,
Abandoning with its own Acts
The Just it would found,
Betraying its ground
In innumerable judgements and facts.

But failing to fail its own test
Would break law across its own chest –
For how could it function
If not by disjunction,
Compounding the worst with the best?

Imagining law that departs
From such sophistical arts
Demands the distraction

Of counterfeit action –
Like boring false wholes in your parts.

But what kind of thing could that be,
That's neither law nor *anomie*?
Especially when this
Looks like the abyss
Of what could never not be?

It seems we are wound in a coil,
Whose bound complications will foil
Essays to escape
This grimy landscape
And bring us back up to the boil.

Not-have-to-nor-can-do-nor-should
Is the only way out of this wood:
But all these negations
Inspire divagations
That cannot be understood.

So: nonsense as logic of sense
Becomes a granular lens
Through which one can see
A nomothete-free,
Post-cameral vision of *mens*.

28

WAITING FOR LAW

A play in one act

Stacy Douglas

X, sitting on the ground under a tree, trying to take off his boot. The tree is covered in sheets of unmarked paper. Although X is outside, the backdrop is plastered in large print copies of legal cases between the Estate of Samuel Beckett and numerous stage companies. X pulls at his boot with both hands, with difficulty. X exhausted, tries again. Gives up. Enter Y.

X: Nothing to be done.
Y: You can't say that.
X pulls at his boot with both hands, panting.
Y: You can't do that!
X looking confused.
X: We always find something, eh–
Y excitedly cutting off X; scared.
Y: Shhhhhhhh! [*Looking around. Ensuring no one has heard*] They might be listening. You have to choose your words very carefully.
X tries for boot again. Y stops X.
Y: And your actions!
X: But what are we to do then? Just sit here?
Y: Just sit here.
X: And wait?
Y: And wait [*Fidgeting; anxious*]
X: But nothing is happening.
Y: That's the point.
X: That's the point?
Y: That's the point.
X: That doesn't seem like a very good point.
Y: It is a profundity which you would not understand.
X: [*Looks confused*] Oh. Okay. [*Pause*] I'm hungry.

Y: That isn't relevant.

X: Isn't relevant to what?

Y: The point.

X: I am really beginning to not like the point.

Y: You don't understand the point.

X: Are we waiting for the point?

Y: You can't ask that!

X: Why not?

Y: Because the point is a profundity. [*Sighs in exasperation*] You wouldn't understand.

X: Well, I am going to get something to eat [*Begins to walk away*]

Y: [*Desperately*] Wait!

X: No!

Y: [*Physically stopping X*] I mean, wait! You can't leave. [*Reluctantly*] I can find you something to eat. [*Searching the area haphazardly; finds an apple on the ground under the tree, gives it to X*] Here.

X: I'm allergic to apples. You know that.

Y: Well, then just sit down and … just sit down!

X: I will not sit down! I will not wait! I will not not take my boot off! [*Standing on one foot, X violently takes one of his boots off and throws it out of sight. X and Y hear a loud "Ow" from someone hit by the boot*].

Z: [*Muttering as they enter. Rubbing head from boot wound*] No, no, no, I'm afraid this won't do at all, won't do.

Y: [*Speaking to X*] Oh, now you've done it.

Z: My friends, this is not in the script. This isn't in the script at all. No, no, it won't do.

X: I'm sorry. Did I hit you with my boot?

Z: [*Not acknowledging X and Y; walking around stage, looks at tree*] Oh dear. I'm afraid this is out of control. I don't see permission for any of this.

Y: Look, we're sorry. We were just waiting … my friend here was just about to start waiting.

Z: Oh dear. That's part of the problem. I'm afraid you're in violation of both waiting and not waiting.

X: What?

Z: Oh dear. I'll have to give you notice [*Writing on a clipboard*].

X: Notice of what?

Y: But, we weren't even waiting!

Z: Yes, that's part of the problem. I see you were both waiting without permission and not waiting, which is also not allowed.

X: This is absurd.

Z: Yes, that's right. That is the proprietary name for it. Which is also copyrighted.

X: Who are you?

Y: He's in charge of the waiting …

Z: [*Clears throat*] Executor of the waiting, to be clear.

X: I thought we were making a profound point? What does he have to do with making a profound point?
Y: He ensures it's just the right point. That it's just the right amount of profound.
X: How does he know?
Y: It's there on his clipboard.
Z: It's here on my clipboard.
Y: He has a long history of ensuring such things.
Z: That reminds me. No insurance here. I'll have to add that to the notice, I'm afraid.
Y: [*Looking like they might be sick*] Oh …
X: He can't do this. He's not in charge of us. We have rights! We're not beholden to a clipboard.
Z: I'm afraid you are.

X looking at Y for support.

Y: I'm afraid we are.
X: [*Grabbing the clipboard to the shock of Y and Z; throws it out of sight*] Hah! Take that, Executor! [*pronouncing it as ex-ah-cute-or. X, Y and Z hear a loud "Ow" from someone hit by the clipboard. Enter a burly character, W, with the clipboard in one hand and a baton in the other*].
W: What seems to be the problem here?
Y: Oh … [*Trying to appease*] We were just waiting.
W: With permission?
Y: Well, we were trying to make a point, but then …
W: Without permission.
Z: I'm afraid they were both waiting and not waiting, without permission.
W: That is a problem. Someone threw this [*Raising the clipboard*].
Y: [*Standing in front of X, attempting to defend him*] I can explain …
X: I'm sorry, did I hit you with the clipboard?
Z: [*Taking the clipboard from W*] You can't just go throwing clipboards.
W: No, I'm afraid not. I'll have to give you notice [*Tapping the baton in his hand*].
X: Notice of what?
W: Your violation.
X: What violation?
W: For throwing the clipboard.
Z: On top of both waiting and not waiting.
X: This is absurd.
Z: Oh yes, and copyright infringement [*Makes a note on their clipboard*].
X: [*Rolling eyes*] Okay, go ahead, write me a notice.
W: Oh no. I don't write notices.
Y: Thank God!
W: You'll have to wait here for the Investigator [*Begins to leave*].
X: What?
Y: Wait? Here?
W: Yes. To make a point. You can't go throwing clipboards around.

Y: How long will we have to wait?

W: Don't know.

X: What if we don't want to wait? What if we refuse to wait!

W: Wait here.

X: What if we're hungry?

W: [*Looks around haphazardly, sees an apple on the ground, offers it to X*] Here's an apple.

X: I'm allergic to apples.

W: I'm afraid that's all there is while you wait.

Z: [*Also getting ready to leave*] I'll leave this notice here for the Investigator … [*Pinning notice on tree*].

W and Z begin to leave on opposite sides of the set.

X: That's it. I've had enough of these spurious charges! I want a lawyer!

W and Z stop.

X: Do you hear me? [*To no one in particular; grabs apple from W and throws it off stage in protest*] I WANT A LAWYER! [*Nothing happens*].

Pause.

W: Wait here.

X: I will not! I am not doing anything until I get a lawyer! [*Looking at Y, with pleading eyes*].

Y: [*Unsure*] Uh … that's right. [*Unconvincingly*] We want a lawyer [*Takes X's hand*].

Z: Oh dear. [*Looking through his notes*] I don't see any permission rights for this …

Y, taking X aside.

Y: You do realise … um …

X: We await the mighty hand of justice, which is swift and precise! [*Sits down defiantly*]

Y: [*Pause*] Yes! [*Defiantly sits down with X; pauses, then less convinced*] All the same, we'll be in violation of …

W: [*Interrupting their aside*] I'm afraid your waiting will make you in violation of …

Z: [*Taking over from W*] … you're now in violation of two counts of waiting without permission from the Estate, and two counts of waiting improperly [*Putting second notice on tree*].

W: The Investigator will be along [*Exits*].

Z: [*Takes a long look at X and Y*] Oh dear [*Exits*].

[*Long pause*]

Y: [*Looks around*] You do realise … um …

X: We await the mighty hand of justice, which is swift and precise!

Y: … but we're *waiting.*

X: Yes, I know.

Y: But you said before …

X: There once was a man. This man was very hungry, but all he had to eat were apples and he was allergic to apples …

Y: [*Sarcastically*] I think I've heard this one before …

X: he saw apple after apple on the ground, sometimes others even offered him apples, but each time he refused. And yet he grew hungrier and hungrier. After several days of having nothing to eat, he was ravenous, but still he did not eat one of the many apples at his feet. Then, one day, when the man was nearly dead from starvation, a woman came by with an apple pie and offered it to the dying man. And he ate it. He ate it with such happiness and such satisfaction. And when he was done, a light returned to his eyes, showing the woman that her apple pie had saved this man's life. The woman said to the man: "But if you were so hungry, why did you not eat one of the many apples at your feet?" And he said that he needed another story. He needed to think he was eating pie, not apples.

[*Long pause*]

Y: But did the man have an allergic reaction anyways?

X: Oh yes, quite severe. Buried him that day.

Y: Oh dear.

[*Long pause*]

Y: But what are we to do then? Just sit here?

X: [*Defiantly*] Just sit here.

Y: And wait?

X: [*Confidently*] And wait.

Y: But nothing is happening.

X: That's the point.

Y: That's the point?

X: That's the point.

Y: That doesn't seem like a very good point.

X: It's a profundity which you would not understand.

[*Curtain*]

29

THE PROTOCOL OF MOBILE ROOMS

Aristide Antonas

Article 1

1.1 The Protocol of Mobile Rooms applies to those areas crossed by moving populations who have had to abandon their homes and/or countries permanently. Such migratory flows, which entail large numbers and move across long distances, compose the State of Mobile Rooms.

1.2 Other, unforced, migratory people are not barred from subscribing to the Protocol of Mobile Rooms. The only constitutive condition is that they are willing to become citizens of the State of Mobile Rooms.

Article 2

2. A specially designed room is provided to any subscribing person from the Bank of Mobile Rooms, upon request.

Article 3

3.1 A person who uses a mobile room is accountable under the Protocol of Mobile Rooms. The Protocol of Mobile Rooms is superior to all other protocols as it grants constitutive status under the State of Mobile Rooms.

3.2 Such status grants power to the person using a mobile room to move between states, irrespective of the laws of the countries through which they pass.

3.3 The Protocol of Mobile Rooms guarantees sustainability in the auspices of the provisions secured by the Bank of Mobile Rooms.

Article 4

4.1 Transit across countries does not necessitate any change to the mobile room in use. Each room is guaranteed security and permissibility in material and legal terms: its free international movement is facilitated by the novel legal framework of the State of Mobile Rooms. While its geographical location changes, the mobile room remains attached to the State of Mobile Rooms. The state defines itself as a stable "elsewhere" and immaterial space to which the state's material name and manner refers and only. The State of Mobile Rooms is, thus, defined as "an agglomeration of mobile rooms".

4.2 The mobile room is transported by train (for long transits) or truck (for shorter transits).

4.3 Each mobile room is identical to others and corresponds to each moving resident nominally; though there are rooms that suit accompanying children. The room functions as the identity of everyone who moves with it.

Article 5

5.1 The mobile room is equipped so to enable a user to virtually view and to be viewed via the live satellite network it forms a part of. From the mobile room the user can oversee the network via a satellite connection –wherever it may geographically move to – while the user remains also visible to the virtual community of the moving people of the State of Mobile Rooms.

5.2 Every mobile room is technologically equipped and frequently updated. Most of its functions are controlled by a user-friendly computerised network system which can be interacted via smart touch screens on any surface of the room. The room is equipped with a series of reservoir mobile phones that remain permanently connected on the satellite network, through the use of high-end rechargeable batteries.

5.3 A mobile room is formed by welcoming spatial characteristics despite being minimal in size. The room contains a flexible-size sleeping mattress and pillows and a smart kitchen area. Each room stores enough water for ten days on the move, a bathing area and sufficient quantities of food.

5.4 During transit the toilet converts to a chemical mode. When a stop is made within the facilities of a city, the toilet can be connected to the urban sewer network.

Article 6

6.1 New civic infrastructures which are collectively formed to allow for the shorter- or longer-term settlement of mobile rooms are defined as "counter-cities". When a mobile room settles, for however long, it is defined as a counter room.

6.2 Counter-cities are designed like large resorts, reminiscent of new hotel complexes. There is no limitation on the settlement period and technically the infrastructural blocks can be moved to any destination and as often as the user-resident wishes.

6.3 On resting in a counter-city, the counter rooms are connected with electricity, their batteries are recharged, their systems updated and they are topped-up with a supply of fresh water for as long as they reside in the counter-city.

Article 7

7.1 The relation between resident user and counter room corresponds to the formal identity of citizenship but acts as a counter identity. The room certifies the existence of the resident and ensures their rights within the framework of the Protocol of Mobile Rooms.

7.2 The counter room is a permanently accessible and secure status as identified by the International State of Mobile Rooms.

Article 8

8.1 The mobile room is constantly recorded: their movement is always registered.

8.2 Residents are expected to sleep every night in the room. Leaving the room vacant for more than two nights locks the room and cancels the user's identity and associated rights.

8.3 Upon the event of a lock-out residents are no longer recognised as a citizen of any Member State to the Protocol of the State of Mobile Rooms.

Article 9

9.1 The Bank of Mobile Rooms is a cooperative bank, which produces, distributes and sustains the mobile rooms. The bank remains independent of other economies and currencies.

9.2 The Bank of Mobile Rooms is founded upon two functions: to host people and transmit and circulate currency applicable to the location of each monitored room.

9.3 The Residential Plan of the Bank of Mobile Rooms refers to a warehouse of mobile rooms. As the rooms have no wheels of their own, they are driven exclusively by special means that the bank charters for transportation.

9.4 In transit, the mobile rooms are arranged on special scaffolding, with the infrastructure of water and electricity supplied by special cranes.

9.5 The currency which itself acts as an identity-monitor for every resident of the mobile rooms is provided by a cash pool of money gathered cooperatively by all resident-users.

9.6 Each user of a mobile room has his/her debts cancelled by the Bank of Mobile Rooms.
9.7 The Bank of Mobile Rooms funds those cities which continuously provide the infrastructure for the network and any other special spaces and facilities reserved for the use of mobile rooms.
9.8 The Bank of Mobile Rooms manages the agglomerated property of the counter rooms.
9.9 The Director of the Bank of Mobile Rooms is elected by the residents of the counter rooms through a virtual democratic procedure on the condition of submitting a manifesto outlining the benefits to every resident.
9.10 The monetary flow of the Bank of Mobile Rooms is associated with property redevelopment, according to the voluntary work undertaken by any resident-user who wishes to contribute to the bank's capacity and stock.

Article 10

10.1 Every person has the right to a room on the condition that any account with another bank is rendered void.
10.2 The residents of host cities have the right to acquire a room in the State of Mobile Rooms if they wish. Once this takes place, they acquire the right to occupy a holding spot in the counter-city of their city as any other resident-user of a mobile room.
10.3 The transfer to the State of Mobile Rooms does not describe a mere transit in space, but a civil transformation in the system of representation which grants every resident their new identity and financial security.
10.4 The transfer to the State of Mobile Rooms and the attribution of all property to the Bank of Mobile Rooms relieves the inhabitants of any city from any tax obligations, as they can be formally associated with and financially contributing only to the State of Mobile Rooms.

Article 11

11.1. The Bank of Mobile Rooms aims to the gradual decline of privately-owned properties in existing cities and its constitutive scope is to introduce a replacement rural-dwelling system.
11.2. A city is to be replaced by the agglomeration of counter rooms which are owned by the Bank of Mobile Rooms. This new functional system succeeds the historical city and constitutes a new urban form.

30

LAW NO. 9321/2028

Exceptional Regulations for Communal Living and Use on the Ground of Higher Order Natural Sites

Thanos Zartaloudis

The President of The New Hellenic Republic

We hereby issue the following law passed by Parliament:

Article 1

1.1 Paragraph 17 of Article 7.2 of the *Code of General Supervisory Powers – Penalties of Law in the Post-Covid-19 Era* (4582/2027) amending Section 2, Article 5 of *Exceptional Regulations for Circulation, Isolation and Distantiation and Other Provisions in relation to Higher Order Natural Sites* (OGG 18/A/19.7.2020), as amended by Law 776.4/2021 (OGG 67B), is hereby amended as follows:

7.2 (henceforth: 17.4) The installation of civic lifestyles, identities, personalities and the use of proprietary essences and associated claims is forbidden at the security-designated exclusive "*Higher Order Natural Sites* (HONS)", including seashores, public forests, woodlands and aligned public areas of exceptionally declared "higher natural order", equal and equivalent to those designated by law as of "divine or sacred" historical heritage.

17.5 Private individuals are not permitted to occupy and/or interact with such HONS in any commercial, personal or other substantial way.

17.6 Civic violators of HONS shall be punished with imprisonment up to three (3) years or fined, or both, unless a higher penalty is elected under another provision, as ordered by the Criminal Court, ordering their violent expulsion and deportation.

17.7 The civic process to be satisfied is described in Articles 6–18 of the *Pandemic Resilience Procedure Code 2020*, for the investigation and adjudication of "misdemeanour anti-natural acts".

17.8 "Higher Order Natural Sites" are juridically designated for the meeting of natural needs by communes of self-negating individuals. For every juridical action there must be according to natural necessity an equal and opposite juridical reaction.

17.9 As it is impossible, by any recognisable finite process, to arrive at an absolutely zero degree of natural existence, self-negation by such individuals unveils a natural self of the higher order, who remains a body of compositions outside of earlier naturalised proprietary forms, whether as assumed essences or delegated identities; and whose components are no longer contractual properties attached to civic rights.

17.10 The satisfaction of "natural needs" requires seamless and free access to the universal network of common and communally-shared areas as designated under OGG 18/A/19.7.2027, waiving proprietary rights over common goods designated as "natural communes" when situated in HONS.

17.11 "World" is hereby defined against non-scientific misdescriptions, according to *The Pandemic Resilience Scientific Guidelines*, Para. 27C as "Living in the World", which is premised on at least one world, that is generally of a natural kind. Creatures or things of the natural kind interact continuously on their essential natures, akin to fundamental laws of nature, as scientifically proven and legally instituted, such as the Law of Natural Conservation, the Symmetry Principle of Equality Compensation and the Law of Higher Order Relativity, all of which are based on essential properties of the natural and not logical kind.

17.12 Definitive scientific proof that all natural laws are concerned with the interaction of creatures and things and not with qualifications of "the kind of the world this is", necessitate hereby the installation of a new *Juridical Framework of Release*, for the establishment and protection of the Right to Self-Negation on the grounds of being an entity or thing of the, generally, higher order natural kind.

17.13 In the absence of any natural differentiation between worlds and the, now, religious-scientific establishment of the "at least one world principle", henceforth "this world", as one of a natural kind which may be disjoined but only so because of its correlated unity, the conventional differentiating "essential properties" of any natural creature or thing are to be no longer those upon which its identity depends for its determination, but those upon which it evades its earlier claimed identity or self.

17.14 For self-replicating, evolving and complex substances like human beings, essences are agreed to be of a general genotype. Nomic necessities no longer conform to conventional "natural necessity"; and in designated "Natural Sites of the Higher Order" can be so declared null and void by a negation of the will to will.

17.15 A "natural necessity of the higher order" is to be, henceforth, understood as a "higher-order universal" that is unindependent, yet free, of anything other to it.

Article 2

2.1 An "'area of communal natural use of the Higher Order" is, hereby, defined as the site (or realm, in the case of an agglomeration of such sites), where the way of life of commune-participants is determined as communal.
2.2 A "communal way of life" is defined as the individual and collective negation of self and of any attached ownership claims and rights.
2.3 A "network of communal goods" is defined as the non-proprietary, non-reversible construction, or system of constructions for the satisfaction of communal natural needs as a matter of higher order necessity.

Article 3

3.1 A "self-negating individual" is defined as the individual who self-negates his or her or other private form and personality (as defined in Article 5, 57 *CC*) and any associated contractual or proprietary claims or rights.
3.2 "Self-negation" is defined as a legal act of the Natural Higher Order that negates the ordinary, in order to fully, and permanently, exercise material and/or immaterial unresilience of Natural Living.
3.3 "Unresilience" is not the opposite of resilience but what resilience policy deforms in order to justify its supposed necessity. Precedents to this, that a court may consider in adjudicating disputes, include "security policy" which deformed social security in the fight against "global terrorism"; and "freedom-policy" that deformed socio-economic freedom in the fight against those who believed that freedom could not and need not materialise in an ideal society where everyone remains relational to themselves and others at all times.
3.4 The "enjoyment of HONS" is defined as a constantly shared, evolving, non-commercial, common use of natural, material and/or immaterial goods.

Article 4

The self-negation of a private form and personality shall be orally declared in song, under oath, if so and upon request by the Supervisory Public Health Resilience Authorities (SPHRA).

Article 5

5.1 The "Higher Order Natural Way of Life" is defined as the maximal expression of the constitutional right to the environment (Article 24 A).
5.2 The maximal realisation of this right renders the right itself negated, surpassed and transformed into a permanent way of natural life.

Article 6

6.1 Whilst acknowledging the jurisprudence (CFI of Athens. 10691/1997) and Articles 966–968 CC, "communal goods" are defined as such material and immaterial goods that cannot be the object of profit, trade, appropriation or expropriation.

6.2 A "permanently unappropriated good" is hereby defined as the communal good that is no longer subject to individual or collective appropriation and/or expropriation.

Article 7

7.1 The stipulated right to Communal Natural Use of the Higher Order is of a fundamentally exceptional character and is to be initiated by, as defined in Article 4, the self-negation of the individual form, identity and personality of any participant in the commune.

7.2 The right to self-negation in Communal Living of the Higher Order negates, through its exercise, its own past "nature" derived as a matter of civic or other form and right.

7.3 A "free use of HONS" is defined as the non-private and non-proprietary use of such sites.

7.4 HONS are common goods on Higher Order Natural Law grounds (*ius naturale et profanum*), according to which the *Higher Order Natural Uncondition* does not require juridical authorisation (civic or otherwise) and does not and cannot establish a new legal regime (*quia necessitas non habet legem*).

Article 8

As a "natural need or necessity of the Higher Order" is thereby defined any communal use of material and immaterial goods in the Natural Way of Higher Order Living.

Article 9

9.1 Any prohibition of such natural use and exercise amounts to a violation of the Higher Order Natural Rights of self-negating human and other beings and things.

9.2 HONS hereby compose the fundamental ground of the maximal realisation of Article 24 of the Greek Constitution and of Article 4.2 of the Equality of General Rights and Duties.

9.3 The Right To Have No Rights within HONS remains a juridically recognised right, for all purposes of adjudication, when outside the bounds of HONS.

31

A CONFIDENTIAL PRIVATE PLACEMENT MEMORANDUM

By Pierre Schlag

RE: Heads Up

* Associate Dean Taylor <taylors00@su.edu>
To: * Susan J. Tremain

Hi Susan,

I just got an email from Strong Arm Futures. *See attachment* (I got it because I've done business with Strong Arm before.) Should we do anything about this? Should I send it to the Appointments Committee or to Evaluations? Maybe both? See especially pages 4–5.

On a different topic, I spoke to university counsel yesterday about our ongoing pending matter. I'll fill you in at our 3:00 meeting. Also, Daniel wants to make a small presentation at the faculty meeting next Friday. (I said no.)

All the best,
John

P. S. How did Sam like camp?

RE: Heads Up

* Dean Susan J. Tremain <SJTremain@su.edu>
To: * John F. Taylor

John,

Glad you're back! Sam loved summer camp!

Thanks for the attachment. I had heard something like this was in the works, but it's good to have the details. Talk to you about it (and everything else!) at our meeting. See you at 3:00.

Kind regards,

S.

CONFIDENTIAL PRIVATE PLACEMENT MEMORANDUM

Respectfully Submitted
On behalf of Strong Arm Futures, LLC,
A Delaware Limited Liability Corporation
In compliance with Protocol VII of The American Association for Premium Business Ethics

An Illusory Offer for Prime Investors

Tenure Assist V.C.

(Founders: Strong Arm Futures, LLC)

$3,500,000
10,000 Shares of Class A Stock

Closure Date: March 1, 2027

EXECUTIVE SUMMARY

Each year, across the globe, thousands of the brightest young professors at top universities reach the final stages of an arduous journey to tenure. Some began this journey in kindergarten. Some a bit later. Many will succeed. Some will not.

Nearly all have already devoted hundreds of thousands of dollars and untold time to their professional quest. With everything these tenure candidates have to gain and all they have to lose, both financially and emotionally, *Tenure Assist V.C.* (hereinafter called, "The Company") wants to help. Our new revolutionary platform, *Tenure Assure!* promises to capture this untapped market.

For a modest $20,000 one-time fee, each candidate can maximise his/her/their chance of success. With so much riding on the tenure decision, this is one consumer base that cannot afford to pass up our product line and services. We will shepherd tenure candidates through the various hoops, hurdles and gates. Armed with our advanced product line and services, we will take the guesswork out of the tenure process.

This prospectus is addressed to prime investors. The Company *ultimately aims to serve the entire consumer base for tenure at accredited universities throughout the world.* We will start small, by introducing our product line and services at law schools in the US.

Initial funding aims at an initial sum of $3,500,000 with a dual stock structure.[1]

Eligibility

Given recent political events, the requirements of the Foreign Agents Registration Act, 22 U.S. C. § 211 *et seq.* and our legal responsibilities under 22 U.S.C. § 611(c); 28 C.F.R. § 5.100, prudence advises that all initial round investors in The Company be limited to natural persons – either born or naturalised US citizens. For those investors interested in their suitability, please see the section on Ethical Considerations below.

In addition to the usual matters (e.g., terms of offering, tax implications, team, etc.) provided in the Appendix , we provide the following information:

Primary Product Line – Tenure Assure!

This prospectus describes the initial form that our primary product *Tenure Assure!* will take – servicing the needs of pre-tenure candidates, primarily in the US (and looking to expansion in Canada, Europe, as well as strategic locations throughout the world). This servicing will involve the licensing of access to *Tenure-Assure!* – a user-friendly data-gathering, analytic, tenure counselling, and a software platform (augmenting the power of existing CRM technology for the academic marketplace).

Software platforms

Analytics (measuring impact and calibrating success of a publication strategy)
Data gathering (confidential)
Manuscript sales and placement (templates, texts and strategies)
Blog strategies (including access to our patented SEO)

Market penetration: understanding and meeting the tenure standard

The tenure standard (what does "outstanding excellence" really mean?)

1 Further information concerning the terms of the offering and the eligibility of subscribers are contained in the *Appendix*.

Networks, nodes and memes (how to signal your way into the top publishing venues)
Conferences (from impact ratings to psycholinguistics and everything in between)
Virtual/IRL sales team creation (how to leverage friends and colleagues)
Getting noticed I (the "cinch fight" – choosing your enemies carefully)
Getting noticed II (entourage! entourage! entourage!)
Getting noticed III (optimise! optimise! optimise!)
Optimal virtue signalling (when too much is just enough)
Creating your own centre and programme (the "Potemkin effect" and other multipliers)
Branding (all top three brands represented: Evolutionary Super-Economics, Neoliberal Critical Theory, and STEM-FUSION).
Mastering the academic *quid pro quo* (achieving asymmetrical advantages in dealing with Chairs and Deans)
Perilous zones – demographic black holes and topological dead zones (e.g., the faculty lounge)
Departmental tenure home (including how to transfer out of sociology!)
Macro-strategy (when everyone is cynical, there's no one left to fool – so what's *your* business model?)

Secondary product line—Review-Certain!

In this second wave, after establishing a secure hold on the market for our primary product line, *Tenure Assure!* and no later than five years from the closing of initial round investments, we will embrace an "arms-race" approach and turn to servicing the hiring and evaluation processes. Our secondary product line, *Review Certain!* will thus be targeted at university institutions – evaluation committees, appointments committees – to enable them to render competent judgments and decisions about candidates.

The *Review Certain!* product line will offer and market a *Star-Predictor Index* that will assess and rate the probable career success of academic candidates based upon a continual update of the candidate's scholarly production and our 24/7 aggregated competitive profile. (User-friendly variable specification included). It is anticipated that *Star-Predictor Index* will lead to smooth separation decisions for pre-tenured candidates without requiring the often costly, awkward, and divisive process of full tenure deliberations. And, of course, *Star-Predictor Index,* can also be used in department or college-wide merit-pay determinations. (Liability avoidance is a plus).

As for hiring, both at the entry and lateral level, *Star-Predictor Index* takes the guesswork out of the equation. *Star-Predictor Index* will become a must—a game changer in terms of competitive advantages.

Ethical considerations

The Company is committed to the highest ethical standards maintained by the American Association for Premium Business Ethics. In order to avoid any conflict of interest between *Tenure-Assure!* and *Review Certain!* in the case of candidate-institution overlap, The Company will not disclose to either party the existence of the other contract. This conflict of interest provision will also apply fully to any competing institutional purchasers of *Review Certain!*

The securities offered here are highly speculative, involve a high degree of risk, and should be purchased only by investors who can afford to lose their entire investment. No representation besides those above have been made.

Copies of all documentation which is material to The Company and this offering are available for inspection by qualified investors at the offices of The Company upon request. In addition, The Company will, in its sole discretion, make available to qualified investors any other information concerning The Company that an investor requests to evaluate the investment. Representatives of The Company are available to answer any questions or inquiries from qualified investors concerning The Company and the investment.[2]

Appendix

Further information concerning the terms of this offering (e.g., terms of offering, tax implications, team, etc.) and the eligibility of subscribers are described above.

2 The last two paragraphs have been adapted and modified from language made available by the "Start Up Garage", https://thestartupgarage.com/tsgwiki/sample_private_placement_memorandum_ppm/#Confidential_Private_Placement_Memorandum.

32

THE STATUTE OF SNOUTS – AN ACT FOR THE ELONGATION OF NOSES

Peter Goodrich

> The "shine on the nose" – was in reality a "glance at the nose". The nose was thus the fetish, which, incidentally, he endowed at will with the luminous shine which was not perceptible to others. (Freud, "Fetishism", 1927)

Be it enacted by her most regal and rugose majesty, *nasus enormis*, upon the advice of the lords wrinkled of trunk and stooped of nostril, with the consent of the common snubs and sniffers, the puisne and pugnozzled, in the parliament of snoutfigs, as follows:

Preambulation

It is well established by tradition, contrition and erudition alike that the nose is the instrument of equilibrium. The proboscis is the tip and tiller of the face, the harbinger and foghorn of the person, so much so that antiquity teaches that the longer the prow the closer the subject is to the divine. *Ora pro boscis*, pray for the bugle, is more parlously needed today than ever before.

Noses are being lost in terrifying numbers to cosmetic surgery, to rhinoplasty, to poor dentistry and to bicycling accidents. The consequences are inopinate, extreme and most unfortunate. Circumcision of the other Priapus, nasoectemy of the most barbarous ilk is being permitted, particularly in Pinewood, Sandalwood, Hollywood, Bollywood, Lollywood, Tollywood, Nollywood, as well as in boxing venues worldwide. Let it be noted, inscribed, tabled and fined, that the law of nature has assigned to the ears the quality of never closing, to the eyes the penthouse lids of choice, to the mouth both lips and language, while the divine attribute of the muffler is that it grows. To shorten the nose in a vandalism of symmetry is not simply *contra naturam*, an outrage against the order of things, but a deranged unbalancing of the equilibrium and judgment of the proper person –

ideona persona – or the *propositus* upon whom the legal pendulum depends. A denasified law is one which has excised what Catullus coined as *imaginosum*, meaning that now, lacking, castranosed, it is stuffed with nothing, it has no direction.

A tremendous trumpet, Roman, aquiline, cogitative, mine for example, is a manifestation of an equitable judgment and well-balanced method. The rhinoceros parchment proboscis of the jurist, with its egalitarian nostrils, rims flaring at every injustice, nasopharynx aligned perfectly with the sinus of reason, is the pride of the bench and the mark of the scholar. A firmament of a flute adds spectacularly to the power of well-directed vision as it settles upon the subject of judgment in its necessarily unerring and laser-tipped exercise. There is a judge, a scholar and a jurist, the ancients would proudly say of the grandly proportioned and well-directed pince-nez of legal reasoning, the schnoze of the statute. *Homo emunctæ naris*, the judicial proboscis free of all interferences and the varied deformations of cosmetic surgeons, plastic practitioners, barbers and barbarians, is an essential attribute of the *corpus iuris* and a boon to the polity. Be it noted that gnosis is nasal, and if only erudition were still a shared property, septum and scholarship would already be bonded together in the nostrils of mutual augmentation, as this enactment proposes.

O tempora, o mores, o nares, but how the times have conspired to diminish and unbalance the instrument of scent, the trunk of tracking, the jug of judgment and all other olfactory lucinations. But precedent can make the case conclusively and provide a foreground to this legislation by indicating the mischief that it aims to abrogate, and the flute of reason that must be restored.

The reference, and it can hardly be lost on one so erudite as yourself, *un nez retroussé*, a celestial conk, is to the decision in *Rex v Harris* from 1836. The defendant, Ann, in an altercation with a neighbour, bit off the end of her beak. Narry a native nose remaining. She was indicted under the Statute 9 Geo. IV. c. 31, s. 12 which makes it an offence for anyone to shoot at or draw a trigger upon another, "or [who] shall unlawfully and maliciously stab, cut or wound any person ..." The long and short of it, the snub of the decision, based upon the precedential deliberations, because such is how their regal and inherently choral honours, the plurality of proboscators, used to express themselves, of 15 judges, was that Ann must go free, and this despite the wild attack on her neighbour's nostrils, and the calumny of her erstwhile friend. The ostensive reason was that biting off the nose could not be deemed to fall within the words "stabbing, cutting or wounding". Thus, *ergo* as we used to like to say, in that most stochastic and singularly symptomatic language of determination: "Verdict – Not guilty".

The case has been taught, the rule elaborated, students entertained or bamboozled, for the ensuing 182 years, and counting. It is said to be an instance of the black letter of the law: the wounding must be read as consequent upon stabbing or cutting which involves an instrument. The teeth, for reasons undisclosed, do not stab, or cut or wound in law, but rather, and it must be confessed that this has to be made up, because the learned brethren and tribe of parchment probnosticators were silent as to their reasons, they bite.

If the genius of the law is in its smeller, the decision, the disequilibriation of this particular proboscation, might be opined to be an instance of projection. That Ann Harris, with her snappers, removed the better portent of her friend's nose, led the court in traumatic empathy to imagine itself lacking both *pince* and *nez*, and thus to proffer a decision lacking entirely in equiparation. The defendant was freed by a conjunctive, as opposed to disjunctive, "or". *Sans nez*, the court in counter-transference lost its balance, it tripped and fell for an interpretation that refused to conceive the masticated part-loss of an organ as a wound. It is as if the Siniatic camel's nose of irrationality got under the tent and into the chambers of law.

In conclusion of preamble, the Act is aimed at eliminating the savagery of nasal mutilation and the offence to nature and law that such dismemberment, brutal buttism, occasions. The ill effects of such *contractio ad fundamento*, this making of the face into an ass, proboscicide, are not simply metaphysical but foolosophical. The phallus has no sense of humour, the ass makes its demands, and the nose may occasionally, of necessity, lie down with the bum as a 'sucke fist', kissarse or lickspittle, according to Judge Rabelais, butt such is a matter of tumult and exception. The nose, let us conclude, should not wander, there is no happy nasal exodus, it belongs *per naturam*, on its owner's face. Collegiate Assessor Kovalyov, recollect, had to hunt for the missing organ, being left with only 'an idiotic flat patch of skin'. So no asses here. The Statute of Snouts, as enacted herewith, is in preservation, promulgation and propagation of proboscation:

Lex

1.1 The policy of the statute and the principle of interpretation to be applied to all ambiguities, enigmas or other riddles in the legislation is *procedere ad naso* and in favour and furtherance of the extension wherever possible of the proboscatory instrument.

1.2 Judgements in all cases prosecuting proboscicidal reduction are to be before the Court of Augmented Noses and to be tried according to the tip of an alar law that carries the sinus of judgment upon the wings of the nostrils to the turbinate of decision.

1.3 The case of *Rex v Harris* is to be disinterred and reversed without audience or appeal. The judges are reprimanded for their helpless *gravitas* and subjected herewith to the penalty of *damnatio naris* – they are to be deemed noseless, witless asses, for a period of two weeks, or a fortnight, while their other judgments are reviewed for lack of *levitas*.

1.4 Denasification of any sort, whether occasioned by snappers or surgeons is in the former instance calumny and in the latter instance to be adjudged mutilation, grievous and mulcted nasal harm. *Contractio nasi* is a crime committed by any party, single or several, who endeavours to punch, break, cauterise, shorten, unnecessarily straighten, rigidify or otherwise to reduce, circumscribe or restrain any dimension of the proboscis from the tip of the nose, to the depths of the nasopharynx.

1.5 All medical, theological, legal, musical or pornographic facilities, whether private, public, aquatic or anarchic are to provide, free of charge and upon request, nose stretching implements appropriate to the size, design, contours and colours of the client's proboscis.

1.6 Augmentation is understood in this Act to reference an entirely imaginary expansion, accolade, stroking, approbation, stretching and laudation of the fullness of nose that is in the best spirit of judgement. No surgical instruments, incisions, knives, teeth or pharmacotropic libations are to be used in the expansion of the trunk. Blowing one's own trumpet is the primary therapy, to be followed by aesthetic, spiritual, theological and poetic remonstrations of collective identity and the commonality of thought through the twin tunnels of insufflation.

1.7 Where nose augmentation is undertaken as an in-patient at a registered columbarium, sanatorium, bureau, archive or restaurant, the facility is to provide counselling and support from trained probiscodologists who are to perform exercises in foolosophical reasoning for the edification and advancement of the now enhanced equilibriation and judgement of the recipient's jug.

1.8 Those with enhanced nostrils and extended prows are upon completion of augmentation qualified therewith to sit as jurors and in juggerment upon cases commercial, combative, civil, celestial, creative and criminal, at their own instigation, in any court of noses, augmented or natural, scented and always *au jus*.

This Act shall be known in well-equilibriated company, amongst proboscators generally, and snoutfigs in particular, as *Lex Slawkenbergiensis*.

33

SCIENCE AND SCHOLARSHIP RESTORATION ACT

Bernhard Schlink

Preamble

The decline of science and scholarship has one main cause: too many unsubstantial, irrelevant and unimportant publications. The pressure to publish keeps too many scholars and scientists from researching, thinking and writing about what matters, and the pressure to keep up with what is being published makes too many scholars and scientists waste time and energy on reading what does not matter. Even publications that matter could regularly be edited drastically.

Both the experience of everybody working in the field and psychological and epistemological long-term studies demonstrate that a scholar and scientist can, in one year, come up at best with new ideas or new results that fit onto 20 pages. Acknowledging scholars and scientists' inability to eliminate redundancy, the act allows every scholar and scientist to publish 15 pages per year.

Penalties for breach of this limit are severe. Strong incentives are needed to break with old habits. General awareness of publications' dispensability did not make scholars and scientists kick their excessive publishing addictions but indulge them even more – as the book that you are right now reading illustrates.

The act is compatible with freedom of expression. Since scholars and scientists, as scholars and scientists, do not have more to say per year than what fits on 20–25 pages, they are not deprived of expressing any scholarly and scientific thoughts that occur to them. They are free to express their scholarly and scientifically unsubstantial, irrelevant and unimportant thoughts in whatever form they like, e.g., as novels, paintings, sonatas – just not in the guise of scientific and scholarly publications.

§ 1

Every scholar and scientist is entitled to publish 15 standard pages per year, a standard page being 1800 characters.

§ 2
Pages that have not been published in one year may be transferred to subsequent years.

§ 3
Co-authored pages count for each co-author with proportionate fractions.

§ 4
Publishers report each publication and its author to the Agency for Scholarly and Scientific Efficiency (ASSE).

§ 5
Authors who violate this act, and publishers who facilitate violations of this act by authors, will be banned from publishing.

Olympus, July 1, 2020
Pallas F. Athene, President

34

CONSTITUTIONAL EXHAUSTION

Pierre Schlag

"A letter always arrives at its destination."
January 30, 2050
Official Motto of the U.S. Postal Service

At the 2048 conference of U.S. federal appellate judges, the assembled judges faced what is now generally recognised as a momentous problem calling for immediate and decisive action. Indeed, many academic commentators back then viewed it as something of a scandal that the federal judiciary had not acted sooner.

As we all know, the problem of "constitutional exhaustion" (which had featured in numerous law review symposia including at top law schools such as Harvard Law and NYU-Bermuda) was about to reach a head. Indeed, peak US constitutionalism exhaustion had been predicted by many to occur as early as 2030. In retrospect as in many other predicted peaks (peak oil, peak natural gas, peak beef) this one was a bit premature. At the same time, however, the slope of the curve on the downside turned out to be hell.

By the time the 2048 judicial conference convened, peak exhaustion had long been reached in constitutional law and the situation was truly dire.

Even though the crisis had been long foretold, its arrival was nonetheless brutal. Indeed, by this point, the sort of fatal contradiction exemplified in the two opposed religion clauses (freedom of exercise/establishment clause) had pretty much metastasised to other clauses of the Constitution.

The equal protection clause was viewed as a "right-remedy paradox" where discrimination and reverse discrimination claims were quite clearly cancelling each other out on an almost daily basis – provoking huge conflicts (and not a little hostility) between the 5th and the 24th Circuits.

Similarly, the First Amendment was widely understood as a deadlock between speakers' and listeners' rights and their respective doctrinal strains.

Other clauses of the Constitution were not so much deadlocked as deflated. The Fourth Amendment collapsed on itself as advancements in cyber-surveillance gradually reduced the expectation of privacy to virtually nothing. Procedural due process likewise withered—as state legislatures enacted global statutes declaring that all property and liberty entitlements included as an "integral and non-severable part" of their identity, the processes appended to defeat them.

Other forms of deflation also contributed to constitutional exhaustion. The elimination of the limits of the commerce clause was a done deal. First presaged in expansive readings of the concurrences in the famous Obamacare case of *National Federation of Independent Business v. Sebelius*, the commerce clause was soon ailing. The terminal state was pretty much achieved in the *West Coast Hair Salon* cases where it was firmly established that the federal prohibition on the "retro hirsute look" was constitutional in so far as the look had a depressing effect on commerce – particularly once "all hirsutes were aggregated".[1]

In short, by the time the judicial conference of 2048 was held at NYU-Bermuda, it was pretty much a given that virtually every constitutional clause was in utter internal deadlock or terminal deflation. What truly cinched the realisation of the impending disaster came in a Harvard Law Review article making out the nearly unimpeachable case that any effort to "scale back" on doctrinal deadlocks and deflations would not work. "Scaling back" would not extinguish, but merely shift the deadlocks or deflations to different doctrinal locations thereby failing to overcome exhaustion. The clincher in the argument came from a meticulous demonstration (some called it brilliant) that the precedents of constitutional law had over the years migrated (apparently all on their own) into numerous statutory schemes—where the same kinds of deadlocks and deflations had been steadily flourishing. "Scaling back" was thus out of the question for all except the most ambitious scholars.[2]

But let us not digress nor be distracted.

At the judicial conference, some argued that a defunct constitution was not the worst thing in the world. Edgar Kennedy (unrelated to Duncan Kennedy, but of somewhat similar views) pointed out that constitutional law was essentially a random jurisprudence effectively introducing interstitial free radicals into the *corpus juris*. Kennedy added,

> That the Constitution is now a mess owes a lot to the fact that it has always been a mess – a document not only ignorant of Rousseau's constitutional

1 It is to be noted that many hirsutes objected to being aggregated and some found the idea profoundly offensive.

2 It was pointed out by a young scholar that this was an ironic role reversal – the radicals pushing for "scaling back" the constitution, while the conservatives wanting to "let it all hang out."

> paradoxes, but given to a ridiculous pretence that the Constitution is constitutive merely because it says it is.

At some conference, someone said, "But it works!" To which Edgar Kennedy famously responded. "Yeah sure – the Constitution works, monarchy works, everything works until, of course, it doesn't." He also added:

> The point is that the Constitution was since the beginning a shameless projection of private law into a corporate charter masking as a founding political document. In short a double oxymoron.

Edgar Kennedy's view, of course, drew a lot of support, but also a great deal of opposition from the Super Patriotic Federalist Society (a right-wing offshoot of the original Federalist Society). The latter also opposed Edgar Kennedy's views, but more mildly and mostly out of habit.

One solution discussed at some length at the conference was to appeal to the UN to conduct an investigation of the United States in order to determine whether the international norms of democratic self-determination (under the New Charter of 2026) had been violated. The argument was both elegant and compelling: a sclerotic constitution meant a defunct constitution. A defunct constitution meant no constitution. And no constitution meant no self-determination. It was argued that the new pre-emption provisions of the New Charter could be used to displace domestic law – *even if* this entailed displacement of domestic constitutional law. It was conceded, and this may have been politically ill-advised, that this displacement would only apply in the event of "fundamental pre-emption" —that is to say, only where fundamental guarantees or prohibitions of the New Charter were at stake.

Of course, it was soon noted that "fundamental pre-emption" had already evolved into its own deadlock – with one side arguing that all pre-emption is fundamental while the other suggesting that the use of the term "fundamental" implied that at least *some* pre-emption was not itself fundamental. And as soon became clear, when the advocates meant "some" they meant "most", which under the canons of construction, meant "nearly all". The arguments have been theorised under a rubric that distilled the arguments into two paradigms: Mostly and Mostly Not (apparently very influential in U.S. Supreme Court decisionmaking).

When all this came up at the judicial conference, Chief Justice Louise M., who served as chair at that moment, managed to bracket all of it in favor of what many at the judicial conference took to be the right question: "what should we do?"

The posing of that question was met with long and sustained applause.

"She really cut to the chase," one judge said. "She is really terrific," said another. And this was true because the Chief Justice's brazen formulation of the question had effectively cut through its tiresome derivatives: "What should we do to answer the what should we do question?" often followed by "So then—should we do it now or later?"

When the applause died down, a relatively unknown judge from the 18th Circuit called "George" proposed the radical step of invigorating a little-used (and thus still potentially vital) constitutional power – notably, the postal power – to perform all essential constitutional tasks and functions.

This was summarily dismissed as passing weird by Chief Justice Louise M. Nonetheless, covering all bases, she cautioned that—weird or not—if the "postal power gambit" were invigorated and made to do serious constitutional work, it would soon encounter the same arresting deadlock and deflation difficulties. "We've become acculturated to deadlock and deflation," she said. "They have become integral aspects of our informal norms. It is not so easy to move beyond these sorts of socially engrained propensities. A modicum of humility is advisable."

Again the room burst into fevered applause—soon followed by a standing ovation. One judge was overheard to say, "She's got it. She has really got it."

The Honourable Judge George, however, was having none of it. Unfazed by the authority and obvious charisma of Chief Justice Louise M., he pressed on. "It matters not" he said, "that the precedents of the old constitution have migrated in informal norms. The fact is that the postal power is in virtue of its pristine, which is to say, largely unused character, a source of sweeping authority to reconstruct the old constitution and its creeping colonisation of the legal and social fabric."

He paused for effect. "Think about it—what isn't covered by the postal power? This is the veritable power to 'establish Post Offices and Post Roads.' That is the United States in a nutshell, right there." He went on: "speech, communication, interaction, democracy, the will of the people, our very institutions, and the state itself—all implied by the postal power.

At that point, pandemonium broke out as Judge George was called variously a "constitutional thug", a "Thurman Arnoldian", and "a left fascist". A faction of judges immediately left the room waving their Super Patriotic Federalist Society pamphlet chanting, "What does a Constitution looks like? This is what a constitution looks like". Also later: "Whose law? My law".

At exactly the same time, another faction of appellate judges, spearheaded by Judge George, also left the room with manifest determination. This was the famous "activist faction". They were going out, as everyone now knows, to look up the postal power and to prepare a legal memorandum in support of Judge George's proposal.

The first thing they found was an Am Jur entry, going back all the way to the second edition. What they discovered cheered them beyond all reasonable expectations. (We have added emphasis below to indicate the sources of their enthusiasm.)

> [The] postal power, like all of the other enumerated powers of Congress, *is complete in itself, may be exercised to its utmost extent, and acknowledges no*

> *limitations, other than those that are described in the Constitution*. Thus, under the postal power, *Congress may regulate the entire postal system*.[3]

The obvious solution (and they hit upon it almost immediately) was to declare the United States, an implication of the Postal Power. (This became known as the now famous "institutional implication doctrine" – later deployed in other fields.) The idea – elaborated in suitable hashtag-sites such as "constitution# expounding" and "broad#outlines" – was that the United States would have to be viewed as an institutional implication and thus subdivision of the postal power because that was the only remaining functioning aspect of the US Constitution. This made a certain amount of sense: many commentators noted that it would stretch all interpretation beyond good sense (and valid precedent) to suppose that the US could somehow survive as the product of a deadlocked and deflated constitution. This would be contrary to history, reason, and law itself. The only plausible conclusion was that if the Postal Power was the only real generative source of constitutional meaning, then it had to be completely constitutive in its authorizing and delimiting power. It was a compelling argument. And while it was not ironclad, its minor shortcomings were immediately repaired by judicious invocation of the Necessary and Proper Clause.

Judge George's faction immediately published its conclusions to the conference.

The Super Patriotic Federalist Society meanwhile declared that the newfangled institutional implication doctrine was judicial imperialism of the worst kind. The young Super Patriots pointed out that if the US were considered an outgrowth of and subordinate subdivision of the US Postal Service, there would be no end to what government might do. The Q-Anon judges in attendance vigorously supported this view, duly noting that the US postal system was filled with second and third generation paedophiles and first-generation cannibals.

At this point the ultra-activist faction, picking up on the tactics of the Super Patriotic Federalist Society, pointed out that not only was the Postal Power plenary, but that almost surely, it now made sense to remove the Postal Power from the states.[4] This, of course, was how the "dormant postal clause" was born—later aggressively expanded to the "dormant postal clause with bite." The latter ultimately led to the invalidation of all state services to private postal endeavors.

3 § 1 **Postal Power, Generally**, Am. Jur., Second Edition Noah J. Gordon, J.D. (*citing* State v. Jones, 958 P.2d 938 (Utah Ct. App. 1998)). Earlier case law, not surprisingly, read the postal clause somewhat narrowly. *See, e.g.*, United States v. Railroad Bridge Co., 27 Fed. Cas. 686 (No. 16,114) (C.C.N.D. Ill. 1855). These precedents became of questionable value—affected as they were by antiquated conceptions of federal-state relations.

4 There is reason to believe that, in contrast to the Articles of Confederation, the U.S. Constitution did not create an exclusive monopoly in the United States in regards to postal matters. Most commentators believe this is accurate. But as Justice Thompson famously wrote, even if in a different context "That was then. Now is now."

What happened next to UPS and Fed Ex was pretty much a foregone conclusion. By contrast, Inyourfacebook Delivery did survive.

In any event, so it was that the judicial conference of 2048 voted its overwhelming support for the institutional implication doctrine as well as the sustained and deliberate use of the Postal Power in conjunction with the Necessary and Proper Clause.

The rest is history.

Today, the intrepid figure of the unknown postman graces not only the US flag, but all official documents of the federal government. In 2052, a gigantic blue mailbox, some 36 stories high, was built next to the Washington Monument. Every year, in June, the universal postal carrier begins a trans-continental journey via horseback from Concord, Massachusetts, to the shores of the San Francisco Bay.[5]

There, from the Golden Gate Bridge, he or she drops a ceremonial letter into the bracing waters of the San Francisco Bay.

All is well.

5 A number of media influencers have noted that this ritual is yet another example of fiction made real. *Cf. The Postman* (2013).

INDEX

For Product Safety Concerns and Information please contact our EU representative GPSR@taylorandfrancis.com
Taylor & Francis Verlag GmbH, Kaufingerstraße 24, 80331 München, Germany

www.ingramcontent.com/pod-product-compliance
Ingram Content Group UK Ltd.
Pitfield, Milton Keynes, MK11 3LW, UK
UKHW022021180926
475701UK00005B/958
9780367566586